MAKING JUDAISM SAFE FOR AMERICA

THE GOLDSTEIN-GOREN SERIES IN AMERICAN JEWISH HISTORY

General editor: Hasia R. Diner

We Remember with Reverence and Love: American Jews and the Myth of Silence after the Holocaust, 1945–1962
Hasia R. Diner

Is Diss a System? A Milt Gross Comic Reader
Edited by Ari Y. Kelman

All Together Different: Yiddish Socialists, Garment Workers, and the Labor Roots of Multiculturalism
Daniel Katz

Jews and Booze: Becoming American in the Age of Prohibition
Marni Davis

Jewish Radicals: A Documentary History
Edited by Tony Michels

1929: Mapping the Jewish World
Edited by Hasia R. Diner and Gennady Estraikh

An Unusual Relationship: Evangelical Christians and Jews
Yaakov Ariel

Unclean Lips: Obscenity, Jews, and American Culture
Josh Lambert

Hanukkah in America: A History
Dianne Ashton

The Rag Race: How Jews Sewed Their Way to Success in America and the British Empire
Adam D. Mendelsohn

Hollywood's Spies: The Undercover Surveillance of Nazis in Los Angeles
Laura B. Rosenzweig

Cotton Capitalists: American Jewish Entrepreneurship in the Reconstruction Era
Michael R. Cohen

Jewish Radical Feminism: Voices from the Women's Liberation Movement
Joyce Antler

Making Judaism Safe for America: World War I and the Origins of Religious Pluralism
Jessica Cooperman

Making Judaism Safe for America

World War I and the Origins of Religious Pluralism

Jessica Cooperman

NEW YORK UNIVERSITY PRESS

New York

NEW YORK UNIVERSITY PRESS
New York
www.nyupress.org

References to Internet websites (URLs) were accurate at the time of writing. Neither the author nor New York University Press is responsible for URLs that may have expired or changed since the manuscript was prepared.

Library of Congress Cataloging-in-Publication Data
Names: Cooperman, Jessica, author.
Title: Making Judaism safe for America : World War I and the origins of religious pluralism / Jessica Cooperman.
Description: New York : New York University Press, [2018] | Series: The Goldstein-Goren series in American Jewish history | Includes bibliographical references and index.
Identifiers: LCCN 2017060986 | ISBN 9781479885008 (cl : alk. paper)
Subjects: LCSH: World War, 1914–1918—Jews. | Jewish Welfare Board. | Jewish soldiers—United States—History—20th century. | Jews—Cultural assimilation—United States. | United States. Commission on Training Camp Activities. | World War, 1914–1918—Social aspects—United States. | Americanization. | United States—Ethnic relations.
Classification: LCC D639.J4 C56 2018 | DDC 940.3089/924—dc23
LC record available at https://lccn.loc.gov/2017060986

New York University Press books are printed on acid-free paper, and their binding materials are chosen for strength and durability. We strive to use environmentally responsible suppliers and materials to the greatest extent possible in publishing our books.

Manufactured in the United States of America

10 9 8 7 6 5 4 3 2 1

Also available as an ebook

To Hartley

CONTENTS

Introduction

On April 2, 1917, President Woodrow Wilson went before Congress to ask for a resolution of war against Germany. Wilson had held off domestic and international pressure to bring the United States military into World War I for nearly three years, arguing for American neutrality in the battle between Europe's great powers. Now, provoked by Germany's pursuit of unrestricted submarine warfare and by the infamous Zimmermann Telegram, which revealed German attempts to lure Mexico into the war in exchange for the return of its lost territories in Arizona, New Mexico, and Texas, Wilson felt compelled to abandon neutrality and bring the United States into the fight.

Nearly a year later, in March 1918, Chester Teller, the executive director of the Jewish Welfare Board (JWB), spoke at the annual meeting of the Jewish Publication Society of America. US involvement in the war was well under way, and Teller represented the only Jewish organization with the authority to give social, spiritual, and moral support to the soldiers. In his comments, Teller did not focus on the burdens of war. Instead, he gave an uplifting address that offered hopeful news about the state of American democracy and the status of Jews in American society. Teller stated,

> We do the work of the larger American community when we remind them that America permits them to be Jews—nay, as we, wants them to be Jews for what they *as Jews* may contribute to the permanent culture-values of America in the making. . . . Thank God we understand now better than ever before what America means. . . . The democracy for which we are fighting now is not a democracy that merely tolerates distinctive culture values—it insists upon them. . . . It challenges every man to be himself and to look to his neighbor likewise to be himself.[1]

In this speech, and on other wartime occasions, Teller and his colleagues at the JWB articulated a vision of American society that celebrated distinctive cultural and religious values as an inherent part of true democracy. Looking back at Teller's comments, it seems that he significantly overestimated early twentieth-century American society's readiness to see Jews, or other minorities, as positive contributors to the culture, strength, and well-being of the country. Yet Teller was not wrong. World War I did in fact usher in changes that moved the country toward an embrace of certain kinds of diversity, particularly the "tri-faith" model of religious pluralism that would come to characterize the second half of the twentieth century. Over the course of the war, through the efforts of the JWB, the US military and the War Department became agents of profound change to the structures of American religious life and helped bring about a redefinition of American religion.[2]

The decision to enter the war served as a catalyst to change in virtually every area of US domestic and military policy. The United States had long resisted entanglement with foreign conflict and the profound expansion of the federal government that such entanglement seemed to necessitate. As President Wilson worked to stir patriotic support for the social and political transformations the war would create, he assured the American public that this battle was necessary for the preservation of freedom across the globe. Wilson believed that World War I would lead to the creation of a new world order that would affirm the superiority of American-style democracy over European imperialism, within which the United States would naturally assume the mantle of global leadership.[3] As he prepared to bring the United States into battle, Wilson's description of the country's war aims reflected the grandeur of his vision of the American future. In terms that sounded humble and yet clearly proclaimed American moral and political superiority, Wilson told Congress,

> Our object . . . is to vindicate the principles of peace and justice in the life of the world as against selfish and autocratic power and to set up amongst the really free and self-governed peoples of the world such a concert of purpose and of action as will henceforth ensure the observance of those principles. . . .
>
> The world must be made safe for democracy. Its peace must be planted upon the tested foundations of political liberty. We have no selfish ends to serve. We desire no conquest, no dominion. We seek no indemnities

for ourselves, no material compensation for the sacrifices we shall freely make. We are but one of the champions of the rights of mankind.[4]

Most Americans fell in behind Wilson's stirring charge to make the world safe for democracy and accepted the changes to both government and daily life that came with it, although many did so while recognizing the ironies built into this international crusade for justice. In 1917, the United States placed powerful constraints on the freedoms of its own citizens. As the country geared up to champion the rights of mankind, American women could not vote, and African Americans faced harsh discrimination, humiliating Jim Crow laws, and, at times, unchecked violence.[5]

Immigrants, too, had only tenuous access to the freedoms Wilson sought to defend abroad. Nearly fifteen million immigrants had entered the United States in the twenty years before the war. Unlike earlier waves of immigration from northern and western Europe, many of them came from places in southern and eastern Europe. Their arrival in the United States changed the demographic makeup of the country and challenged its cultural norms. As their numbers increased, immigrants faced suspicion about their loyalties, intelligence, and ability to assimilate into American society. Influential political figures such as former president Theodore Roosevelt demanded that the newcomers quickly and completely embrace "100 percent Americanism" and cast off "hyphenated identities" that tied them to other nations and countries. Those who either could not or did not want to abandon the languages and cultural practices that they had brought with them to the United States faced anger and even violence. German Americans, once celebrated as model immigrants, faced particular hostility as the country prepared for war against their former homeland, but nativism haunted all immigrant communities and raised significant questions about what wartime American democracy would mean to those with roots outside of the United States.[6]

As the war effort ramped up, each of these different and diverse groups had to make decisions about how and whether to support the country's call to defend democracy abroad, even as they chafed against its limits at home. There were dissenters—pacifists who refused to fight on principle and others unwilling to throw unconditional support behind a government that seemed to take freedom in Europe far more seriously than freedom at home—but the majority of Americans from all communities accepted Wilson's call to duty in the name of democratic values.[7] But just as Wilson entered the war hoping to advance an American agenda even while fighting for the rights of others, disenfranchised communities hoped that through their contributions to the country's war effort, they might gain ground in their own struggles for rights within American society. As historian Chad Williams argues in his study of African American soldiers in WWI, the war offered a chance for these men to stake their claims to the rights promised by democracy and to take a decisive step forward in the struggle for justice.[8] For some Americans, service in the war thus became a domestic battle to make America safer for democracy, as well as a crusade to bring American-style democracy to the world.

Americans struggled to agree over whether and what kind of freedoms should be extended to women, immigrants, African Americans, and others, but freedom of religion had long been seen as one of the cornerstones of American democracy. Jews and Catholics, however, fit uneasily within early twentieth-century definitions of religion. They were heavily represented among the masses of new immigrants to the country and, sometimes, were specifically targeted by anti-immigrant agitators. Jewish and Catholic Americans from earlier waves of migration, however, could point to congregations and communities established during the colonial era.[9] Generally categorized as white, they did not suffer the sort of legal segregation and discrimination inflicted on African Americans, but Jews and Catholics still faced unanswerable questions about their identity and whether they should be viewed as members of distinct races or simply as religious communities.[10] Religion offered a means of describing Jewish and Catholic identity that seemed to transcend questions of race or national origin and that appeared to be protected under American law, but it proved to be an unstable mechanism through which Jewish and Catholic citizens could assert their freedom as Americans.

From the colonial period into the twentieth century, "religion" in the United States was generally understood to be Protestantism. Indeed, for much of American history, Protestantism seemed so naturally intertwined with the institutions of American life that it was almost invisible, appearing only as the seemingly neutral ground on which society rested.

Protestantism exerted such a profound influence, scholar of American religion Tracy Fessenden argues, that it came to serve as the unperceived underpinning not only of what Americans understood to be Christian but also of what they saw as secular. "Far from being a neutral matrix," she writes, "the secular sphere as constituted in American politics, culture, and jurisprudence has long been more permeable to some religious interventions than to others. The co-implication of secularism and Reformed [Protestant] Christianity has meant, for example, that Christian religious polemic could remain compatible with America's vaunted history of religious liberty and toleration by being cast in strictly secular terms."[11] This veneer of secularity allowed Protestantism to exert profound influence over the dominant institutions of American cultural and civic life while appearing as if it were simply American.

The "co-implication" of Protestantism and Americanism helped to cement the cultural power of the "Protestant establishment," which historian of American religion William Hutchison describes as "a network of Protestant leadership that extended across the churches, controlled most of the nation's political life, and managed virtually all of the major secular institutions and entities in American society."[12] The ability of Protestantism to pass as religiously neutral allowed this Protestant establishment to dictate the norms and standards of enfranchised American society without appearing to violate commitments to religious freedom and equality. Such an arrangement, however, had profound implications for non-Protestants. If Protestantism was American, then other traditions were implicitly rendered un-American according to the degree by which they deviated from Protestant norms. Exhortations that immigrants embrace identities of "100 percent Americanism" were, therefore, not religiously neutral. Definitions of "Americanism" sanctioned by established cultural, intellectual, and political institutions were entangled with a national heritage of Protestantism. This arrangement made it difficult for Jews and Catholics to inhabit spaces of cultural or political power or to be seen as fully embodying American ideals.

In the Wilson administration, the influence of Protestantism on the seemingly secular institutions of the state was not entirely invisible. In many ways, it was central to the president's understanding of his, and the United States', mission to the world. According to scholar of American religion Cara Lea Burnidge, Wilson understood his work in the secular spheres of government and public service through the lens of his own deeply felt personal commitment to the Presbyterian Church. Burnidge writes, "Wilson's performance of civic duties was not exclusively a matter of politics or government but a sustained effort to Christianize the culture in which he lived. If he and other social Christians Christianized the United States as they intended, then they assumed Americanizing the world would follow."[13] Wilson felt confident that the foundations of the country corresponded to his own moral and spiritual foundations. By embodying his Christian values and imbuing his office and administration with them, he would lead the country to live up to its own highest ideals and thus make the righteousness of the American cause apparent to the world. Burnidge argues, "Wilson and his elite white social Christian coterie believed this war could usher in a new world order fashioned after what he believed to be true and universal Christian principles."[14] He and his administration spoke in nonsectarian terms, she notes, but "firmly stood upon a Protestant foundation."[15] Wilson's Protestant convictions did not necessarily mean that his administration sought to evangelize the country and convert non-Protestants to his own true path. It did, however, mean that the president and many of the men who served under him could not always perceive the ways in which their assumptions about religion, as well as about the supposedly secular realm of the state, were shaped by Protestant norms that did not accommodate Jews and Catholics.

The effect of this entanglement of Protestantism and Americanism could be felt not only in the Wilson administration's vision of the country but also in many of the policies put in place during the war. As the United States geared up for battle, War Department officials, including Secretary of War Newton D. Baker, believed that the military should serve not only as a fighting force but as a kind of laboratory for engineering a more moral and high-minded citizenry. During WWI, the US government began a multifaceted experiment in "improving" Americans, particularly the young men drafted into the armed forces. The IQ testing of nearly two million soldiers, conducted under the auspices of the American Psychological Association, is perhaps the best-known example of this wartime project, but it is not the only one.[16] Historian Christopher Capozzola demonstrates the different ways in which the wartime state used its vastly expanded powers to persuade or coerce citizens to accept and participate in a culture of political obligation. Historians Nancy Gentile Ford and Nancy Bristow, in their scholarship on the War Department's Commission on Training Camp Activities (CTCA), have explored the agency's role in promoting social improvement—Ford, in an examination of how the government met the challenge of transforming a conscription military with an unprecedented number of foreign-born soldiers into a cohesive fighting force; Bristow, in a history of Progressive-minded "social hygiene" policies intended to educate soldiers in appropriate white, middle-class conceptions of masculine behavior.[17] These studies and others note that religiously affiliated organizations played a significant role in official experiments with social improvement, but until recently the implications of attempting to improve Americans by exposing them to the guidance of religious organizations have not been adequately considered. As historians of American religion Kevin Schultz and Paul Harvey have argued, religion has often been mentioned in histories of America, but it has rarely been engaged as a serious category for analysis.[18] In his examination of American religion during WWI, Jonathan Ebel similarly notes that "studies of America's wars tend to ignore religion. Studies of American religion tend to ignore war."[19]

This book takes up the charge that these scholars make regarding this important gap in our understanding of both American religion and the impact of World War I on American society. As part of the fight to make the world safe for democracy, the Wilson administration, Secretary Baker, and the CTCA initiated important structural changes within the military and government that were designed to enhance the moral, physical, and spiritual welfare of American servicemen. They created new programs intended to imbue soldiers with seemingly neutral American values and ideals. In order to implement these all-American programs, however, they turned to the evangelizing Young Men's Christian Association (YMCA) on the assumption that, as a nondenominational Protestant organization, it would easily meet the spiritual and social needs of all American servicemen. By end of the war, the War Department had changed its stance and had recognized the JWB and the Catholic Knights of Columbus as equal partners to the YMCA in its soldiers' welfare programs.

How did such a change take place? As scholar of American religion Mark Silk notes in his study of religious pluralism, "It was the case that, before the middle of the twentieth century, non-Protestants remained outside the de facto American establishment. General Christianity," widely seen as the necessary moral undergirding of the state, "was pan-Protestantism. . . . Non-Protestants were relegated to a second tier."[20] How then, within the deeply Protestant Wilson administration, did Catholics and Jews come to serve as partners to a wartime program for enhancing the moral welfare of American soldiers and sailors? What led the War Department to offer recognition to communities that, to a striking extent, were composed of immigrants whose loyalties it saw as suspect and whose religious traditions had long been seen as standing at odds with American values?

What, moreover, were the implications of this shift for both policy and state structure? Theorist Talal Asad argues that "defining what is religion is not merely an abstract intellectual exercise. . . . When definitions of religion are produced, they endorse or reject certain uses of vocabulary that have profound implications for the organization of social life and the possibilities of personal experience."[21] By selecting religious organizations to serve as partners in the government's project for building better citizens, the War Department engaged in a significant act of defining which groups, and which traditions, had a place within the American religious landscape. If, as Tracy Fessenden argues, Protestantism had long served as the de facto basis for American definitions of both religion and the secular, how did those definitions change with the inclusion of non-Protestant agencies within these officially sanctioned state programs? This book addresses these questions and, in doing so, considers the ways in which American definitions of religion shifted as a result of new policies instituted by the federal government during World War I. It argues that although these policies were not implemented with the intention of challenging the cultural force of Protestantism or of the Protestant establishment, they unintentionally created space for Judaism and Catholicism to enter the pantheon of American religions.

The book focuses on the work of the Jewish Welfare Board, which became the only Jewish agency to work under the Commission on Training Camp Activities in the War Department's soldiers' welfare programs. The JWB represented the old guard of American Jewish leadership, not the multitudes of new immigrants who had arrived from eastern and east-central Europe in the years before the war. It was founded and largely run by wealthy, well-established men with a patrician sense of their own role in determining and protecting Jewish interests. When faced with the challenges and possibilities created by the war, they fought to make room for Judaism within official structures of power, as well as to shore up their own influence over the Jewish public. Partnership in the War Department's soldiers' welfare programs gave them exclusive access to the nearly 250,000 Jewish men who served in the US Armed Forces during World War I. It afforded them a unique opportunity to control expressions of Judaism in the US military and thus to shape the identity of a generation of American Jewish men.

That is not to imply that the JWB was insincere in its efforts to support the country's war aims and to care for the welfare of Jewish soldiers—quite the contrary. But it is worth noting that the JWB's involvement in the work of soldiers' welfare was also deeply connected to broader concerns about the future of American Jews and Judaism. Through their role as the military's exclusive Jewish partner in the soldiers' welfare programs, JWB leaders were able to promulgate a particular vision of what they considered to be appropriate American Jewishness, one they believed would both enhance the Americanness of Jewish men and make Judaism more palatable to the larger society. Their work laid the foundations for a more religiously pluralistic America in which Jews could be seen as equal partners to Protestants and Catholics. Indeed, it was, at least in part, through the instigation of the JWB that the United Service Organizations, better known as the USO, emerged as a joint Jewish-Protestant-Catholic effort to raise the morale of members of the armed services in the run-up to World War II.

Like African American soldiers, immigrants, advocates for women's rights, and even President Wilson himself, the men behind the JWB brought multiple agendas to their participation in the country's war effort. They fought to make the world safe for democracy, to change the structures of democracy at home, and to shape the future of American Judaism and the lives of American Jews. Policies put in place during the war sometimes led to unexpected results, as has been made clear by scholar Christopher Sterba's study of how WWI shaped Jewish and Italian communities' participation in American public and political life and by historian Jennifer Keene's examination of the ways that conscription gave American doughboys unexpected power to demand changes within US military policy.[22] All of the religiously affiliated organizations that worked with the government to promote soldiers' welfare did so, at least in part, for their own distinct purposes and, by partnering with the War Department, they gained leverage to use in ways the government had not accounted for.

In looking at the wartime experiences of the JWB, we are able to consider a unique moment in the history of American religion, one in which the US War Department empowered a Jewish organization to serve as an officially recognized agent of the state, in a program intended to improve American citizens and servicemen. In doing so, it created an opportunity for American Jews to shift the country's definition of religion, moving away from a Protestant establishment and toward the idea of a Judeo-Christian America in which Protestants, Catholics, and Jews stood as equal partners. This does not mean that World War I marked the end of anti-Jewish and anti-Catholic biases any more than it marked the end of discrimination toward women, African Americans, or immigrants. Indeed, while women succeeded in gaining the vote in 1920, the interwar years witnessed a startling rise in racist violence, restrictions on immigration, and anti-Jewish and anti-Catholic agitation. Service in the war did, however, create new bases from which soldiers and civilians demanded that the rights and freedoms American democracy promised to the world be delivered at home.

This book examines the complicated relationship between the US War Department, the JWB, and the Jewish soldiers that both institutions sought to improve during World War I. Chapter 1 focuses on the 1916 Punitive Expedition into Mexico, which both inaugurated Secretary of War Baker's experiments with moral reform in the military and revealed the need for new structures and policies through which a morally uplifting program of soldiers' welfare services could be implemented. Chapter 2 traces the establishment of the CTCA and examines the strategies through which the JWB managed to gain an appointment as a CTCA partner agency while keeping other Jewish organizations from challenging its authority. Chapter 3 explores the ways in which the JWB sought to combat the invisible sectarianism of the soldiers' welfare programs by claiming that Judaism was as fully American as Protestantism and thus was equally deserving of representation in government and military policy and on military bases. Chapter 4 examines the JWB's plans to Americanize and improve the masculine character, behavior, and religious practices of Jewish soldiers, while chapter 5 turns to Jewish servicemen's responses to and protests of the JWB's religious and social programs. Chapter 6 looks at the achievements and perceived limits of tri-faith religious cooperation during World War I, and the conclusion offers reflections on the establishment of the USO and on some of the longer-term changes to American ideas about religion created by the soldiers' welfare programs of World War I.

This book argues that the World War I military offers a critical site for studying twentieth-century definitions of American religion. Broad popular acceptance of the idea of a tri-faith America, in which Protestantism, Catholicism, and Judaism were equal partners, did not fully take hold until the second half of the twentieth century, but later developments relied upon the critical structural transformations that occurred during World War I.[23] We can understand the mechanisms of these changes by exploring the challenges that the JWB faced as it navigated the demands and opportunities that arose as it became one of the three most-prominent religiously affiliated partners of the WWI-era War Department. By 1918, when Chester Teller delivered his optimistic speech at the annual meeting of the Jewish Publication Society, the JWB officially represented American Jews in the shared work of boosting the morale and morals of nearly five million American servicemen. The process through which the JWB attained that position and the compromises it made in order to retain it provide a unique window into the relationship between religion and state power, as well as the process of defining American religion and democracy in the twentieth century.

1

Border Conflicts

Looking back on his experiences leading the American Expeditionary Forces (AEF) in Europe during World War I, General John J. Pershing lamented what he saw as a dangerous lack of military preparation. In an article published after the war, Pershing wrote, "Our plunge into the World War, in the face of all our handicaps, was extremely courageous, but quite pathetic. . . . Only he who has witnessed the result of throwing half-trained officers and men into battle . . . and he who has been directly responsible for the employment of such troops in battle can appreciate the wickedness of unpreparedness."[1]

General Pershing had a point: The United States was not entirely prepared for entry into WWI or for the enormous changes that mass mobilization would bring to American society. As late as 1916, two years after war exploded in Europe, President Woodrow Wilson remained committed to keeping the United States on a path of neutrality. As the war ground on to deadly stalemate in 1915 and 1916, Wilson argued that, by staying out of the fight, the United States could gain the moral high ground necessary to position itself as the world's peacemaker while simultaneously building the financial and industrial bases that would allow it to challenge war-ravaged Europe's economic dominance.[2] The president had enough support on the issue of neutrality to win reelection in 1916 with the slogan "He kept us out of the war," but while Wilson and his supporters preached the virtues of peace and neutrality, other voices raised alarms that the United States Armed Forces were not ready for modern military conflict.[3] Some supporters of US military "preparedness" focused on the need to expand the size of the standing army, reorganize the National Guard, and increase the development of military technology. Others, however, saw military service as a means to fortify the health and character of American men. In 1916, unexpected conflict on the Mexican border forced preparedness advocates and members of the Wilson administration, as well as religious organizations anxious to prove what they could contribute to the moral well-being of American men, to take a hard look at the US military and assess its ability to safeguard the country and the character of its citizens.[4]

The Punitive Expedition

As early as 1911, prominent political and military leaders advocated for the reorganization and modernization of the American military and for the creation of a system of universal military training for white American men. Theodore Roosevelt, former US president and lieutenant colonel of the famous Rough Riders volunteer cavalry unit, was perhaps the best-known supporter of military preparedness. Yet many others, including former army chief of staff General Leonard Wood, worked doggedly to persuade the Wilson administration that the United States needed to reform its military and institute programs of civilian military training, which would both prepare soldiers to fight and uplift the character and morals of American citizens. General Wood had graduated from Harvard Medical School in 1880 and entered the army as a physician. Scholar Michael Pearlman, in his study of the military preparedness movement, argues that Wood saw military training as a therapeutic device that could be used to cure both social and physical ills. Wood subscribed to a school of thought that Pearlman calls "Christian pathology," which understood disease to be caused primarily by sin. Building upon the medical wisdom of seventeenth-century Protestant clergy who considered virtue to be the primary source of vigor, Wood believed that universal military training could promote both physical and spiritual improvement. According to his supporters, the hardy "physical culture features of military training [would] develop a new and better [form of] American manhood," while attention to "character building" within programs of military training would sustain and encourage the virtue required of truly American men.[5]

Historian Nancy Gentile Ford notes that General Wood and his political allies saw military training as necessary to the proper development of the moral, physical, and social health of the nation as a whole, as well as to that of the individual.[6] Concerns about the health of American society were thus embedded within the project of military preparedness, and its supporters focused particularly on the physical and moral decay that they saw spreading within the United States' increasingly foreign-born and urban-based citizenry. Roosevelt spoke and wrote widely about the need to protect the "virile fighting virtues" of white American manhood. Where once these virtues had been sustained through conquest of the American frontier, he argued, men now needed to pursue moral and physical health though a "strenuous life" defined by military service. Historian Gail Bederman has argued that Roosevelt understood the health of the country as resting upon the ability of white men to take up the "burden" of civilization and, in the absence of a frontier to conquer and natives to subdue, its forceful promotion through American military imperialism.[7] To preparedness advocates such as Roosevelt and Wood, the military offered a means through which the country's power could be asserted while developing the manly virtue of its white, male citizens.

President Wilson was no less concerned with the United States' ability to wield power in the world than his predecessor, but he saw the strength of the country in its ability to offer moral and ideological leadership rather than in its military might.[8] As World War I devastated Europe, President Wilson and his supporters rejected the call for preparedness as an unnecessary and even dangerous embrace of the sort of militarism that had led to the European conflict in the first place. Many members of his administration, however, shared the concern that, in order to protect the moral welfare of the country, its citizens needed to be better educated in the virtues of Americanism.

Massive waves of immigration since the late 1870s had made the United States more racially, ethnically, and religiously diverse and divided than ever before. Social Progressives such as Wilson embraced the idea that rational government operating for the good of the country could cure society's ills and uplift the nation through a combination of technical expertise and what historian Steven Diner describes as a "powerful if vaguely defined faith in Christian morality."[9] Wilson's administration resisted the overt militarism of Roosevelt and the preparedness movement, but it mirrored both their belief that Protestantism served as the underlying basis of American morality and their desire to improve the health and character of American men.

Revolution in Mexico, which had destabilized successive governments and threatened American investments in the region, challenged

Wilson's reluctance to engage in military conflict. On March 9, 1916—in retaliation for US support of his rival for power, President Venustiano Carranza—Francisco "Pancho" Villa led a small group of men in an attack on the border town of Columbus, New Mexico, and the unit of the Thirteenth US Cavalry stationed there. By March 11, the *New York Times* reported, twenty-three American soldiers and civilians had been killed in the raid, and Congress was "practically unanimous" in its support of military action against Villa. Senator Henry Fountain Ashurst of Arizona was quoted as proclaiming, "I think the army ought to be sent into Mexico to bring Pancho Villa and his murderous cutthroats back dead or alive. They should be brought to Columbus, where they made a funeral pyre of American men and women, and there be shot on the spot. In other words, I favor using grape shot and not grape juice."[10] The attack on Columbus outraged the public and raised concerns about border security. Wilson felt compelled to exercise American military power in order to seek justice for the Americans killed and to safeguard both the United States' reputation and American property.[11] With both Congress and public opinion demanding immediate action, Wilson sent Brigadier General John J. Pershing into Mexico with orders to capture or kill Pancho Villa.[12]

Pershing had been promoted to brigadier general by President Roosevelt in 1906, and he seemed to embody exactly the sort of military manhood that Roosevelt held up as an American ideal. He had fought against Geronimo and his Apache fighters on the frontier, earned his nickname "Black Jack" by leading the segregated African American Tenth Cavalry Regiment in the Spanish-American War, and rose to national prominence by subduing rebellion and serving as military governor of Moro Province in the Philippines.[13] Pershing led ten thousand Regular Army soldiers into Mexico in pursuit of Villa, while nearly one hundred thousand National Guardsmen were called to the border to defend against further attack.

The so-called Punitive Expedition against Mexico produced little by way of military glory. Villa was never captured, but the expedition bolstered the cause of military preparedness by revealing profound gaps in the army's state of readiness. Aside from the obvious lack of border security that had allowed Villa to successfully carry out his raid, the conflict exposed flaws in the army's ability to arm, transport, feed, house, and care for its men. Motorized trucks, for example, were used to carry military supplies, but little attention had been paid to their maintenance or to the training of drivers and mechanics. These oversights, combined with poor roads, no railroad lines to fall back on, and resentful local populations, meant that Pershing's forces inside Mexico often lacked supplies, including food for both soldiers and horses. One history of the expedition quotes an officer as saying, "I have been in three wars, and for unmitigated hardships, the Punitive Expedition was worst of all."[14]

The conflict with Mexico assured the passage of the National Defense Act of 1916 in June. The bill fell short of achieving the full range of reforms that preparedness advocates had hoped for, particularly universal military training, but it did expand the size of the Regular Army and the National Guard, provided federal funding for summer camps to train sixteen thousand civilians, and created a Reserve Officers' Training Corps, or ROTC, on college campuses in order to maintain a ready pool of trained men and officers.[15] Beyond these immediate changes, the Mexican Expedition convinced key members of the Wilson administration that the United States needed to prepare for military conflict. National security, it seemed, required policies and mechanisms designed to facilitate the fast and efficient mobilization of the country's military, industrial, financial, and social resources.

Among those persuaded was the newly appointed secretary of war, Newton D. Baker. Baker was new to Washington, DC. Wilson had tried to lure him to federal office earlier, but Baker insisted on first fulfilling his term as mayor of Cleveland, where he strove to eliminate vice and crime by building alcohol-free dance halls and amusement parks and by sponsoring pageants and programs that would provide Cleveland's citizens with entertainment wholesome enough to deter them from immoral behavior. With his term completed, the well-respected mayor arrived in Washington and was sworn in as secretary of war on March 7, just days before the mobilization of troops against Villa. Baker brought a deep commitment to Progressive social reform with him. Although he had previously supported American neutrality, in his new office, he embraced both the need to prepare for the possibility of war and the unique opportunities that the military created for promoting the moral and physical welfare of American citizens.[16]

The Welfare of Soldiers

Baker had no experience in the military or with military administration when he took over the post of secretary of war, and he was deeply disturbed by what he learned of the realities of army camp life. Reports of deplorably low moral conditions along the Mexican border poured into his office. The American Social Hygiene Association, an organization formed in 1914 by John D. Rockefeller Jr. and other social- and moral-reform advocates in order to combat the spread of venereal disease, sent accounts contending that bars and brothels surrounded the camps and that incidents of drunkenness, debauchery, and sexually transmitted infection ran high among the troops.[17] Baker saw the presence of alcohol and prostitution in military camps as a threat to the effectiveness of the army, as well as a moral and physical danger to soldiers and the women and children to whom they might return after their service.[18] He responded by appointing Raymond Fosdick of the Rockefeller Foundation to investigate conditions in the camps.

Fosdick came from an old-stock American family. Both his mother and father could trace their lineage to English immigrants who had arrived in the American colonies in the 1630s. They kept a deeply religious home, and Fosdick recalled that "from our earliest days, religion was for us children a vital part of the air we breathed."[19] His older brother, Harry Emerson Fosdick, became one of the twentieth century's most noted liberal Protestant theologians. Raymond Fosdick studied at Princeton University, where he first met the charismatic professor Woodrow Wilson. After completing his law degree at New York University, Fosdick went to work for the Bureau of Social Hygiene, which Rockefeller had founded to conduct research and influence public policy on venereal disease, crime, and delinquency. After World War I, he would go on to serve as president of the Rockefeller Foundation and long-term adviser to Rockefeller. Both he and his brother would work with Rockefeller to create the ecumenical Interchurch World Movement.[20]

By 1916, Fosdick had made his mark at the Bureau of Social Hygiene by investigating European and American police systems, and through this work he became acquainted with Baker.[21] Fosdick was an able investigator, and he shared Baker's profound concern for the deleterious impact of loose morals among the troops. He admired Baker, whom

he described in his memoirs as possessing a "deep social insight, a supreme ability to articulate his ideas in felicitous words, and a superb
courage . . . [with] a singularly serene and gracious mind," and was eager
to work with him on confronting the issue of vice among the troops.[22]

To social reformers such as Baker and Fosdick, conditions on the Mexican border revealed dangerous problems within the military and convinced them of the need for effective government intervention to promote
character building among American soldiers. For some reformers, in fact,
this opportunity almost made the entire Mexican Expedition worthwhile.
According to biographer Frederick Palmer, Baker thought about preparing soldiers in "broader terms than sheer material efficiency." He hoped
that "some good might be wrought out of the evil of war through the effect
of the right kind of army régime on the recruit. If he escaped permanently
disabling wounds and disease, then proper nutrition, exercise, and regular
hours might improve him physically; the tone of his associations might
give him a sounder and broader sense of civic duty and human fellowship."[23] Baker and Fosdick approached their work with a commitment to
advancing reforms that would protect America's soldiers from vice and
take advantage of the possibilities that military life created for increasing
virtue among American soldiers and citizens.

After several weeks of inspecting conditions in and around military
camps, Fosdick testified before the House Committee on Military Affairs
that his tour of the Mexican border revealed "an almost unrelieved story
of army camps surrounded by growing batteries of saloons and houses
of prostitution."[24] More privately, Fosdick and Baker were concerned
that the United States might soon enter a far larger military arena, and
they began discussing ways to address the disorder on the border and
create a cleaner and more wholesome atmosphere in the American military. In a letter to Major General Frederick Funston, commander of
the army's Southern Department based in San Antonio, Texas, Baker
brought up the problem of loose morals among the troops and stressed
the pressing need to address it, particularly "in view of the possibility of
our shortly having to undertake the training of large bodies of men—
men selected probably from the youth of the country, who have not yet
become accustomed to contact with either the saloon or the prostitute,
and who will be at that plastic and generous period of life when normal
and wholesome outlets for exuberant physical vitality will be readily ac-

cepted as substitutes for vicious modes of indulgence, if the former be made accessible."[25]

In keeping with their backgrounds as Progressive social reformers, both Baker and Fosdick felt sure that the morally debased conditions present on the Mexican border could be improved through effective intervention by the government. If young men were driven to vice, the former mayor reasoned, it was the result of neglect, a lack of guidance, and insufficient recreational activities. Finding ways to suppress more "vicious" indulgences while making wholesome ones accessible to soldiers became a central component of Baker's plans to prepare the military for future conflict. As Baker insisted in his annual report for 1917, "The significant thing about a true civilization is its spontaneous upward tendency and the young American instinctively prefers sound and healthy occupations and recreations, if the opportunity to enjoy them be but offered."[26]

As the Mexican campaign continued, the Wilson administration's War Department unexpectedly found itself promoting goals similar to those advanced by many preparedness advocates. While Secretary of War Baker never embraced Roosevelt's or Wood's vision of military service as a force for good in itself, when faced with the reality of having to oversee the country's armed forces, he became determined to use the military as means to promote what he and his staff saw as neutrally defined good morals and good character among the troops. They began a two-pronged assault on the degeneracy of the camps in the hope of promoting both vigor and virtue among the young men stationed there. Baker brought the considerable pressure of the War Department to bear on local leaders as he requested that they close down red-light districts near military bases and prohibit the sale of alcohol to soldiers. To build the characters of American men, however, he made the provision of healthy recreation—including sports, reading, singing, and theatrical performance—and the promotion of morality and clean living central to the work of the US War Department.[27]

Baker used the financial and legal powers of his office to fight the first part of this battle on degeneracy. Most local leaders complied with Baker's request to make alcohol and prostitution inaccessible to soldiers, rather than risk having him make good on his promise to remove military bases, and the income they generated, from towns and cities that resisted his plans for reform.[28] Baker had a harder time leading his second line of attack, however. Neither the War Department nor the military was prepared to implement the sort of wide-scale program of "sound and healthy occupations and recreations" that Baker advocated. Prior to the Mexican Expedition, only the military chaplaincy explicitly concerned itself with the moral and spiritual well-being of American soldiers, but in 1916, the chaplaincy found itself neglected, understaffed, and internally divided over questions concerning rank and salary.[29]

No existing branch of the government or the military possessed the staff or the skills to quickly implement a vast new program of social and moral uplift among American troops. Religiously affiliated civilian organizations, however, were eager to help. The Protestant Young Men's Christian Association leapt at the opportunity to send YMCA secretaries to the border to provide American soldiers with wholesome recreational activities and a healthy dose of spiritual guidance. The YMCA had first instituted welfare programs for American soldiers during the Civil War and had started to offer services to National Guardsmen along the Mexican border as early as 1911. The mobilization of troops and the friendly attitude of Baker's War Department toward its work and organization led to a rapid expansion of YMCA soldiers' welfare programs.[30] By August 1916, the YMCA employed approximately three hundred secretaries and clergymen, who organized entertainment and recreational activities, particularly sporting events, and put together "a constructive program of religious work . . . including Bible classes and religious meetings."[31]

American Catholics were also eager to support the troops. The Knights of Columbus, a Catholic fraternal order founded to provide mutual aid to its members and defend them against the accusations of anti-Catholic nativists, headed to the border. They estimated that Catholic men might make up as much as 45 percent of National Guard units from the North and felt that, without necessary services, these "thousands of Catholic men at the border were precariously situated so far as spiritual ministration entered into their lives."[32] The Knights did not possess as much experience working with soldiers as the YMCA, nor did they have close ties with Secretary Baker. Yet they saw the situation along the Mexican border, in which servicemen were compelled "to seek recreation . . . in the little border towns that were rife with dishonest and immoral camp followers profiteering at the expense of the boys," as urgent enough to mobilize their civilian volunteers.[33] The Knights' Supreme

Board of Directors called upon its members in border towns to create a "haven for men of Catholic faith."[34] The first order of business was to provide adequate opportunities for religious practice among Catholic servicemen. The YMCA, they argued, was an "essentially non-Catholic organization." The Catholic men at the border, they claimed, longed for recreational facilities similar to the ones that the YMCA provided, "but in an environment to which they were more accustomed."[35]

Jews Fighting on the Border

The presence of approximately 3,500 Jewish soldiers among the men fighting with Pershing and stationed at the border similarly drew the attention of Jewish organizations. They were also interested in helping to promote the welfare of the troops and in offering a Jewish alternative to the YMCA.[36] The Young Men's Hebrew Association was the first to stake its claim in the emerging field of soldiers' welfare work. The YMHA had been founded in the 1850s as a literary society designed to aid in the intellectual development of young Jewish men. It had aspired to be a national organization representative of all American Jewry, without regard for differences in religious practice or political affiliation. However, it had found that in the United States, where religious affiliation was entirely voluntary, Jews shared little consensus on communal representation. Regional, denominational, economic, and ideological divisions often trumped any desire for broad communal unity.[37]

By 1916, as the YMHA organized a branch near the Mexican border, massive waves of immigration had altered the demographics of the country and had made the American Jewish community more diverse than ever before. In terms of sheer numbers, Jews in the United States had grown from a population of perhaps two hundred thousand in 1860 to nearly two million in 1910, and like other European immigrants, their points of origin had shifted away from western and central Europe to the south and east.[38] These newer Jewish immigrants came overwhelmingly from the lands of the Russian and Austro-Hungarian Empires, and they brought with them theological, political, and cultural perspectives that challenged those of the more established American Jewish community.

Newer immigrants often understood their Jewishness differently from their American coreligionists, sometimes more traditionally, sometimes less, and the chaos, diversity, and disorder of this mass immigration created deep anxiety within more Americanized corners of the Jewish public. American Jewry had never been a united or monolithic community, but by the 1910s, Jews in the United States embraced a wider range of perspectives and affiliations than ever before. Some adhered to socialism or communism and thought of their Jewishness as a cultural rather than religious identity.[39] Others held fast to what they saw as traditional Judaism and rejected the openness to religious reform that they saw among established American Jews.[40] Some embraced claims of Jewish racial and national distinctiveness, and many joined the growing Zionist movement.[41]

In Jewish communities across the country, and particularly in the large cities where the highest numbers of immigrants were settling, more established and Americanized Jews embraced the ethos of social reform and worked earnestly to help support the new arrivals as they adjusted to life in their new home. There was, however, often an Americanizing agenda in these efforts. Wealthy philanthropists such as Jacob Schiff gave generously to settlement houses and visiting nurse services, which provided aid to new immigrants, but Schiff also supported aspects of the military preparedness program as a more forceful means of training eastern European Jewish immigrants in American cultural standards.[42] Cultural organizations such as the YMHA worked to promote education and acculturation to the norms of American society, but like other Progressive Era projects, they were not immune to the passion for social uplift. Efforts to help new immigrants were often intended to improve them by hastening their path toward appropriate Americanization. The help was welcome and sometimes desperately needed, but the condescension of established Jews toward their greenhorn brethren was not necessarily appreciated.

As troops mobilized on the Mexican border, Jews who had come to the United States as part of this massive wave of immigration represented a segment of the American Jewish community that was both large enough and stable enough to challenge the authority and presumed superiority of their would-be mentors. Eastern European Jews established their own synagogues, newspapers, and philanthropic and mutual-aid societies, and they resisted the advice and guidance of their Americanized, central European coreligionists. As the Jewish landscape of the United States grew more complex, Jews from different backgrounds and perspectives fought over who had the right to speak for all American Jews and to define what it meant to be a Jewish American.[43] It seemed impossible that any one organization could represent the character-building virtues that Judaism had to contribute to the US military, yet the YMHA set out to try. It established an army and navy branch and headed to the Mexican border to offer wholesome and uplifting activities to the Jewish men stationed there in the National Guard and Pershing's army.

Organizational insiders described the establishment of the Army and Navy YMHA in 1916 as a natural outgrowth of the association's other activities for the benefit of young Jewish men. In a retrospective history of the Mexican conflict, they claimed that the YMHA "soon felt called upon to lend its attention to the needs of Jewish men in the military services. An 'Army and Navy Branch' took shape, and, in 1916, when the United States sent a military expedition to the Mexican border . . . [a] special Army and Navy Committee was formed, and [YMHA general secretary] Samuel A. Goldsmith . . . was entrusted with the direction of Army and Navy work."[44] YMHA leaders, however, had far more pointed concerns than this account suggests. An article in the *YMHA Bulletin* of December 1916 praised the YMCA for the good works it had undertaken among American soldiers but made it clear that national YMHA leadership was concerned about the implications of an avowedly Christian organization working to improve the morals and the morale Jewish soldiers. As the article in the *Bulletin* put it,

> No sooner did they [the militias] reach their destination than the Young Men's Christian Organizations began making plans for their comfort. Christian influences were brought to bear everywhere in camp, and no efforts were spared by the chaplains of the army and the YMCA to surround the boys with all the Christian influence possible. . . . [I]t is not difficult to imagine the feelings of our Jewish boys, who saw on all sides the thought and care bestowed upon their Christian comrades and nothing for themselves. It would be hard to expect enthusiasm and loyalty for Judaism from those whom we neglect in times when they need us most, away from home, lonesome, and subject to possible danger. And so the National Council decided to have a YMHA at the border . . . and arranged to take care of the Jewish soldier boys who sought recreation without temptation.[45]

Initiatives to promote the welfare of soldiers thus brought potential dangers with them. YMHA leaders worried that if Christian organizations were allowed to be the only visible providers of such care, then Jewish boys would feel neglected and suspect that Judaism lacked the spirit of both patriotism and generosity that they saw in the YMCA. More worrisome still was the possibility that, without a guiding Jewish influence, the unmediated interaction of Jews and Christians would lead to assimilation and Jewish self-destruction.[46] Writing in the *Bulletin* about the need for civilian YMHAs, Rabbi A. G. Robison described the situation in stark terms:

> When we find that we can play with our Gentile neighbors we will begin to pray with them; . . . when the time comes when there will be no distinction between Jew and Gentile, either in their civic or their social life, we Jews will begin rapidly to disappear. Religious assimilation will go hand in hand with social assimilation, for the reason that the religious life is built upon and conditioned by the existence of a separate and distinct social group. When the Jew ceases to be a differentiated social organism, his religious life will absolutely vanish.[47]

If the threat of Jewish social and religious extinction seemed dangerously near on the home front, where young Jewish men could remain tied to their families, attend religious services, and make independent choices about how and where to spend their time, then the situation must have appeared desperate for Jewish men in the military, where the preservation of "separate and distinct social groups" lay in direct contradiction to military norms.

On the Mexican border, the Army and Navy YMHA strove both to provide services through which the Jewish soldier could preserve his cultural and religious distinctiveness and to promote the sort of wholesome atmosphere that the War Department increasingly deemed necessary to American military preparedness. It moved quickly to establish a field headquarters in Douglas, Arizona.[48] In a tribute to its director, Falk Younker, the *YMHA Bulletin* described his work with soldiers: "In a building set aside for the purpose ["to provide the proper spiritual leadership and entertainment for the hours of leisure"], he established writing-rooms with abundant material, game rooms for those inclined to spend an hour at play, libraries for the studious, meetings for the comrades of thought, religious services for all Jews at the various posts, and established a good feeling and respect for those of our faith by the force of example."[49]

The YMHA seemed confident that the creation of a distinctly Jewish social space, in which soldiers might relax and find entertainment away from bars and brothels, advanced both American and Jewish ideals. The YMHA could build character and promote virtue among young Jewish soldiers while protecting them from what its leaders saw as too much contact with their non-Jewish compatriots. "The Jewish soldier was a gentleman, a Jew and a soldier because of the work done by the Army and Navy Branch," the *YMHA Bulletin* proclaimed, carefully noting that its work advanced both the War Department's goal of turning soldiers into "gentlemen" and the YMHA's own goal of making sure that they continued to identify as Jews.[50]

By the summer of 1916, however, YMHA representatives at the army and navy branch in Douglas and members of local branches found themselves struggling to maintain their activities and provide "spiritual leadership" to Jewish soldiers scattered all along the border. Despite their best efforts, the YMHA men found that, as representatives of a fraternal organization without government or military support, they could neither reach nor accommodate all Jewish soldiers. By the fall of 1916, members of the local YMHA in Brownsville, Texas, complained that they had exhausted their funds and had yet to figure out the nature of their relationship to the Jewish soldiers stationed in their town. Far from being able to create the broad program of wholesome activities that the War Department desired, the Brownsville branch could barely convene meetings, elect officers, or agree on a mission. On behalf of the frustrated soldiers, YMHA member Percy Weisman wrote to the association's Civilian Advisory Committee: "The Officers elected Sunday a week ago were . . . more or less temporary. The representatives were self-appointed in part, as not all of the Military Organizations in Brownsville were represented. Incidentally, we have no Constitution or By-laws, but the most important feature we can [g]rasp, is that there has been no meeting of the entire or major portion of the male Jewish community, both civilian and Military, to determine their wishes in this matter."[51]

As the Jewish High Holidays approached, it became clear that local YMHA branches would be hard pressed to provide even basic religious services for Jewish soldiers and that they now faced competition from other Jewish organizations. The Central Conference of American Rabbis (CCAR), which represented the rabbis of the Reform movement, was also interested in the War Department's plans for promoting soldiers' welfare programs among American forces fighting in Mexico. But rather than bolster the efforts of the Army and Navy YMHA, the CCAR made its own plans to provide for the spiritual welfare of Jewish soldiers.

In spite of Secretary Baker's concerns over the morals of the troops, the provision of services intended to improve their character suffered from the same lack of preparedness as other facets of the armed forces. Little coordination existed between the War Department, the military, and the various groups attempting to offer services designed to promote virtue among soldiers, and there were no systems or mechanisms through which these entities could effectively communicate with one another. The YMCA, the largest and best-organized group involved, maintained the closest ties to the government. YMCA chairman John Mott was a personal friend of President Wilson's, and YMCA representatives built relationships with military officers and chaplains in lieu of a straightforward chain of command or administrative policy.[52] Jewish groups lacking those connections had no obvious means of making their presence known to the troops or of coordinating their services with soldiers, officers, the government, or apparently with other competing Jewish organizations.

In the summer of 1916, the CCAR expressed concern about soldiers' observance of the upcoming Jewish High Holidays and inquired with Secretary Baker about the appointment of a Jewish chaplain for the purpose of conducting services at the Mexican front. The possibility of such an appointment had existed, in theory, since 1862, when President Lincoln had amended military policy to allow rabbis to serve as chaplains in the Union army.[53] In practice, however, the War Department noted that it assigned chaplains in accordance with the faith of the majority of men in any given regiment. The 3,500 Jewish soldiers among Pershing's regulars and the National Guard along the border may have been significant in number, but Jews did not predominate in any single regiment, and thus no Jewish chaplains could be commissioned. When CCAR representatives suggested that a Jewish chaplain-at-large might be appointed to tend to Jewish soldiers' religious needs during the holidays, the War Department informed them that no provisions existed within army regulations for such an appointment.[54] The CCAR thus decided to send a rabbi to the front to organize religious services for the holidays of Rosh Hashanah and Yom Kippur under its own auspices.[55]

The CCAR selected Rabbi Isaac Landman of Temple Keneseth Israel in Philadelphia to be its representative at the front. Landman was a member of the Executive Committee of the CCAR and went on to an impressive career not only as a rabbi but as an author, a playwright, an educator, an advocate of Jewish-Catholic relations, the editor of the *American Hebrew and Jewish Messenger* newspaper, and the founder of an annual institute on Judaism for Christian clergymen.[56] Under his direction, the CCAR initiated a fund drive among its members and their congregations in order to support Rabbi Landman's services and the printing of prayer books for soldiers. A letter sent by CCAR president Dr. William Rosenau on September 1, 1916, to the organization's members emphasized the shameful neglect from which Jewish soldiers at the front suffered and indicated how poorly this compared to the care provided by other religious denominations.[57] The appeal requested assistance in providing Jewish soldiers on the Mexican front with the means to celebrate the holidays, but it also took care to mention that recognition had been extended to the CCAR by Secretary Baker. References to the secretary of war no doubt strengthened the impact of the fundraising appeal, but it also served to bolster the CCAR's claim to be able to minister to Jewish soldiers—a claim that quickly became a point of conflict.

In a letter sent to Rabbi Landman in August 1916 by Rabbi Samuel Marks of the Reform Temple Beth-El in San Antonio, Marks noted the existence of several good centers from which CCAR-sponsored religious services might be organized. He urged the CCAR to move ahead quickly, as delay might play into the hands of the YMHA, whose work he had recently discovered:

> It would be advisable for the Conference to send a representative here and have him look over the situation. He will have my hearty co-operation. There are several centres where religious services might be held on the holy days. . . . The Army and Navy Department of Federation and Council of Young Men's Hebrew and Kindred Association, New York ["New York" added in pencil]—whatever that may be—have representatives

of the ultra-orthodox type operating here with a view of pushing to the front students from the New York Seminary. It goes without saying that I should like to see our college students in charge of the above mentioned camps, at least among the soldiers who incline toward Reform.[58]

In a second letter to Landman, written just a few days later, Marks made his point even more clear. He wrote, "Would it not be wise to communicate with Mr. Freed at once relative to sending a college student before the New York divines get a foothold?"[59]

The "New York divines" expressed equal displeasure when they learned that another Jewish agency wished to establish its own bases for work with Jewish soldiers. In an exchange of letters, Morris Stern of the YMHA and CCAR president Dr. Rosenau each firmly assured the other that the rival organization's services would not be necessary. Stern suggested that perhaps the CCAR should attend exclusively to soldiers already identifying themselves as Reform. Rosenau, relying upon the authority given to the CCAR by Secretary Baker, replied, "The Central Conference of American Rabbis appreciates the welfare work that the YMHA has done. [But] the organization of religious services belongs entirely to the Central Conference of American Rabbis, and you may rest assured that the Orthodox, as well as the Reform elements will be properly taken care of."[60] Stern responded that the CCAR should stay out of San Antonio's business.[61]

Issues regarding the provision of religious services for Jewish soldiers proved to be controversial not only among different Jewish agencies but also within the presumably more-cohesive groups attempting to organize these services. CCAR member Rabbi Leon Franklin, after receiving a request for money to finance the printing of a soldiers' prayer book, refused to support such a project on the grounds that the CCAR Executive Committee had no right to tamper with existing Reform liturgy. He wrote angrily, "You know full well that I am not taking my position out of mere stubbornness, or with a desire to hamper you in carrying out your plans. . . . But here a principle is involved. I definitely hold that the Executive Committee has no right to authorize the publication of this book without the previous sanction of the Conference. . . . Who shall say that the Conference is willing to endorse such a book, when less than half a dozen members have actually seen it?"[62]

The "principles" in question were likely only those governing the actions of the CCAR, but Rabbi Franklin's outburst pointed to a far larger issue. If even the decision to publish a prayer book for soldiers or to offer holiday religious services on military bases proved too difficult to resolve, how would American Jews be able to participate in any wide-scale program for the welfare of soldiers? Who, if anyone, would have the authority to make decisions and implement these programs? And what sorts of spiritual care did Jewish soldiers need in order to improve them? Other agencies, such as the YMCA, might step in to offer help, but if the YMHA was correct that Jewish soldiers needed Jewish guidance and Jewish spaces in order to be made into gentlemen while remaining Jews, then this lack of order and agreement could leave them in danger either of failing to live up to the War Department's expectations of soldierly virtue or of forgetting their Judaism. The chaos on the Mexican border did not bode well for American Jews' ability to contribute to this crucial new field of military preparation.

Rabbi Landman did finally manage to hold Yom Kippur services for General Pershing's troops at Colonia Dublán, Mexico, in 1916. CCAR publicity materials described the services as the "crowning achievement of the remarkable enterprise undertaken and so successfully carried out by the Conference . . . to carry the message of Israel to the Jewish boys, wearing American khaki and marching under the American flag."[63] In a publicity piece entitled "Pershing's Column at Colonia Dublan," the writer described the magnificent scenery, the moving solemnity of the service, and Rabbi Landman's sermon on the theme of "Let Us Reason Together." He noted the acclaim of the men in attendance. The services, and particularly the sermon, received high praise both for the fine impression of Judaism they conveyed to the non-Jewish men present and for their success in bringing many of the Jewish men "back to the faith." The article stated that "some of the [Jewish men in attendance] later confessed to Rabbi Landman that these were their first religious services since their enlistment; one of the men had not attended a religious service in 23 years" and claimed that

> this undertaking of the Central Conference of American Rabbis, brought back to the faith many who had drifted away entirely and it effected a great number of family reunions. Boys who had left their home in anger

and had severed themselves entirely from all their family ties, were so moved by the spirit of the day and the influence of the service, that they were inspired to write to the parents whom they had well nigh forgotten, giving their families the two-fold joy of the reunion and the knowledge that their sons and brothers had once more came back within the camp of Israel."[64]

CCAR records offer no clues about what actually motivated these men to attend religious services or what had led them to "drift away" from the "camp of Israel" and enlist in the army in the first place. Some may indeed have been "moved by the spirit of the day" and pleased, after months—if not years—as a religious minority in Pershing's regulars, to congregate with other Jews and celebrate their Judaism. Some, as the article claimed, may even have decided to reembrace their faith and to reconnect with their families. But the disorganized conditions in Mexico may point to other reasons for their enthusiasm for Rabbi Landman's services. Indeed, the CCAR estimated that only 150 of the 500 men who attended Rabbi Landman's services were Jewish. It is possible that after seven months in Mexico, with limited services and difficulty receiving even food and basic supplies, these Jewish men—like the 350 non-Jewish men who attended Yom Kippur services with them—may have come to hear Rabbi Landman speak out of sheer boredom and an utter lack of other things to do.

The Commission on Training Camp Activities

Despite the publicity that the YMHA and the CCAR each gave to their own accomplishments with the troops, the tensions between and within the groups, the lack of coordination with other Jewish organizations and communities, and the absence of any official structure within which to operate led to limited success in instituting morally uplifting programs for Jewish soldiers on the Mexican border. The War Department, in fact, judged the entire experiment in providing character-building welfare services to soldiers engaged in the Mexican conflict to have been a failure. Raymond Fosdick praised the "imaginative beginnings of the work of the Army and Navy Branch of the YMCA," but he admitted that the task went "far beyond their limited funds" and that the work accomplished remained "totally inadequate to the need."[65] He reported with disappointment that "our army on the Mexican border was demoralized; that their morale was shot to pieces; that all sorts of vicious influences had been allowed to surround them and these boys were coming back home, many of them with scars not won in honorable conflict."[66] When called to testify before the House Committee on Military Affairs about the conditions American troops had experienced when stationed on the Mexican border in 1916, Fosdick told Congress, "The fellows went to the devil down there because there was absolutely nothing to do. . . . [O]ut of sheer boredom they went to the only places where they were welcome. . . the saloon and the house of prostitution."[67]

In April 1917, just months later, the United States entered World War I. Baker and Fosdick agreed that if they wished to achieve their goal of creating a wholesome environment in American military camps, their tactics would have to change in order to meet the demands of this far larger mission. In an address given in 1919, after the end of the war, Fosdick explained that as they had faced this new and far bigger conflict, "the President, the Secretary of War, and the Secretary of the Navy made up their minds that the conditions that surrounded our men on the Mexican border were not going to be repeated."[68]

They realized that, as with more material military supplies, the provision of welfare services had been far too disorganized and decentralized to meet the needs of either the men or the War Department and that in the coming conflict the need would be much greater. The number of troops involved in the conflict with Mexico paled in comparison to the nearly five million American men mobilized during World War I. Moreover, Fosdick noted, "the men heretofore volunteered their services." In World War I, following the implementation of the Selective Service Act on May 18, 1917, "they were to be drafted" and thus were both more diverse in the habits and values they brought with them to military camps and often less enthusiastic than their predecessors about the discipline of military service.[69]

The enormous numbers of men, the diversity of the troops (which would include large numbers of immigrants), and the likelihood that most soldiers would serve far from the stabilizing influences of home convinced Secretary Baker and President Wilson "that new social conditions must be created in connection with the military environment;

camp life must be made wholesome and attractive," and the men must be surrounded with "clean and wholesome influences."[70] General Pershing, back from his frustrating pursuit of Pancho Villa and named to lead the AEF in Europe, agreed. In his memoirs, he explained that he too had seen "the necessity for controlling the use of strong drink among our troops . . . [as] the habit of drinking was not only detrimental to efficiency but it often led to other indiscretions."[71] Like Baker and Fosdick, Pershing envisioned the American military camps as a sort of laboratory in which American men could be improved. Pershing, echoing the language of preparedness advocates such as Leonard Wood and Theodore Roosevelt, described them as places where "a rigid program of instruction is carried out daily with traditional American enthusiasm. Engaged in healthy, interesting exercises in the open air, with simple diet, officers and men, like trained athletes are ready for their task. Forbidden the use of strong drink and protected by stringent regulations against sexual evils and supported by their moral courage. . . . American mothers may rest assured that their sons are a credit to them and the nation, and they may well look forward to the proud day when on the battlefield these splendid men will shed new luster on American manhood."[72]

Eager to assure the success of their plans to add luster to American manhood, Baker sent Fosdick on another fact-finding mission, this time to Canada, to study military training camps.[73] When he returned to Washington, Fosdick reported that the key to efficiency in soldiers' welfare services lay in greater centralization and government control. Otherwise, he warned, they would be faced with a wasteful duplication of work. "In New York City, for example," he warned, "no fewer than seven different agencies are actually preparing to play some part in connection with this question and unless their endeavors are centralized and co-ordinated through some clearing committee, infinite confusion is bound to result."[74]

Baker, in accord with Fosdick's recommendations, established the Commission on Training Camp Activities (CTCA), a new federal agency intended to oversee soldiers' welfare services, and named Fosdick as its chairman.[75] The commission represented an impressive list of Progressive social reformers, including: Lee F. Hanmer, former field secretary of the Playground Association of America and director of the recreation department at the Russell Sage Foundation; Joseph Lee, president of the

Playground and Recreation Association of America; Malcolm McBride, a friend of Baker's and member of the Distribution Commission of the Cleveland Foundation, which supported the establishment of public parks and recreational facilities; Charles P. Neill, formerly of the US Department of Labor; Lieutenant Colonel Palmer E. Pierce of the US Twenty-Seventh Infantry and liaison between the CTCA and the general staff; Joseph Raycroft, chairman of Princeton University's Department of Health and Physical Education; and John R. Mott, general secretary of the International Committee of the YMCA.[76]

Baker and Fosdick felt confident that through the CTCA they would be able to effectively centralize and streamline soldiers' welfare programs in order to realize their goal of creating a clean and wholesome American military. The failures they perceived in the Mexican campaign convinced them that soldiers' welfare work needed to be conducted on a far larger scale, with more direct governmental involvement than had been tried previously. But the War Department also learned from what they perceived as the successes of the Mexican campaign, and the first lesson among these was the importance of the work of the YMCA. As the CTCA took shape, YMCA chairman John Mott's inclusion on the committee seemed like a foregone conclusion. What agency could be better situated to raise the spirits and improve the moral character of soldiers?

Jews and Catholics, however, remained deeply uneasy with the implications of turning this work over to the avowedly Protestant YMCA. They had also learned from their experiences in Mexico, and as the United States prepared for war, Jewish and Catholic organizations made plans of their own to protect soldiers' welfare and to combat the influence of the YMCA on "their boys." Jewish leaders involved with both the YMHA and the CCAR prepared for battle by strategizing ways to secure positions on the CTCA while fighting off competing forces within the Jewish community. For the War Department, for the YMCA, and for American Jews and Catholics, the United States' entry into World War I initiated a struggle not only to win the war but to define the sort of values that made good Americans.

2

Going to War

"I daresay," Cyrus Adler, the well-known scholar and acting president of the Jewish Theological Seminary of America, wrote to a colleague, "that some Army discipline would improve the whole House of Israel."[1] Yet as the United States began the massive task of gearing up for military engagement in World War I, army-style discipline did not prevail among American Jews. They remained divided by class, by country of origin, and by religious, ideological, and cultural differences, and they had little consensus about who, if anyone, had the authority to represent Jewish interests in the United States. During the Mexican conflict, these divisions had hampered Jewish participation in the War Department's plans for creating a program of morally uplifting social services in the military, but disorganization and lack of preparation had plagued the entire expedition, not just the small Jewish contribution. Given the contained scope of the conflict and the relatively small number of Jewish soldiers involved, disputes between Jewish organizations over how to arrange holiday services for soldiers serving in Mexico and on the border remained an issue of limited communal concern. Entry into World War I, however, made the need for Jewish soldiers' welfare services a far more serious matter.

World War I affected every community and transformed virtually all aspects of American society. When he spoke to Congress on April 2, 1917, to ask for a declaration of war, President Wilson warned that US entry into World War I would "involve the organization and mobilization of all the material resources of the country to supply the materials of war and serve the incidental needs of the nation." Wilson predicted that the army and navy would need vastly expanded supplies and new, more modern weaponry and that at least five hundred thousand men would be called into military service.[2] The realities of the war demanded far more.

After the passage of the Selective Service Act in May 1917, the Wilson administration implemented the largest draft the country had ever seen.

Drafted men eventually represented 72 percent of the US Armed Forces in World War I. During the Civil War, by comparison, only 8 percent of the Union army was drafted.[3] The government also established an array of new federal agencies led by men dedicated to Progressive reform and the implementation of policies designed to promote centralized, scientific management, efficiency, and civil and social improvement. Under the guidance of Treasury Secretary William McAdoo, head of the US Food Administration Herbert Hoover, chairman of the War Industries Board Bernard Baruch, Secretary of War Newton Baker, and others, the Wilson administration restructured the country's railways, highways, food production, shipping and ship building, industrial and munitions production, finances, international trade, and national defense. The government called upon citizens to become agents of the state by contributing to liberty loan campaigns and by voluntarily restricting their diets and use of manufactured goods, such as metal and rubber, in order to send supplies to the troops. It asked them to volunteer their time and energy to support the country's war aims by doing everything from knitting socks for soldiers to imparting patriotic lessons to their fellow citizens. It even asked average men and women to serve as the state's eyes and ears as it strove to root out political dissidents and foreign agents on the home front through the enforcement of the Espionage Act of 1917.[4]

No group of Americans felt the expanded power of the state more acutely than the nearly five million men who served in the WWI armed forces. They were a captive audience, subject to whatever training and guidance their superiors deemed most necessary and appropriate. Soldiers' welfare projects represented only one part of the War Department's massive push to ready its troops for battle, but both Secretary of War Baker and General Pershing believed that the protection of servicemen's moral and spiritual well-being was of vital importance to the country's war effort. The newly formed Commission on Training Camp Activities (CTCA), led by chairman Raymond Fosdick, took up the task of improving the welfare of soldiers and sailors and sought to enhance the common good by shaping the ideals and behaviors of a generation of young American men.[5]

The CTCA reflected the biases of the men behind it. To Fosdick, Baker, President Wilson, and others in his administration, the common good was rooted in Protestantism. While they described the CTCA's mission as strictly American and nonsectarian, its Protestant leanings quickly became apparent to Jews and Catholics. In Mexico, efforts to promote wholesome values among American servicemen had been disjointed and unorganized. Now they would be part of a coordinated, federally sponsored program that would affect all of the men in the armed forces, Jewish and Catholic soldiers and sailors among them. If American Jews and Catholics wanted to exert any control over the sorts of moral guidance these young men would receive as part of their military training, they would have to persuade the War Department that Judaism and Catholicism had something meaningful to contribute to the welfare of the country. But before they could do this, American Jews had to unite the disparate parts of their community in order to effectively represent Jewish interests to the US government.

Nonsectarian Soldiers Services

As with the Punitive Expedition, the War Department's World War I program for soldiers' welfare had both coercive and persuasive aspects. Coercive measures focused primarily on restricting soldiers' access to alcohol and prostitutes by pressuring local leaders for more stringent antivice legislation and arresting women suspected either of working as prostitutes or of carrying venereal disease—regardless of whether or not they were in fact prostitutes.[6] To bolster these efforts, the Selective Service Act also contained provisions prohibiting the sale of liquor to men in uniform and gave the president discretionary power to establish special zones around military camps in which prostitution was outlawed.[7]

The persuasive facets of Baker and Fosdick's program, those that would promote soldierly virtue by providing wholesome and compelling alternatives to the saloon and brothel, still suffered from a lack of government and military resources. Baker and Fosdick therefore decided to officially empower the civilian agency they saw as most suited to the job of promoting the welfare of the troops: the Young Men's Christian Association. Within days of the United States' declaration of war, the War Department recognized the YMCA as a partner to the CTCA and made John Mott, general secretary of the International Committee of the YMCA, a CTCA member. The YMCA established a National War Work Council and named Mott as its head. On April 26, 1917, President

Wilson issued an order describing the qualifications of the YMCA for this post, noting that its work was "so beneficial and bears such a direct relation to efficiency . . . happiness, content, and morale of the personnel" that he was granting it official recognition "as a valuable adjunct and asset to the service." Wilson enjoined military officers to "render the fullest practicable assistance and cooperation in the maintenance and extension of the Association."[8]

Baker and Fosdick assumed that the YMCA would be the only civilian agency necessary to the CTCA's program for building military morals and morale. The YMCA promised that its programs would be conducted on a "broad basis . . . the facilities and privileges being open alike to officers and men of all arms of the service, regardless of religious affiliation," but such assurances belied the organization's origins and mission.[9] The YMCA had been founded in 1844 in London by two young Englishmen, George Williams and J. Christopher Smith, who hoped to protect workingmen from the sordid life of the city through prayer groups and Bible study. Branches of the organization soon appeared throughout England, Scotland, Ireland, and Wales and, by 1851, in both the United States and Canada. During the Civil War, the YMCA provided Bibles and social services to Union soldiers, and the association flourished in the United States after the war. Membership in the YMCA was initially restricted to young men belonging to evangelical Protestant churches. Catholics, Unitarians, and Mormons were expressly excluded. By end of the nineteenth century, the YMCA had begun to redefine its mission. It positioned itself as an ecumenical Protestant organization and chose to emphasize activities that would complement, rather than compete, with membership in mainstream Protestant churches. It placed particular importance on sports and physical education as means of both developing a balanced Christian character in existing members and luring men to Christianity through the gym.[10]

The promise that the YMCA would conduct a program open to all soldiers was perceived as a threat by Catholics and Jews. Both groups had long been targets of evangelizing Protestant missions and certainly knew about the YMCA's strategy of using recreational activities as a tool for missionary work.[11] John Mott's position as head of the YMCA's National War Work Council, and as a member of the CTCA, only provoked further concern. Mott had presided over the 1910 World Missionary Conference and is remembered, among his many other accomplishments, for his book entitled *The Evangelization of the World in this Generation*, published by the Student Volunteer Movement for Foreign Missions in 1905.[12] Catholic and Jewish organizations immediately began lobbying for their own inclusion on the CTCA and in the War Department's programs for soldiers' welfare.

In his memoirs, Fosdick noted that he and Baker had not initially foreseen any problems in working exclusively with the YMCA: "Baker and I had assumed—and I think that most of my associates on the Commission shared the assumption—that the approach of the YMCA to its work in the camps would be nonsectarian. We thought that it would represent an American contribution without relation to creed or any other divisive factor. . . . It was with real dismay, therefore, that I learned that the YMCA had no real Catholic representation on its newly formed War Work Council. My reaction was that it was an inadvertence, but I was told that the omission was 'a necessity.'"[13]

In this quote from his memoirs, written in 1958, Fosdick expressed surprise and dismay that the supposedly nonsectarian work of the YMCA excluded Catholics, but this YMCA policy had been in place since the Civil War and had certainly been applied as the association built its programs on the Mexican border. It was, in fact, part of the reason the Knights of Columbus felt compelled to create their own soldiers' welfare program. But the YMCA was not alone in defining nonsectarianism in terms of Protestantism. Nineteenth- and early twentieth-century notions of nonsectarianism often masked what scholars of gender and performance studies Janet Jakobsen and Ann Pellegrini describe as "stealth Protestantism," sometimes expressly excluding both Catholics and Jews.[14] As legal historian Steven K. Green has demonstrated in his study of policies regarding Bible reading in public schools, "nonsectarianism was based on shared assumptions about the indispensability of moral and civil education and the interconnectedness of Protestantism and republicanism."[15] Or as constitutional law scholar Noah Feldman argues, nonsectarianism arose as a strategy for addressing Protestant American religious heterogeneity while preserving the centrality of the King James Bible in children's education. As Catholic immigration and anti-Catholic hostility increased over the nineteenth century, nonsectarianism became harnessed to anti-Catholic educational policies.[16] These policies preserved state funding for schools that reflected nondenominational Protestantism, which was deemed necessary for the moral and civil education of children, while defining Catholic education as inherently sectarian and thus ineligible for public funds. Catholic protests against the Protestant bias inherent in these policies made little headway until the second half of the twentieth century.[17]

In 1917, the YMCA was not at all stealthy about its explicit Protestant affiliation or its evangelizing intentions. Fosdick's surprise at the exclusion of Catholics may reflect his sensibilities at the time he wrote his memoirs but not those that initially guided the soldiers' welfare program he had directed during the war. By naming the YMCA as a civilian partner to the CTCA, the Wilson administration's War Department embraced a connection between the moral and civil well-being of American soldiers and the teachings and values of nondenominational Protestantism. The CTCA had significant power to promote programs and policies it saw as beneficial to the common good and to police and punish activities and individuals that it saw as opposing its goals. By naming the YMCA as a partner and its chairman, John Mott, as a member of the commission, the War Department transformed the YMCA into a powerful agent of the state. Military camps offered access to large groups of men who might not otherwise have sought out the sorts of recreational, educational, or spiritual services that the YMCA had to offer. Partnership with the CTCA gave the YMCA the ability to exercise real control over the types of outlets and activities to which these men would have access.[18]

Catholic protests against the appointment of the YMCA, however, began to challenge the easy connection between nonsectarian American values and Protestantism. Catholics represented at least 17 percent of the American population in 1917, and by some estimates, Catholic men were expected to constitute as much as one third of the American Expeditionary Forces.[19] Catholic demands for inclusion in the War Department's soldiers' welfare program and for protection from the missionizing efforts of the YMCA could not be ignored without jeopardizing their support for the draft and the war. Faced with these demographic realities and the challenges of building a conscription military, the Knights of Columbus soon received a position on the CTCA.[20] As Fosdick noted in his memoirs, "Under the circumstances we seemed to have no choice."[21]

Jewish organizations responded just as quickly and demanded that they also needed a seat on the CTCA and a role in caring for the moral and spiritual welfare of American servicemen.

The Jewish Welfare Board

Within a week of the president's call for war, a small group of prominent Jewish men met to form a new organization intended to serve as "a single, all-embracing agency for unified Jewish efforts in connection with welfare work among military personnel."[22] Cyrus Adler, acting president of the Conservative movement's Jewish Theological Seminary of America, spearheaded the effort to create this new agency, which was soon named the Jewish Welfare Board.

The founding of the JWB represented another step in a long history of attempts to create an authoritative national body to represent all American Jews. Adler himself had been involved in attempts like this before. In 1903, after a vicious pogrom in the city of Kishinev, in what is now Moldova, he had been one of a number of Jewish leaders who tried to work with the Union of American Hebrew Congregations (UAHC) and the fraternal Independent Order of B'nai B'rith to form such a body. However, Adler soon withdrew his support and instead partnered with a small group of elite New Yorkers to establish the American Jewish Committee (AJC), which advocated for international Jewish interests and protections.[23]

Adler was an ideal candidate for the job of building an organization to represent Jewish interests in soldiers' welfare work to the US government. He was American born and had excellent Jewish and secular educations. He had started legal training after completing his BA at the University of Pennsylvania but decided instead to pursue an academic career. He earned his PhD in Assyriology from the Semitic Seminary at Johns Hopkins University in 1887. Adler taught at Johns Hopkins for several years, but in 1892, he became the librarian of the Smithsonian Institution and, in 1905, was promoted to the position of assistant secretary of the Smithsonian. Adler was a prolific scholar and a tireless contributor to Jewish cultural, intellectual, and charitable institutions, with incomparable administrative and organizational experience. Through his work at the Smithsonian, he had become well acquainted with Washington society, and he moved easily between Jewish and non-Jewish political and intellectual circles.[24]

The list of other men involved in founding the JWB included a number of prominent Jewish leaders, and many of them, like Adler, were affiliated with the AJC: Judge Julian Mack of the US Court of Appeals for the Seventh Circuit; financiers and philanthropists Jacob Schiff, Mortimer Schiff, and Felix Warburg; Louis Marshall, the prominent New York attorney; Judge Irving Lehman, justice on the New York Supreme Court; and Herbert Nathan Straus, business executive and son of Macy's department store owner Isidor Straus.[25]

Recognizing that participation in the mass mobilization of the county would require the support of Jews outside of the clubrooms of the New York elite, the board's founders reached out to both Samuel Goldsmith of Young Men's Hebrew Association (YMHA) and William Rosenau and Isaac Landman of the Reform movement's Central Conference of American Rabbis (CCAR), in spite of their quarrel on the Mexican border. Leaders of all of the major rabbinical and congregational organizations in the country were also invited to join the new board. In addition to members of the AJC, the YMHA, and the CCAR, the JWB's Executive Committee included representatives from the Conservative movement's United Synagogue of America, the Reform UAHC, the Union of Orthodox Jewish Congregations, the Orthodox Agudath ha-Rabbonim, and the Jewish Publication Society of America.[26]

The establishment of the JWB represented an attempt to head off conflicts and bring all of these different Jewish groups together under one umbrella. As Executive Director Chester Teller reflected a year after the JWB's founding, "It is a commentary upon Jewish life in America, and particularly upon its work of national organization and management, that with 260 years of history behind it, and with literally thousands of organizations, no single agency could be selected as representative of the Jewry of America. True, one or two of them seemed to have some special claim to such recognition, but by reason of their limited constitution or platform, or for some other reason, they failed to secure the endorsement of the Jews as a whole."[27] The JWB, he explained, simply overcame these limitations by inviting everyone to participate in a new agency.

While Teller correctly noted that the JWB invited many groups to participate, it did not secure "the endorsement of the Jews as a whole."

The JWB's significant innovation in Jewish leadership lay in bypassing the support of a fractious Jewish public by securing the endorsement of the US government. If Adler and other JWB leaders could secure a position for their board on the CTCA, then they would be able to represent what they saw as Jewish interests through the authority given to them by the state, rather than by building compromise among the many competing visions of Jewish identity and affiliation that existed in the early twentieth-century United States.

JWB leaders such as Adler realized that the war had created a unique opportunity to assert communal control and to shape the American Jewish future. The reforming impulses of Secretary Baker's War Department and the power vested in the agencies that became part of its program meant that if the JWB secured a position on the CTCA, it would exert tremendous influence over the lives of Jewish men in the armed forces. No one knew for certain how long the war would last or how many men would serve, but few doubted that it would be many and that after their service, with their patriotism proven on the battlefield, these men would go on to become the new leaders of American Jewry. "Indeed," Chester Teller wrote, "in ten or a score of years from now, the eighty or hundred thousand, or possibly one hundred and fifty thousand Jews of our National Army and Navy will be the prominent Jewish citizens, the upholders of our Jewish communities, the leaders and workers of our local Jewries."[28] It was imperative, therefore, that Jewish soldiers and sailors be protected from the Protestant ministrations of the YMCA and trained to be both good Americans and good American Jews.

Nearly 250,000 Jewish men served in the WWI American military. They represented approximately 4 percent of all American servicemen.[29] These men volunteered or were drafted from towns and cities across the country and represented the full diversity of American Jewry. Any man who had filed papers declaring his intention to become a US citizen was eligible for conscription. Draftees thus included both the American born and the foreign born, some of whom spoke little English when they arrived in camp.[30] They included traditionally observant Jews and "reformed" Jews, as well as secular Jews. Some soldiers understood themselves as Americans and endorsed America's war aims, but others did not. Some embraced radical politics or ardent Zionism, while others retained loyalties to the countries and communities from which they had emigrated. The War Department intended for these men to be educated in American values. The JWB set out to make sure that the training and guidance they received in the military also kept them firmly rooted in Judaism and the American Jewish community.

The chance to provide welfare services to Jewish soldiers and sailors was a crucial opportunity to set a generation of young men on the right path toward the American Jewish future. The CTCA was charged with building men's characters by providing them with spiritual guidance, healthy activities, and educational opportunities and, in the case of immigrants, by overseeing their integration not only into the American military but also into American society. Civilian agencies working under the CTCA participated in this broad project of social engineering with the power of the federal government behind them. For the elite group of men behind the JWB, securing a position on the CTCA akin to that of the Knights of Columbus would give them an opportunity to protect Jewish soldiers from the missionizing impulses of the YMCA while shaping the values of a generation of American Jewish men. It would also allow the JWB to cement its claims to uniquely authoritative communal leadership by bypassing the community and gaining government endorsement. These opportunities enticed the men behind the JWB, but in order to achieve their goals, they would first have to convince Baker and Fosdick that Jews, like Catholics, required representation on the CTCA and that the JWB was the right Jewish organization for the job.

"Leading Citizens" versus "Secret Fraternal Orders"

As the war effort got under way, many Jewish groups showed interest in serving Jewish soldiers. As Fosdick warned in his prewar report to Baker, soldiers' welfare groups emerged in every American city and town. Local synagogues, branches of the YMHA, and the B'nai B'rith and B'rith Abraham fraternal organizations quickly declared their own intentions to serve, but the wealth, connections, and political savvy of the men behind the JWB helped them outmaneuver the competition. While other groups held meetings and sought the support of their membership, congregants, or neighbors, the JWB recognized that its success would depend on its ability to "assert and establish supreme authority in its field over all other Jewish organizations."[31] Rather than seeking support from the Jewish public, it went directly to the War Department with its offer of service. In a letter from July 1917, Felix Warburg congratulated Raymond Fosdick on the work being done in the country's military camps and reminded him where the money for such projects came from. "It ought to be a source of great satisfaction," he wrote,

> that as a result of your investigations the suggestions which you made to the War Department are being carried out. . . . [A]s one who was instrumental years ago in the start of this very work, I feel that the time, energy and support given this work was well worth while. . . . So as to save the community unnecessary expenditure and duplication of effort, the Young Men's Christian Association and the Young Men's Hebrew Association has, as you know, reached an agreement that the YMCA shacks will be available to the YMHA secretaries . . . and with that understanding Messrs. Schiff and I have made substantial contributions towards the erection of these shacks. I am very anxious that there should be full understanding and no friction between the YMCA and the YMHA and with that in view Col. [Harry] Cutler of Providence, a leading citizen and a man who has had experience in army life, an efficient, tactful person will be elected chairman of the Board which will have the Jewish Secretaries under him.[32]

Warburg's letter touched upon some of the major concerns of the CTCA. It emphasized the similarity between the YMCA and the YMHA, which would now operate under the control of "the Board," and a cooperation agreement already existing between the two agencies.[33] The CTCA had imagined that it could run a nonsectarian program exclusively through the YMCA. It did not wish to work with any organization that it perceived as representing narrow, sectarian values and ideals. Any Jewish agency authorized to serve American soldiers would have to demonstrate that it could complement the tone set by the YMCA and embrace government standards of nonsectarianism. Warburg, therefore, assured Fosdick that the JWB represented just such an organization. He noted that this new board would be run by the sort of man appropriate to the task: a "tactful person" and "leading citizen" with military credentials.

For this job, the board selected Colonel Harry Cutler. Cutler was a prominent jewelry manufacturer from Providence, Rhode Island. He earned his military title in the Rhode Island National Guard and had served as a state representative from 1910 to 1913. Cutler's family immigrated to the United States from Russia when he was a child, and he often recalled the challenges of learning English and adjusting to American life. He was extremely active in both local and national Jewish life. He served several terms as president of Providence's Temple Beth-El, where he hosted President William Howard Taft, who came to deliver a Passover address in 1915.[34] Cutler participated in local and national committees of the UAHC, the Zionist Organization of America, and the Jewish Joint Distribution Committee, as well as both the AJC and the American Jewish Congress movement, which arose as a challenge to the patrician leadership of the AJC. Rabbi Stephen Wise, advocate of the congress, snidely described Cutler as very much under the influence of "Schiff, Marshall, and the rest" of the AJC leaders who, Wise claimed, liked to "exhibit" Cutler "as a sample Russo-Jewish immigrant."[35] But despite the sniping between Rabbi Wise and leaders of the AJC, Cutler *was* in many ways a model immigrant. A self-educated man who had arrived in the United States as a boy, he had worked his way up from poverty and established himself in business and politics, and he was passionately committed to both his adopted country and the Jewish community. After his years of service in the Rhode Island National Guard, Cutler tried repeatedly to volunteer for military service in WWI but was disappointed to learn that, at forty-two, he was too old to serve. He took on the position of JWB chairman in lieu of his desired military commission.[36]

Warburg stressed that the board, with Cutler as its chairman, would operate with an appreciation of the CTCA's desire for efficiency and its dislike of redundancy. Of course, if this recommendation did not suffice, Warburg also reminded Fosdick that he and the Schiffs had given a significant amount of money to the cause. Fosdick appears to have been somewhat persuaded by Warburg's arguments. He refused to recognize a Jewish partner to the CTCA, but Fosdick did agree to give the JWB informal authorization to carry out soldiers' welfare work. It was an arrangement that fell short of the full recognition the board sought but still offered a first step toward the inclusion of a Jewish representative in this supposedly nonsectarian project. Informal arrangements with the War Department, however, quickly proved inadequate to establishing the JWB's authority over other Jewish groups.[37]

In order to quickly build a national organization, the JWB planned to establish local branches to raise funds, contribute workers, and provide activities and home hospitality for soldiers passing through or stationed near their towns. Members of the rabbinical and congregational organizations that had joined the JWB at its founding were expected to become JWB emissaries in their home communities, as well as to organize the national Jewish soldiers' welfare campaign by spearheading local soldiers' welfare initiatives and calling upon the membership of existing Jewish societies and fraternal orders to work under the control of the national organization. In light of the fact that the JWB had taken control over the work done by the Army and Navy YMHA in Mexico, JWB leaders assumed that local branches of the YMHA would willingly see themselves as JWB subsidiaries.

Many local branches of the YMHA, however, felt outraged at the JWB's claims to nation-wide authority and the suggestion that they should now have to answer to this new board. Albert Hurwitz, president of the YMHA of New England, was insulted by the treatment of his organization at the hands of the national board and declared to Colonel Cutler that he would sever all ties with the board and persuade all the YMHAs in New England to do the same.[38] Local branches of the B'nai B'rith also refused to recognize the authority of the JWB over soldiers' welfare work, and its national office in Chicago began work on its own welfare program. Jewish socialists, equally resistant, held mass meetings in New York City that declared the establishment of yet another soldiers' welfare agency.[39]

Resistance to the authority of the JWB created headaches for the board's national leaders, but ironically, it also helped to secure the JWB's position under the CTCA. In July 1917, Raymond Fosdick, perhaps still hoping that the YMCA might be able to do the job on its own, had made it clear that the board's status would not be equal to that of the YMCA. In his letter to Fosdick, Felix Warburg had suggested that in order to facilitate cooperation, Colonel Cutler could be made a member of the CTCA, like John Mott of the YMCA.[40] Fosdick said no. Swayed perhaps by the realization that if the JWB did not receive the full endorsement of the War Department, the CTCA might have to deal with multiple Jewish agencies demanding recognition of what they saw as Jewish interests in soldiers' welfare work, Fosdick now reconsidered. With Catholic soldiers represented by the Knights of Columbus, Jews had a legitimate claim to inclusion in this supposedly nonsectarian national project, and some of the competing Jewish organizations were not led by men as wealthy and well positioned as those behind the JWB. By comparison, the JWB's claim began to grow more attractive, and this proved crucial to establishing its place as the Jewish partner to the CTCA.

The B'nai B'rith adamantly opposed the JWB's authority to control Jewish soldiers' welfare services. Cutler, a B'nai B'rith member, tried to persuade the group's president, Adolph Kraus, to join forces. But Kraus had quarreled with Cyrus Adler and other JWB leaders in the past over the founding of the AJC, and the split between them created a lasting rift.[41] Now, faced with another attempt by many of the same men to assert control over American Jewish interests, Kraus dug in his heels. In spite of Cutler's attempts to persuade the B'nai B'rith to become a member of the JWB, Cutler and Kraus could not resolve questions about ultimate organizational authority, control over funds, and which group's name would appear at the top of the letterhead.[42] In August 1917, the B'nai B'rith sent a form letter to all its lodges announcing the formation of the American Soldiers' and Sailors' Welfare League of the Independent Order of B'nai B'rith and got to work undermining the JWB.

Cutler wrote to his B'nai B'rith brothers and urged them to give up this mistaken policy. He warned that the international scope of the B'nai B'rith made it an unsuitable partner for the American government in wartime and an inappropriate representative of American Jews: "As a loyal member of the B'nai B'rith, I think it is an imprudent error on the part of that institution, which has lodges in Germany, Austria, and Turkey, to endeavor to head the Army and Navy work in this country."[43] In case the suggestion that the B'nai B'rith's ties to wartime enemies made it an inappropriate representative of American Jews did not prove sufficiently persuasive, Cutler bolstered his argument with some arm twisting from the more influential members of the JWB Executive Committee. He wrote to the powerful philanthropist and JWB founder Jacob Schiff about his inability to make Kraus see the light and requested that Schiff use his influence in the matter:

> You and your friends should take immediate action in order to bring about coordination and co-operation in a work that is so altogether

different from the ordinary social service activities, fraternities and charitable endeavors. . . . If you would present your views, privately or otherwise, whichever you deem best, to Mr. Adolph Kraus, President of the Independent Order B'nai B'rith. . . . I am most anxious that our Board serve the best interests of the government, the men in the service, and our American-Jewish citizens. I am hopeful that as our work develops we may succeed in discharging this patriotic duty with dignity and credit to all concerned. This, however, will never be accomplished unless we can have a central clearing house.[44]

Neither Cutler's warning nor Schiff's arm-twisting, however, had much effect. The B'nai B'rith would not step aside voluntarily, and Cutler soon received reports of ongoing activities and efforts to foil the JWB's attempt to position itself as the sole representative of American Jews to the CTCA. In early September, Rabbi Isaac E. Marcuson of Terre Haute, Indiana, wrote to Cutler, "I had just about gotten things organized for doing something for the Jewish Board for Welfare Work when I was informed that the B'nai B'rith had gotten a letter from a Soldier's and Sailor's Welfare League of the B'nai B'rith. What's the matter, is there opposition again in the camp of Israel? Can we do nothing without fighting? Please let me know as I am chairman of both committees and can hardly work for both. What's the matter with Kraus and the Chicago crowd?"[45]

Another rabbi wrote from Waco, Texas, stating, "Last night the local committee had quite a strenuous meeting. A Rabbi Fox of Ft. Worth came to us with a proposition from Chicago headquarters, I.O.B.B. [International Order of B'nai B'rith] He took occasion to tell the committee that your Board was not doing earnest work for the different camps."[46] Rabbi Davis of "Fort Meyer" wrote, "I was greatly surprised to learn that the B'nai B'rith laid any claims for the local work. They came in at a much later date and expended no money although the authority for expenditure existed."[47] Rabbi Franklin of Detroit, Michigan, wrote,

A week ago last Sunday, I went to Battle Creek at my own expense for the single purpose of attempting to prevent the B'nai B'rith stepping in to a field that I thought was logically yours. Never have I spoken with greater passion than I did on that occasion. . . . [I]t was a hopeless fight. I set up the claim that I believed to be absolutely true, that the Jewish Board of Welfare Work and no other organization has been officially recognized by the government. This was strenuously denied by Rabbi Fox and I could not argue the matter as I did not have facts at my command.[48]

Cutler wrote to Kraus and suggested he "issue a letter to the lodges, urging them to cooperate with the Jewish Board for Welfare Work in the United States Army and Navy," but the B'nai B'rith was unwilling to accept a subsidiary position, and the JWB refused to give another group access to the advantages of controlling Jewish contributions to the War Department's programs for soldiers' welfare.[49]

Raymond Fosdick also received news of the B'nai B'rith's activities on behalf of Jewish soldiers when the fraternal order decided to approach the War Department for authorization to function as another civilian partner to the CTCA's programs. Judge Strasburger of the Municipal Court of the District of Columbia appealed to Fosdick on behalf of the B'nai B'rith. Fosdick responded and explained that the CTCA did not desire the services of the B'nai B'rith: "It has been the policy of the Commission on Training Camp Activities to deal with one agency alone, in connection with specific lines of welfare work. . . . Several months ago after careful consideration, we made up our minds that the organization best fitted for social work among Jewish soldiers was the Jewish Welfare Board, and that Board was recognized to carry on this kind of activity."[50]

By the time he sent this letter in early September, Fosdick may have simply decided to recognize the JWB on a more formal basis, but more likely, the threat of competing Jewish soldiers' welfare agencies helped persuade him of the necessity of doing so. Shortly after writing to Strasburger, Fosdick sent an official letter of recognition to Cutler that stressed the desirability of having all other Jewish agencies unite under the coordination of the JWB:

I am writing to reaffirm the arrangement made informally with your Board some months ago to the effect that this commission recognized your society as the official agency for Jewish welfare work in the military camps of the United States.

It is necessary for us, in each case, to deal with one such agency, so as to eliminate duplication of effort and overlapping of function. I trust that you will be able to co-ordinate all the activities along this special line which are seeking independently to work with Jewish soldiers in the camp.[51]

Fosdick's statement of support still did not put an end to the competition the JWB faced from the B'nai B'rith and other organizations, nor did it put the JWB on equal footing with the YMCA. After having received this letter of recognition, Colonel Cutler again broached the subject of having himself, like the YMCA's John Mott, named a member of the CTCA. Fosdick rebuffed him and expressed exasperation with the request: "As I have repeatedly told you, it will be impossible for us to make any appointments to the Commission on Training Camp Activities for the purpose of sectarian representation. Secretary Baker and I have both made the attitude of the War Department very plain to you in this matter. I am at a loss to understand what you think will be gained by insistence upon this point. My letter to you of September 20th in which I told you of the recognition this Commission extended to your society, is as far as we can go along this line."[52] The YMCA, despite its explicit Protestant affiliation and mission, met Fosdick and Baker's requirements for a nonsectarian agency and, therefore, an appropriate partner of the CTCA. They still saw the inclusion of the JWB, on the other hand, as a concession to sectarian interests, rather than as a desirable and necessary addition to the commission and its work.

Cutler and other JWB leaders, however, knew exactly "what was to be gained" through an appointment to the CTCA, as such an appointment would assure a Jewish presence on the commission and in US military camps and would guarantee that only the JWB would control all Jewish soldiers' welfare programs. The War Department's position frustrated JWB leaders, who remained determined both to fend off challenges from other Jewish organizations in their bid for leadership and to assure that Jewish welfare services would not be relegated to sectarian status in comparison to those of the YMCA.

Members of the JWB Executive Committee, therefore, expressed distress at learning that while Fosdick had rebuffed the B'nai B'rith's efforts to make itself a CTCA partner, Secretary of War Baker had opened another door through which their rivals could enter the field of soldiers' welfare work. On October 29, at the instigation of B'nai B'rith president

Kraus, Baker met with the leaders of Jewish fraternal organizations and announced that he would allow them to "carry on welfare work in the camps to a certain extent," with the intention of "widen[ing] the more or less exclusive privilege which had up to then been accorded the YMCA, and the Knights of Columbus."[53] Did Baker's decision reflect a lack of coherence in the War Department's policies? Did Baker not know of the conflict between the B'nai B'rith and the JWB? Did he want to displace the JWB from its position? War Department correspondence does not reveal the answers, but Cyrus Adler clearly saw this policy as a problem. He wrote to Jacob Schiff, saying, "I am rather disturbed by a statement given out from the War Department to the effect that Secretary Baker has agreed to allow all fraternal organizations to establish headquarters in different camps and cantonments. If this be correct, the Bnai Brith, Brith Abraham, Brith Shalom and all other similar organizations will probably in order to rival each other put up separate establishments and have separate workers and no unity can be maintained. . . . I very much fear that a way to disunion has been opened by the Secretary's ruling."[54]

Disunion, Adler knew, posed a threat not only to the JWB's authority but also to the whole project of Jewish welfare work. The CTCA, unenthusiastic about working even with the well-heeled and well-funded JWB, would not tolerate an uncoordinated field of rival Jewish agencies competing for access to US military camps. Moreover, in addition to the fraternal organizations, other groups sought to take advantage of Baker's decision.

In early November, Leon Goldrich, a JWB field secretary, reported that the socialist-leaning National Workingmen's Association had held a mass meeting in New York City. Seventy-three different organizations were represented at the meeting, and 162 people attended. They agreed to form a new organization, the People's League for Jewish Soldiers of America, intended to "enhance the spiritual life for the Jewish soldiers and to create a Jewish atmosphere for Jewish men in the national camps."[55] The entry of a socialist organization into the field of soldiers' welfare work promised greater disunion and the threat that Jewish soldiers, far from being improved as citizens, would be exposed to political ideas out of line with the government's war aims and with Baker and Fosdick's vision of the common good.

To Adler and Schiff, socialist groups such as the People's League must surely have raised concerns that the Baker War Department would come to see all Jews as potential radicals with views that brought their loyalty to the United States and its war effort under suspicion. Certainly, some among the public, within the Wilson administration, and in military command already espoused such ideas and would have been happy to see sectarian interests, such as those of the JWB, shut out of the CTCA.[56] But rather than weaken the claim of the JWB or cast doubt upon the loyalty of American Jews, the demands of radical groups seem to have strengthened Cutler's hand. Cutler wrote to Fosdick,

> I am enclosing a copy of an advertisement which appeared in the "War-heit."[57] You will observe that this is an attempt to form another organization for work among soldiers and sailors of the Jewish faith. I am informed that its sponsors are members of the socialist group in New York City. . . . [W]ould it not be prudent and advisable at this juncture for a public statement to be made by the Secretary of War, giving the definite recognition to this Welfare Board and urging that in just the same degree as the Catholic element has consented to the Knights of Columbus being its functional agency and the Protestant element, the Young Men's Christian Association, so should all organizations of the citizens of Jewish faith merge and cooperate with the Jewish Board for Welfare Work in the United States Army and Navy as their official agency recognized by the War Department?
>
> If you and the Secretary of War approve of this suggestion, and will immediately make such a public statement, it would, in my judgment, have a salutary effect, not only on the Mass Meeting, advertised for next Sunday, but also on the contemplated propaganda of certain secret fraternal organizations.[58]

Cutler's warnings about socialists, the "elements" they represented, and "secret fraternal organizations" seem to have found their mark. Fosdick responded quickly and assured Cutler that he would be happy to write a letter indicating his support of the JWB, which "could be published as widely as you liked."[59] A week later, Cutler received an official letter from Secretary Baker written on War Department stationery:

> Mr. Fosdick has told me of the effective activity of the Jewish Board for Welfare Work in coordinating the various Jewish agencies which have sought recognition for work inside our military training camps. In order to prevent duplication of effort, it was necessary to deal with a single agency, broad enough in its scope and organization to comprehend other groups seeking to do the same kind of work. For that reason, we were very glad when such men as Mr. Jacob Schiff, Mr. Felix Warburg and yourself, came forward with this plan for a Jewish Board for Welfare Work.[60]

A copy of this letter was printed in the *New York Times* on November 25, 1917, under the title "PRAISES JEWISH WAR WORK; Secretary Baker Writes to Commend Welfare Board." JWB publications dating from after November 1917 often contained copies of both Fosdick's letter of recognition from September and Baker's. The JWB pamphlet *Purpose, Scope, Achievements* featured reproductions of Fosdick's letter inside the front cover and of Baker's inside the back. The decision to display this evidence of the War Department's imprimatur of course made sense. Without the agreement of the government, the JWB could not effectively serve or even access Jewish soldiers stationed in American military camps. Without the full recognition of the War Department, it could not truly stand on equal footing with the YMCA, and without the power of the CTCA behind it, it could never hope to force other Jewish organizations to acknowledge its leadership or cooperate with its plans and programs.

Raymond Fosdick ultimately suppressed the B'nai B'rith's attempt to displace the JWB. On the same day that Baker wrote to Cutler, Fosdick wrote to Adolph Kraus, evidently seeking to establish the superior position of the JWB in matters relating to soldiers' welfare work. Fosdick could not compel the B'nai B'rith to agree to work with the JWB, but he could use the authority of the CTCA to shut it out of American military camps. Reiterating Baker's language about government efficiency, Fosdick wrote,

> For the purpose of preventing duplication and overlapping . . . this Department has recognized the Jewish Board for Welfare Work in the United States Army and Navy as the functioning agency on the cantonments and training camps among the men of Jewish faith. . . . Under

these circumstances it seems unnecessary for any exclusively Jewish organization such as the B'nai B'rith, the B'rith Abraham, and Young Men's
Hebrew Association, etc. to obtain passes to the military camps. I am
confident, Mr. Kraus, that the same end which you seek can be achieved
if you will submit to the Jewish Board for Welfare Work for appointment
under their regulation and employment under their auspices.[61]

Fosdick thus quieted the dispute between the organizations. The B'nai
B'rith never agreed to entirely relinquish control over its soldiers' welfare
programs, but Kraus did agree not to run competing fund drives. He
had no choice but to accept that B'nai B'rith activities for soldiers could
take place in towns near military camps but that the camps themselves
would remain closed to any Jewish group unwilling to work under the
authority of the JWB.[62]

Fosdick's letter, however, did more than just silence the B'nai B'rith.
It also indicated that, at least when compared to other Jewish organizations, the JWB had managed to make the leap to nonsectarian status. For
while he described the various other fraternal organizations—including
the YMHA—as "exclusively Jewish" and therefore inappropriate to the
task at hand, Fosdick no longer described the board designated to direct
and coordinate their activities in the same way. In comparison to the
other Jewish organizations clamoring for access to American servicemen, the JWB clearly emerged as the most suitable, most nonsectarian
among them. Fosdick and Baker may still have seen the JWB as a sectarian agency representing narrow Jewish interests, but by recognizing it as
an official agent of the US government, they shifted American definitions of nonsectarianism further away from exclusive Protestantism. The
decision to include the JWB alongside the YMCA and the Knights of
Columbus in the War Department's program for soldiers' welfare work
was not made with this goal in mind, but granting nonsectarian status
to Jews and Catholics represented a significant shift in the structure of
American definitions of religion.

Using the Power of the State

Throughout the war and the period of demobilization that followed, the YMCA—by virtue of its size, resources, and influence in

Washington—remained the preeminent soldiers' welfare agency, and Colonel Cutler never received a seat on the CTCA. However, along with YMCA chairman Mott and Reverend John Burke of the Knights of Columbus, he did receive a place on the Committee of Six, which advised the CTCA on "religious and moral activities in Army and Navy."[63] Cutler, together with Schiff and Adler, managed to convince the CTCA of the desirability of entrusting the JWB with the provision of Jewish welfare services under the CTCA and thus established the authority of the JWB among American Jews and over other Jewish organizations. The JWB's authority, however, always depended upon the CTCA rather than on popular consensus, and it structured itself as an autocratic institution resistant to popular opinion even within its own ranks.[64] Writing a half century later, the authors of the JWB's official history, *Change and Challenge: A History of 50 Years of JWB*, admitted that although the board expanded in an attempt to include the widest possible range of Jewish communal organizations under its umbrella, "the members of the Executive Committee directed the affairs of the JWB in a manner befitting 'the elders of the community.'"[65]

This preference for centralized and elite control did not always make the JWB a beloved institution with the Jewish public. It often found itself the target of popular resentment. An article entitled "The Problem of Welfare Work," in the December 14, 1917, edition of the *American Jewish Chronicle*, described attempts to set up rival welfare organizations and lamented the lack of unity in the provision of Jewish soldiers' services. It laid blame on the organizations that refused to support the JWB, but it also chided the JWB for acting without the consensus of the Jewish public. Things might have been different, the author claimed, "but there seem to have been very few of the national organizations invited at the start in regard to the formation of the Board. So far as the Jewish public knows, there was no general conference held of all national organizations, representing all elements of our people for the purpose of organizing the new work. The public awoke one day to learn that a new Board had been created, and to find a set of officers, a very excellent set of officers, had been elected. Who did the electing was not known and is hardly know to this day."[66]

The JWB defended itself against charges of elitism by reminding the public that it had managed to do something that had often seemed impossible: It had created an organization which, by popular consensus or not, could claim to represent the interests of all American Jews to the US military and War Department. Of course, it was only by positioning itself as the most suitable Jewish partner to the YMCA and attaining the endorsement of the government that this feat became possible.

Perhaps the best example of how government support sustained the authority of the JWB arose in connection with *Die Warheit*, the Yiddish daily that Cutler had pointed out to Fosdick in connection with ads announcing the mass meeting of East Side socialist groups. In late June 1918, the paper published a series of articles attacking the JWB and its executive committee. Featured among them were reports written by Joel Entin, who had managed to visit two of the US military camps with the largest Jewish populations: Camp Upton, in Yaphank, New York, on Long Island, and Camp Dix in Wrightstown, New Jersey. The paper's editors must have felt sure that they had a scoop with Entin's articles, for an editorial declared,

> When the Jewish Welfare Board was being organized, the "Warheit," after looking over the list of the organizers, called attention to the fact that they will not do anything for the tens of thousands of our sons who will be torn away suddenly from their homes and from their families and placed in strange surrounding. The "Warheit" gave an itemized list of the names of the leaders of the movement and pointed out that although they are patented philanthropists and Jewish "butters in" they still do not understand the Jew and, what is worse, do not care to understand him. The "Warheit" warned continuously that the souls of our children in the American Army must not be entrusted to these charity "butters in" . . . , because even though they will not poison them outright they will let them die of starvation, this being in accordance with their policy of fear and assimilation.[67]

Two days later, the first of Entin's pieces appeared, and the reporter warned his Yiddish-speaking readers: "You are in the power of Jewish-Germany-lackey-like do-nothings. . . . With whose power do these unwanted welfare workers exist?" With a power of the people! With whose money do they operate? With the money of the people! With our nominal consent—since we have not protested—they figure as our representatives, and they became the spiritual caretakers of our soldier boys. The people, having allowed the money collected for war relief purposes to be used for welfare work, these welfare workers rule with an iron hand."[68] The articles continued in the same tone into early July, urging the Jewish masses to reject the leadership of the well-to-do and acculturated men behind the JWB, but by then, Cutler had had enough. Rather than seek to dispute the claims made against the JWB in the press, he wrote to the Military Intelligence Branch of the War Department:

> I enclose herewith three clippings with translations from the "Warheit" of New York, entitled "The Jewish Welfare Kennel in Camp Dix," dated June 30th; "Neighbors with Jesus," dated July 3rd, and a "Letter from the People," dated July 2nd. These articles attacking the Jewish Welfare Board are due to the fact that the "Warheit," a radical paper, has been insistent that the Jewish Welfare Board shall institute recreational programs in the camps out of harmony with the policies laid down by the War Department, under whose supervision this Board is working. . . .
>
> [If the paper is allowed to continue sending its reporter, Joel Entin, into the camps] it will be a direct attack upon an agency recognized by the War Department on the same basis as the YMCA and the K of C and operating under the War Department's directions to enhance the morale of our men. . . .
>
> We respectfully suggest that such steps be taken as will put a stop to the bad influence of this correspondent and his publication.[69]

Concerned that Military Intelligence might not take care of the problem, Cutler also discussed *Die Warheit* with Guy Stanton Ford of the government's Committee on Public Information.[70] He asked Ford about the possibilities for keeping unwanted reporters out of military camps. Ford replied helpfully that he had

> inquired of the News Division about their control over correspondents in the camps. . . . They do not issue permits but . . . their representations would probably be heeded by any commandant and that if any particular correspondent was treating work related to the War Department either directly or through auxiliary organizations, in a way to create false impressions they could easily handle the matter if they had on hand some

examples of his writing. If through other agencies you have not effected a cessation of the articles in the "Warheit," I think we could be helpful if you would send me a translation of any particular contribution of their correspondent.[71]

Later in July, Cutler received a friendly note from Frederick P. Keppel, third assistant secretary of war, which surely made him believe that the Committee on Public Information's help would not be necessary. Keppel wrote, "Dear Colonel Cutler: I have sent you an official letter by today's mail regarding the 'Warheit,' etc. Unofficially I can tell you that the Military Intelligence Branch is throwing a good scare into these folks."[72]

Military Intelligence did manage to take care of the matter for Cutler. Keppel wrote again in August to say "a conference was held with the solicitor of the Post Office Department and he expects to take action very shortly against this paper with a view to revoking its license to publish without furnishing translations. . . . I feel sure that you may expect drastic action shortly."[73] Colonel Masteller of Military Intelligence wrote the next day to let Cutler know that "the action outlined in our recent letter to you . . . has been effected. We are also informed that further action to restrict their present privileges is about to be taken."[74]

In December 1918, *Die Warheit*'s owner, Samuel Untermyer, was called by Military Intelligence to testify in front of the United States Senate regarding his possible involvement in spreading pro-German propaganda.[75] By the end of February 1919, the paper had failed and was bought out by Morris Weinberg, the new owner of the rival *Der Tog* (*The Day*), who promised that the resulting publication, *The Day-Warheit*, would be committed to "militant Americanism."[76]

The example of *Die Warheit* demonstrates the power gained through partnership with the CTCA. On their own, the YMCA, the Knights of Columbus, and the JWB had no access to the coercive powers of the state. They had to rely upon their ability to persuade in order to attract supporters, raise funds, hire staff, and put their plans for the improvement of American servicemen into action. By establishing themselves as CTCA partners, however, they became authorized to use the expanded powers of the United States government to silence their opponents and get their work done. The YMCA was made a CTCA partner based on the implicit assumption that as a nondenominational Protestant organization, it represented the moral values and ideals that the War Department sought to inculcate in its soldiers and sailors. The Knights of Columbus and the JWB, on the other hand, could not rely on any such assumptions. They had to demonstrate their utility to the war effort and their ability to transcend their own supposedly sectarian interests in order to remain in the CTCA's good graces.

Maintaining the support of the War Department and the CTCA did not prove easy to do, but without official support, the JWB lacked the power to impose order and organization upon the diverse and divided interests of American Jewry. Indeed, as the JWB's plans for implementing its soldiers' welfare program took shape, Jewish soldiers and civilians alike balked at accepting the board's wartime leadership. But the Executive Committee remained convinced of the necessity for authoritative and appropriate leadership in order to protect the welfare of American Jewish soldiers and the future of American Jewish citizens. The support of the War Department depended upon the JWB's adherence to Baker and Fosdick's vision of upright American citizenship and the provision of welfare services deemed appropriate to the moral and civil improvement of American servicemen. This meant that the JWB had to navigate carefully between the different components of its mission. It remained crucial to the JWB that it protect the Jewishness of Jewish soldiers rather than exposing them to the ministrations of the YMCA, but it had to accomplish this goal without antagonizing the War Department or transgressing the supposedly nonsectarian nature of the soldiers' welfare programs. As its programs for soldiers' social and spiritual improvement developed, the JWB had to tackle the challenge of acting as a Jewish soldiers' welfare agency within a supposedly nonsectarian governmental program.

3

Making Judaism Safe for America

Speaking at the National Conference on War Camp Community Service in October 1917, Secretary of War Newton Baker discussed soldiers' welfare work and the vital importance of building a vice-free, morally upright national military able to protect young American men from the unspeakable dangers they would face abroad. Baker warned,

> These boys are going to France; they are going to face conditions that we do not like to talk about, that we do not like to think about. . . . I want them armed; . . . I want them to have invisible armor to take with them. I want them to have an armor made up of a set of social habits . . . and a state of social mind born in the training camps, a new soldier state of mind, so that when they get overseas and are removed from the reach of our comforting and restraining and helpful hand, they will have gotten such a set of habits as will constitute a moral and intellectual armor for their protection overseas.[1]

As the war effort progressed, the Commission on Training Camp Activities (CTCA) took on seven civilian partners, all charged with providing American servicemen with the "moral armor" deemed necessary to their training as soldiers and as citizens. These partner agencies comprised the Young Men's Christian Association (YMCA), the Knights of Columbus, the Jewish Welfare Board (JWB), the Salvation Army, the American Library Association, the Young Women's Christian Association (YWCA), and the War Camp Community Service.[2] Dubbed the "Seven Sisters" of soldiers' welfare, they sponsored educational programs and lectures, sports and athletic competitions, camp newspapers, and theatrical performances. They screened movies, invited entertainers to the camps, and organized dances and social events at which soldiers could interact with respectable and well-chaperoned young women. The YWCA established "hostess houses" designed to provide a homey place for servicemen to meet with female friends and family members who ventured to the camps for a visit. The Salvation Army staffed soldiers' canteens, and the American Library Association provided soldiers with reading materials.[3]

According to Baker, the agencies working under the CTCA needed to keep servicemen entertained, out of trouble, and filled with a sense of "righteousness" and the moral values of American civilization. In his aforementioned speech, he encouraged these soldiers' welfare agencies:

> You are the makers of that armor . . . this attitude of mind, this state of consciousness, this *esprit de corps* which will not tolerate anything un-wholesome, this brand of righteousness . . . this pride that they ought to have in being American soldiers and representing the highest ethical type of a modern civilization—all this you are manufacturing in your armories, in the basements of churches, in the lodge rooms of societies, the dinner tables of private homes, the rooms of Young Men's and Young Women's Christian Associations.[4]

The JWB faced a difficult role in this mission to arm young American men. Like the CTCA's other civilian partners, it had to tackle the logistical difficulties of establishing a broad range of new welfare programs for a rapidly expanding constituency of incoming servicemen. But JWB leaders also had to make delicate decisions about how to position their board and its work within the rhetoric of nonsectarianism that guided these programs. Having secured a position as the only Jewish agency among the CTCA's partners, the JWB now had to take on the challenge of demonstrating how Judaism fit within the framework of American values that had long been defined through both explicit and implicit reference to Protestantism. The CTCA had only begrudgingly included the JWB, and through it Judaism, in its armories of righteousness. JWB leaders now had to figure out how to present their representatives in camps and on bases as valuable assets in the construction of America's "moral armor" while also fighting to advance what they saw as the interests of American Jews.

Secretary Baker and CTCA chairman Raymond Fosdick wholeheartedly embraced the idea of using military camps as forges for young men's "invisible armor," and they saw value in this form of moral protection not only for its ability to safeguard American troops but also to effect positive change in the men's lives after their period of service. In both the conclusions and the title of their 1918 book about the CTCA's programs, *Keeping Our Fighters Fit for War and After*, Fosdick and coauthor Edward Frank Allen made clear the connection between wartime social training and American citizenship. Allen ended his review of the CTCA's activities by proclaiming,

> After the smoke of the battle has cleared . . . the men will be mustered out and returned to their former tasks. Those who are spared . . . will be better citizens than they were before they went in. They will have graduated from the "larger university." They will have learned the meaning of concerted effort, obedience, loyalty, cheerfulness, courage and generosity. They will come back with a new set of ideals, as men who have been tried by fire and found good metal.[5]

Secretary Baker expressed a similar sentiment in an October 1917 speech, in which he promised, "When this is all over . . . our soldiers will come back to us better citizens, not merely for the patriotic heroism in which they have engaged, but because of this lesson of social values which they will have learned."[6] Baker intended for soldiers' welfare services both to solve the immediate problem of keeping American servicemen fit to fight and to address the longer-term question of how to turn average men, and particularly immigrant men, into good American citizens. He and Fosdick saw the welfare services provided through the CTCA as a means to encourage Americanization and to promote the seemingly neutral American values of teamwork, patriotism, and sexual restraint, as well as those of "obedience, loyalty, cheerfulness, courage and generosity" listed by Allen.[7] The official rhetoric of the CTCA, historian Nancy Bristow notes, claimed that all of these values expressed distinctly American moral standards that would help to "remake the American populace into a legion of crusaders, better able to act as citizens of the American democracy."[8] The CTCA remained vague on how exactly qualities such as "cheerfulness" would serve to transform the American public, but it was confident that by instilling these qualities in the soldiers under its care, the United States would emerge from the war as a healthier, more united, more virtuous, and more patriotic nation.

The publications and policies of the CTCA stressed that it crusaded exclusively for the religion of Americanism rather than for any sectarian purpose and that all activities held on US military camps and bases must be open and accessible to all men, "regardless of religion or other preferences."[9] But CTCA programs were not open to all men equally. The US military would remain racially segregated until after World War II, so African American soldiers and officers had only limited access to any soldiers' welfare programs, although the YMCA did make some efforts to serve African American troops.[10] Similar to the prewar arguments voiced by military preparedness advocates, the "moral armor" and American values that the War Department wished to instill remained grounded in ideas about white male citizenship and in the seemingly invisible structures and assumptions of what scholar of American religion Tracy Fessenden calls "secularized Protestant culture."[11] But while racial segregation within the military remained the norm throughout the war, the inclusion of the Knights of Columbus and the JWB—and with them Catholicism and Judaism—in the CTCA's programs created instability in the official definitions of nonsectarianism.

Judaism as the Path to Americanism

Even after it became clear that the YMCA would not be the only civilian agency to conduct soldiers' welfare work, the association remained by far the best funded and most politically connected of all the Seven Sisters. As a result, it played the lead role in the soldiers' welfare campaign, running the largest number of domestic soldiers' welfare programs and receiving the lion's share of funds allocated for the operation of such programs. For example, the soldiers' welfare work budget approved by the War Department on September 4, 1918, granted the YMCA $100 million out of a total budget of $175 million. The JWB, in contrast, was granted $3.5 million and the Knights of Columbus $30 million. The allocations reflected both the fact that the YMCA was the largest agency and the War Department's assumption that the YMCA remained the most nonsectarian of them.[12]

While YMCA secretaries did, by all accounts, make their programs open to all soldiers regardless of faith, the organization also remained steadfast in its explicitly Protestant character and purpose. The YMCA's

Manual of Camp Work, which was issued to all YMCA camp secretaries, described the "fundamental objectives" of the association's work in distinctly sectarian terms: "What is the fundamental purpose of Army and Navy work as conducted by the Young Men's Christian Association? . . . It may be said that the simple and yet comprehensive objective in Young Men's Christian Association service is the making of symmetrical and serviceable Christian character."[13] The manual also outlined the basis upon which the efficiency of a YMCA secretary was to be judged: "The final test of his efficiency is how largely he is able to lead men, one by one, through his personal influence, through Bible classes and meetings as well as through the participation of the individual in service for others, to accept and follow Jesus Christ. His crowning service for any man is to lead him to allegiance to Jesus Christ."[14]

As the association readily admitted, and despite the CTCA's insistence that its soldiers' welfare programs represented only nonsectarian American values, proselytizing for Protestantism played a central and even defining role in the YMCA's mission to the troops. After the war, the YMCA remained proud of its record of service and evangelism. In the organization's exhaustive history of its soldiers' welfare programs, *Service with Fighting Men*, published in 1922, the YMCA echoed Secretary Baker's call for the forging of "moral armor" and clearly reiterated its wartime goals:

> The constant central purpose was to send men forth fit to fight, fit to die, and above all, fit to live. Whether to provide armor of defense from moral perils or to strengthen their fighting arm, the resources of religious faith and principles were to be made known to all men who would hear. This did not mean sectarian propaganda, for as will be clearly seen, Association workers cooperated heartily with workers from all faiths to serve all men. It did mean that none should miss a chance to know and avail themselves of all that religion could give. The objectives were stated in a letter to camp secretaries by Mr. Wilder, as follows:
>
> 1. To lead men in Christ.
> 2. To keep professing Christians loyal to their Lord.
> 3. To relate all who come under the Association's influence to the principles and aims of the Kingdom of God.[15]

To YMCA officials, the fact that they opened their activities and fa-cilities to soldiers of all faiths indicated their commitment to nonsectari-anism. That YMCA secretaries also took on the task of spreading news of the Kingdom of God to the men who came under their influence did not raise concerns at either the YMCA or the War Department. Seem-ingly nonsectarian activities, particularly sports, as a means of leading men to Christ played a crucial role in the YMCA's civilian programs, and the organization apparently saw no need to alter either its strategy or mission to suit its new government-sanctioned position. The notion that evangelism and nonsectarianism might represent contradictory goals appears not to have occurred to War Department officials. Indeed, any conflict between the provision of nonsectarian services and Protes-tant evangelism remained largely invisible to them. By the summer of 1918, CTCA chairman Fosdick noted that the Christian character of the YMCA might prove off-putting to some soldiers but argued that, given the pressing need for welfare services and the readiness of the YMCA to undertake the work, his agency would do nothing to alter the situation.[16]

To the executives of the JWB and leaders of the Knights of Columbus, however, the tension between the two parts of the YMCA's mission ap-peared all too clear. If anything, the YMCA's nonsectarian commitment to serving *all* soldiers made it a bigger threat to the spiritual welfare of Jewish and Catholic servicemen than if it ran programs closed to all but professing Protestants. The YMCA's evangelizing intentions concerned leaders of both the JWB and the Knights of Columbus, and they shaped their own programs, at least in part, as a response to the proselytizing ef-forts of the YMCA. Part of their challenge, however, lay in finding ways to protect the sectarian loyalties of Jewish and Catholic soldiers without provoking conflict with the YMCA or appearing to run afoul of the War Department's demands for nonsectarian programming.

Ironically the invisible sectarianism of the YMCA provided both the Knights of Columbus and the JWB with a secure platform from which to launch sectarian projects of their own. Knights of Columbus leaders called on their secretaries in the camps to make sure that "the Catho-lic identity and activity is not submerged" in the provision of welfare services and stressed that "if the YMCA is conducting an Evangelical institute, it is very essential that we conduct a Catholic program."[17] De-scribing the work of the JWB, Cyrus Adler mimicked the language of the YMCA and restated, in a Jewish key, the tension involved in asking religiously affiliated organizations to provide nonsectarian services. At the JWB's annual meeting in 1919, he explained, "It was resolved as a guiding principle to extend the service of the organization to soldiers and sailors without sectarian restriction, but at the same time to make adequate provision especially for the needs of soldiers and sailors of the Jewish faith, whose particular requirements could be fulfilled only by an understanding Jewish organization."[18] Adler's formulation, like that of the Knights of Columbus, lacked the evangelizing tone of the YMCA's mission statement but made clear the dual nature of the welfare agencies' roles. The JWB desired to demonstrate its willingness and ability to serve to all American soldiers and sailors, and indeed the War Department made this a requirement of its position. On the other hand, it remained committed to promoting a distinctly sectarian agenda of its own.

The JWB had fought hard for recognition as a CTCA partner organization. It won this position by convincing Fosdick that the JWB's values fell in line with those of the War Department and that its work would complement the program of the YMCA. JWB leaders could, therefore, afford neither to directly challenge the rhetoric of nonsectarianism nor to complain about the all-too-apparent Protestant bias within the soldiers' welfare program. Its best strategy lay in mimicking the approach of the YMCA by proclaiming its commitment to nonsectarianism while simultaneously defending the values conveyed through its own sectarian services. The praise lavished upon the YMCA by Secretary Baker provided the JWB with the space in which to situate its own programs. If, as Baker claimed, the "righteousness" that American soldiers encountered in "the basements of churches" and "the rooms of Young Men's and Young Women's Christian Associations" made them better citizens, then the JWB did not have to challenge the Protestant underpinnings of the War Department's program for building better citizens but rather had to show that Judaism also offered Jewish men a vital path to virtue and American values.

In seeking to link Judaism and Americanism, JWB executives followed a well-established precedent. Like earlier generations of American Jews, they responded to claims about the Christian nature of Americanism by publicly proclaiming the natural affinity between Judaism and American democracy.[19] Rabbi Louis Grossman, newly named as president of the Central Conference of American Rabbis, spoke on the theme at the group's annual convention in 1917. He declared to his audience of Reform rabbis, "Judaism and Americanism are identical, as in times of peace so now in these ordeals of blood. . . . Our Americanism has been surcharged, as it were, with the moral longings we had cherished through the ages. Our political fealties fused with our historically trained pieties. Jews were democrats long before America was discovered and before the Constitution was framed."[20] Rabbi Hyman G. Enelow, a Reform rabbi later selected to lead JWB activities in France, proclaimed from the pulpit of New York's Temple Emanu-El, "The genius of Judaism has from the first been essentially democratic, and . . . it expressed itself in democratic institutions and personalities even in remote antiquity, when the world at large was predominantly aristocratic. The Decalogue was a democratic code. The Torah was democratic in form and ideal. And no group of men ever were more represented of democracy in every way—in origin, conduct, and purpose—than the Jewish prophets."[21] Likewise, JWB chairman Colonel Harry Cutler assured his audiences that the American values for which they had gone to war represented "the same ideal and the same purpose that was handed down to us from Mt. Sinai."[22]

The English-language Jewish press reiterated these declarations of Judaism's inherent democracy and argued that, as a result, American Jews possessed a particularly strong commitment to America and Americanism. Judge Irving Lehman, Young Men's Hebrew Association president and a JWB founder, paraphrased the Psalms in an article for the *Menorah Journal* entitled "Our Duty as Americans": "In the meditations of our hearts, in the words of our mouths, we have pledged to our country now and at all times an undivided loyalty and support."[23] The *American Hebrew and Jewish Messenger* ran stories offering histories of Jewish military valor and participation in all American wars. It also published editorials arguing that the very tenets of Judaism demanded Jewish support of the American cause.[24] In one, Henry Pereira Mendes, rabbi at New York's Sephardi Orthodox Congregation Shearith Israel, answered the question "Can Jews be Patriots?" by declaring, "We can. We always have been. We always will be. But we must respond to our country's call, not only because our country calls, but because our religion calls to us to fight ever for Righteousness and Justice."[25] In another, the Reform rabbi Joseph Silverman urged his readers to remember that "patriotism with the Jew, however, is not merely a matter of birth or inclination, not merely a nationalistic impulse, as it were, but a sublime ideal fostered by his religion."[26]

Each of these editorials and public statements emphasized the loyalty and reliability of Jews as American citizens. Moreover, they argued that it was Judaism that made Jews instinctively attached to the United States and to American-style democracy. These prominent speakers, writers, and JWB supporters offered up a vision of Judaism that was perfectly in keeping with the values of Americanism. They also stressed that through engaged adherence to the tenets of Judaism, Jews could become better citizens and better Americans.[27]

Seeking to expand the Reform movement's Jewish school system in New York City, the Union of American Hebrew Congregations (UAHC), a JWB member organization, made a similar argument for the civil benefits of Judaism by describing what happened to Jewish children deprived of its influence. The UAHC's Department of Synagogue and School Extension claimed that since the start of the war, juvenile delinquency had been on the rise and Jewish children had appeared in the juvenile courts in unprecedented numbers. As explanation for this shocking behavior, they pointed to these children's lack of an adequate Jewish education. Without it, the UAHC claimed, Jewish children ran the risk of becoming "a menace to society."[28] A fundraising letter sent to UAHC members asking for support of the religious school expansion project explained the goals of the project clearly. The purpose of Jewish religious education lay not simply in teaching children about Judaism; it "was to develop good men and women, and as a necessary consequence, good citizens."[29]

Memos sent to JWB field-workers from the national headquarters in New York followed the same line of argument. They emphasized that "it is the duty of the JWB to assure that the soldier will make an improved civilian after the war," and stressed that keeping Jewish soldiers attached to their faith was crucial to this process.[30] In a 1918 article in the *American Jewish Chronicle*, JWB representative David de Sola Pool explained,

> The prime purpose of our work is to help the morale of the army by preserving among our own men ethical and religious values and the finer aspects of personality. This means stimulating all that is Jewish in our men, and offsetting the mechanizing effects of army life. . . . Such suppression of personality would be harmful to army spirit and morale. Therefore the Government has not only given its sanction to, but it has actively called for the work of the semi-religious YMCA, Knights of Columbus, and the Jewish Welfare Board, for them to bring to expression the depths of personality in the individual soldier.[31]

Assertions of the inherent Americanness of Judaism allowed the JWB to defend its sectarian goals in nonsectarian terms. Inspired by the War Department's mission of instilling American values in the servicemen of the American Expeditionary Forces, the JWB followed the lead of the YMCA and reconfigured its sense of purpose. It dubbed its work "semi-religious," based on the argument that if religion played a crucial role in building up the character and personality of the individual soldier, then Jewish soldiers required Judaism in order to live up to their full civil and spiritual potential. Soldiers' welfare work, despite all protestations to the contrary, would require a markedly sectarian component, as one could only reach the necessary "depths of personality" in each soldier by ministering to him from within his own tradition. The observance and practice of Judaism, JWB representatives claimed, would inevitably enhance American Jewish soldiers' commitment to their country and to the righteousness inherent in American civilization. This contribution to the larger project of stirring the moral and civil conscience of each soldier would more than justify the presence of distinctly Jewish aspects in their work.

Like the YMCA and the Knights of Columbus, the JWB provided welfare and recreational services to all American servicemen. But also like the YMCA and the Knights of Columbus, it promoted a distinctly religious and sectarian agenda based upon the assumption that men needed to practice their *own* religion in order to maintain their spirits, enhance their sense of virtue, and promote their development as both soldiers and citizens. As JWB chairman Harry Cutler explained at the board's school for training and preparing field-workers, "the Catholic priest, no matter how well intentioned, cannot lead our men in *Kad-*

dish [the mourner's prayer], nor can he lead our men in [the memorial service of] *Yiskor*, nor can he give that spiritual stamina which we must ourselves give to our men. . . . There is a definite thing in connection with our welfare work, that is to add to the morale of our men in camp, and this Board is doing that definite thing thru its religious and spiritual ministration."[32]

Indeed, the JWB touted its program for providing religious services to Jewish soldiers not only as a means of instilling American values in the men but as an example of American democracy in action. As JWB executive director Chester Teller explained in an article for the *American Jewish Year Book*:

> As official representatives of the Government, we are called to minister to *all men*. This by no means implies that religious work has no place in the American welfare program, or that the welfare agencies must reduce their efforts to that colorless, meaningless something which frequently goes by the name of non-sectarianism. On the contrary, the Jewish Welfare Board would not truly represent the American Government, unless it also represented the organized Jewry which created it. Indeed, specialized ministrations of each group to its own men in the camps are implied in the very organization which the War Department created.[33]

Given the War Department's initial reluctance even to include sectarian agencies like the Knights of Columbus and the JWB in its welfare work program, it seems unlikely that Teller's description of its intentions regarding "specialized ministrations" is entirely accurate. But by choosing to turn the soldiers' welfare program over to sectarian agencies, starting with the YMCA, the War Department began an unintentional process of redefining what the US government meant by "nonsectarian."

Decisions regarding the outsourcing of the CTCA's programs to the YMCA reveal the invisible sectarianism that led Baker, Fosdick, and others in the Wilson administration to perceive the Protestantism of the YMCA as religiously neutral, in spite of the association's explicitly evangelical agenda and biases. The inclusion of the JWB and the Knights of Columbus made those biases visible and revealed a flaw in the War Department's approach to improving the character of American soldiers. The War Department had argued that allowing Catholic and

Jewish agencies to enter the field of soldiers' welfare would create an unnecessary duplication of efforts and an un-American sectarian division between servicemen. The JWB responded with claims that Jews could only be improved by appeal to their own tradition. The promotion of good values and good citizenship required the free expression of religious difference. JWB leaders thus offered a new definition of nonsectarianism, one that refuted the easy association of American values and Protestantism and instead argued that Protestants, Catholics, and Jews all had equal claim to American values. Secretary of War Baker did not initiate the soldiers' welfare program in hopes of dislodging Protestant norms, but the seemingly necessary presence of both Jews and Catholics in the work of the CTCA led the War Department toward a tentative embrace of religious pluralism. As scholar of religion and Jewish studies Sarah Imhoff notes in her recent study of masculinity and American Judaism, however, American ideas about "good" religion were still shaped by reference to Protestantism. Religious practices or beliefs that did not conform to Protestant norms could not easily be understood as contributing to good citizenship.[34] In order to effectively insist that Judaism was vital to the moral development of American soldiers, the JWB needed to be sure that the Judaism it presented in the US military resembled the structures of Protestantism.

The Kosher Food Controversy

No issue tested the JWB's arguments for pluralism or its ability to work within both Jewish tradition and the parameters for soldiers' welfare work set by the CTCA more than that of kosher food. Around this issue, the JWB found its claims for the Americanism of Jewish religious practice pitted against both the demands of military life and the definition of religion recognized by the US War Department.

JWB executives understood that the provision of kosher food would become a pressing issue as soon as Jewish recruits began arriving in military training camps. For traditionally observant Jews, strict dietary laws regulating procedures for slaughtering animals, preparing meats, cooking, and determining which foods are kosher (permissible to eat) and which are *tref* (prohibited) played a central role in their daily lives and did not allow for laxity on the part of soldiers. The authoritative text on the matter was *Mahaneh Israel* by Rabbi Israel Meir Kagan, known as the Chafetz Chaim. Published in 1881 as a guide for Jewish soldiers serving in the Russian army, it urged soldiers to make every effort to obtain kosher food. (In 1943, Rabbi Moshe Yoshor would publish in English-language version for American soldiers fighting in World War II. He reiterated the Chafetz Chaim's position and suggested that should it prove impossible to get kosher food, Jewish soldiers should adopt a vegetarian diet.[35])

The Selective Service Act of 1917 drew Jewish American men from across the religious spectrum into military service. For the Orthodox among them, the question of what they could or would eat had to be addressed immediately. Orthodox representatives on the JWB saw the provision of kosher food on military bases as a matter of necessity and an obvious extension of the JWB's other "semi-religious" Jewish welfare activities. For them, the only question lay in how to assure an adequate supply of kosher food. For other members of the JWB, however, the provision of kosher food strayed too far from normative American definitions of religion to be either practical or advisable in the US military.

The provision of kosher food on military bases across the country would have presented daunting challenges under any circumstance. In 1917 and 1918—and indeed until after World War II—no centralized standard for kosher certification existed in the United States. Different cities organized their own systems for certifying foods as kosher and had little interest in working together. Even within cities with large Jewish populations, such as New York, kosher certification was chaotic and sometimes unreliable as different rabbis, slaughterhouses, and butchers competed for the right to claim authority over the provision of kosher meats and hurled accusations of corruption at one another.[36] Without uniform national standards, questions of who could supply and supervise the provision of kosher food to the US military would have almost certainly proved impossible to resolve. But even if it had been possible, not all board members agreed that providing kosher food fell under the JWB's purview.

Dr. Bernard Drachman of the Union of Orthodox Jewish Congregations raised the matter at a JWB Executive Committee meeting a few weeks into the war. The ensuing debate revealed the ideological and logistical challenges that kosher food provoked. A letter written to the

Reform rabbi George Zepin described the scene that took place at the meeting:

> Dr. Drachman brought up the question of *Kashruth* [kosher observance]. He proposed to have the government supply kosher food to Jewish soldiers, as is being done in Austria. Mr. Rosenstamm objected on the ground that emphasizing this matter officially would be objectionable to a great many Jews and would interfere with the securing of financial support. Dr. Adler suggested that if the government could not do so, this Board could undertake the matter of supplying kosher food wherever it was requested at its own expense, provided that a specific fund was raised for this purpose. He volunteered to ascertain unofficially through Congressman Siegel of this city if the government would cooperate in this matter. It was also thought advisable that the suggestion should be made to the Hebrew National Sausage Factories to attempt to secure government contracts for supplying to the army their various canned products, of which they have a great variety.[37]

The enclosed report of the JWB Executive Committee meeting indicated that Drachman and other Orthodox leaders felt that the JWB should move swiftly to demand that the government provide Jewish soldiers with kosher food based on the logic that if Austria could do it, the United States could do so as well.[38] In making such an argument, however, Drachman seemed remarkably tone deaf to the implications of drawing parallels between the needs of Jewish servicemen in the American Expeditionary Forces and those of Jews serving in an enemy army. Presumably, for him and other Orthodox leaders, Jewish religious practice—in this case the observance of dietary laws—outweighed national divisions and even wartime enmity, but this focus on the ways that Judaism unified Jews across boundaries and in spite of the war flew in the face of the JWB's goals and its conception of American Judaism. The board's work emphasized the perfect agreement between Judaism and American democracy. It could not then point to imperial Austria as an example of how Jewish needs might be better served. To do so would raise the specter of international Jewish conspiracies and allegiances and the suggestion that Judaism might not complement Americanism as perfectly as the JWB claimed. Historian Joseph Bendersky, in his study of anti-Semitism in the US Army, argues that many military officers were already inclined to accept anti-Semitic tropes about the conspiracies of "international Jewry," including those found in the notorious forgery *The Protocols of the Elders of Zion*, which was translated into English in 1918 and circulated among Military Intelligence Branch officials.[39] In such an atmosphere, the JWB could not afford to suggest that American Jews placed any loyalty above that of citizenship.

To Reform Jewish members of the board such as Rosenstamm, arguments like Drachman's also raised concerns that the JWB catered too much to Orthodox opinions and "*goluth* [diaspora] sentiments," rather than the actual needs of American Jewish servicemen.[40] While many American Jews certainly continued to observe traditional Jewish dietary practices, many others did not, likely due to their desire to embrace American norms, the lure of nonkosher foods, and the challenge of assuring access to reliably kosher products. Expending JWB funds and energies on the provision of kosher food, let alone arguing that the American military should base its own policies on those of Austria, would not draw American Jews together, Rosenstamm warned. Instead it ran the risk of alienating Reform Jews who were uninterested in having their financial donations used to promote traditional religious practices.[41]

JWB founder Cyrus Adler did not focus on the religious or denominational aspects of the debate over kosher food but, instead, on what JWB demands for kosher food might mean for the board's crucial relationship to the government. He hesitated to press the matter directly and preferred to work through back channels to ascertain whether such a demand would be received favorably before making the politically risky move of asking for special treatment for Jewish soldiers. To some Executive Committee members, including Chairman Harry Cutler, it seemed clear that by demanding kosher food, the JWB would push the boundaries of nonsectarianism beyond the limits of what the War Department would tolerate. Religious services could be defended as the Jewish equivalent of YMCA services or Bible study sessions, but pursuing a religious program for Jewish soldiers that had no parallel in the programs of the YMCA carried with it the risk of affirming suspicions of the JWB's sectarian nature and Judaism's incompatibility with the goals of the War Department.

These concerns dictated the JWB's approach to discussions with various military and government agencies regarding the possibility of providing kosher food on military bases. In a letter to the paymaster general of the Department of the Navy, Colonel Cutler reiterated the JWB's claim that only through adherence to their own religious traditions and practice could Jewish men be made into better soldiers and citizens. Cutler refrained, however, both from making demands and from indicating that Jewish tradition was inflexible on the question of kosher food:

> As to the question of feasibility, the Navy Department must of course decide; and this Board has no intention or desire to embarrass the government in any way, in the prosecution of the War; moreover, all of the great Jewish legal authorities have declared for many hundreds of years, that religious laws may be set aside in the defense of one's country. We believe, moreover, that the morale of the men in the service is strengthened and improved by the maintenance of their religious customs and practices.[42]

Cutler's gentle request reveals the delicacy of the JWB's position. The board depended upon the continued good will of the government and could not afford to jeopardize its position with the CTCA. There were limits to what the military was either willing or able to do in order to support the religious practices of a small minority of its men. Cutler, Adler, and other Executive Committee members therefore opted to tread lightly on the question of kosher food in order to protect their special status under the War Department. Religious customs and practices that corresponded neither to more natural-seeming Protestant norms nor to the attitudes and policies of the military and the War Department could, Cutler implied, be abrogated for the national good.

Orthodox Jews disagreed, and they grew increasingly frustrated with the timidity of the JWB's approach. Letters of complaint came in to JWB offices, and the Yiddish press published reports of Orthodox soldiers living on nothing but bread and water rather than eating nonkosher food.[43] Orthodox leaders became impatient with the JWB and demanded that the need for kosher food be addressed. Albert Lucas, secretary of the Union of Orthodox Jewish Congregations and antimissionary crusader, wrote to Cutler and asked him to try harder to make the government understand the urgency and importance of requests for kosher food:

We turn to you as head of the one organization, which has been officially recognized as authorized to do religious work in the army and navy of the United States. . . .

We need not point out to you that Kosher food is a matter of vital importance to conscientious Jews. You as a Jew know this perfectly well. . . . We do not think that the Government is fully informed concerning the matter or quite realizes the attitude of the Orthodox Jew in regards thereto . . . We desire to cooperate with you and we do not desire to undertake any independent action recognizing that the Welfare Board is authorized to deal with these matters. But we do ask and hope that this matter will be properly settled; namely; by arrangements providing for such Jewish soldiers and sailors who desire Kosher food.[44]

Lucas remained somewhat restrained in his request to Cutler. He took care to acknowledge the leadership of the JWB, of which the Union of Orthodox Jewish Congregations was a constituent member, and he assured Cutler that his organization had no plans to defect. Instead, he appealed to Cutler's sense of Jewish solidarity and religious responsibility to spur the JWB to action, rather than threaten its authority to represent American Jews and American Judaism in the US military. He suggested that perhaps the problem resulted from a lack of knowledge on the part of a government that could not appreciate the importance of dietary laws in traditional Jewish religious observance. If Cutler could make this clear, Lucas suggested, then the problem might be easily resolved.

Lucas may have guessed correctly that many in the government did not fully understand the significance of kosher food, but he did not see the issue through the eyes of the JWB Executive Committee. The JWB justified the religious components of its program through an appeal to the role of religion in creating better soldiers and citizens, and it used the government's acceptance of the evangelizing aspects of the YMCA's work as evidence that religion had a place in the CTCA's supposedly nonsectarian mission. If Protestantism was the only truly invisible form of sectarian practice in the military, then Judaism needed to resemble Protestantism in order for the JWB to avoid charges of sectarian divisiveness. Religious services, even those held on Saturday rather than Sunday, clearly resembled Protestant religious practice. However, dietary restrictions, no matter how central to traditional Jewish practice, did not. Adler and Cutler worried that emphasizing the ways that Judaism differed from Protestant Christianity would raise concerns that the two religions espoused different values, that Judaism did not sufficiently reinforce Americanism, and that Jewish men differed in crucial ways from their non-Jewish compatriots. As they debated how to fulfill their responsibility to Jewish soldiers, represent Jewish interests to the military and the government, and maintain their position under the CTCA, they concluded that demanding kosher food took them a step too far.[45]

Other Jewish organizations took a more aggressive stance. Stung, perhaps, by their exclusion from the JWB Executive Committee and less interested in defining Jewishness with reference to Protestantism, Zionist groups saw the debate on kosher food as an opportunity to assert their own claims to American Jewish leadership. In a call to Cyrus Adler, Rabbi Drachman of the Union of Orthodox Jewish Congregations reported that "the Zionist organization [of America]," despite its secular orientation, had decided to take up the cause of kosher food.[46] Drachman claimed that American Zionist leader and Supreme Court justice Louis Brandeis had been asked to use his influence in Washington "in the matter of procuring Kosher food for the soldiers."[47] Moses Hyamson, rabbi of the Orthodox Congregation Orach Chaim in New York City and former acting chief rabbi of England, called Adler with a similar report, adding that Rabbi Margolies, president of the Orthodox Agudath ha-Rabbonim and himself a member of the JWB Executive Committee, had also contacted Justice Brandeis. According to Hyamson, Brandeis and Zionist leader Jacob de Haas had proposed to Secretary Baker that "Jewish organizations would provide the sum of $25,000 for additional kitchen utensils" if "the War Department would endeavor to have a kosher kitchen for each two companies in which there were a sufficient number of Jewish men who desired kosher food, the experiment to be initiated at Camp Upton."[48]

Brandeis was no fan of the established Jewish elites behind the JWB, and they returned the sentiment. JWB founder Louis Marshall and Justice Brandeis, in particular, had little love for each other. The religiously orthodox and politically conservative Marshall resented what he saw as the more liberal Brandeis's intrusion into the domain of Jewish communal politics in spite of his lack of engagement with Judaism. Brandeis was a new convert to Zionism, which Marshall opposed, and even more galling, he had recently been named as the first Jewish Supreme Court justice, a position for which Marshall had once been considered. During the war, they were engaged in bitter conflict over the proposal to create an American Jewish Congress, which Brandeis supported, as a challenge to the authority of the American Jewish Committee, which Marshall led.[49]

Drachman urged Adler to take up the cause of kosher food in earnest and without delay, rather than allowing Brandeis and the Zionists to claim it as their own, but Adler disagreed. "So far as I am concerned," he wrote to Colonel Cutler, "I believe that it would be a matter of the highest interest if Mr. Brandeis should arrange Kosher food for Jewish soldiers."[50] Indeed, if a powerful man such as Brandeis, who had no love for or affiliation with the JWB, could have solved the problem of kosher food on his own, it would have offered an ideal resolution to the JWB's conflict. It would have meant that Jewish soldiers could have kosher food if they wished, while keeping the JWB out of the debate between Orthodox and Reform Judaism and away from accusations of sectarian activity. Unfortunately for the JWB, however, no such solution appeared. JWB, government, and military records offer no evidence that Brandeis ever took up the challenge of arranging for the provision of kosher food on military bases, nor is there any indication that the resolutely secular Brandeis, who did not keep kosher himself, would have been interested in such a project or successful in accomplishing it.[51]

The debate between the JWB and its Orthodox constituents grew more acrimonious, leading the Union of Orthodox Jewish Congregations and the Agudath ha-Rabbonim to threaten to provide kosher food to the soldiers on their own initiative.[52] But the JWB remained the CTCA's only official Jewish partner and the only Jewish agency with authorized access to US military camps and bases. Concerned groups could provide kosher meals to soldiers on leave, and they could both threaten and cajole the JWB to take a more aggressive stance. Nevertheless, the JWB retained control over the types of Jewish services it would present as necessary to Jewish soldiers' moral development, and its position regarding kosher food remained both deferential to the demands of the War Department and cautious about challenging American religious norms.

Behind the scenes, JWB executives grew annoyed with the kosher food debate. They became frustrated with their Orthodox coreligionists' insistence that Jewish religious observance should trump military practices, CTCA policy, and the larger project of establishing Judaism as a force for promoting Americanism. JWB Chairman Harry Cutler wrote with apparent irritation to Jacob Schiff, arguing that "ghetto Jews" simply could not understand either the realities of the board's position or what was at stake in conducting Jewish welfare work:

> I presume that you have sensed that there are certain groups in New York who claim that no Jew is good enough for this work unless he is a ghetto Jew, living on the East Side of the city. Well, that may be their opinion.... Then there are other elements who feel the only thing worthwhile in this welfare work is the question of Kashrith, one man going to the extent of making an application to be appointed Chief Shochet [kosher slaughterer], with commission of Major or Colonel, and a regiment or division of Shochtem under him.[53]

Schiff responded with sympathy to Cutler's position and his frustrations with the ongoing debate: "I can sympathize with the desire of many of the men to have Kosher food, but that is of course not feasible. These men must realize that they are units in a large organization and that they must adapt themselves to the necessities of the situation. The sooner these elements become thoroughly Americanized the better it will be for all concerned."[54] For Schiff, as for Adler and Cutler, Jewish religious practice needed to adapt to the conditions at hand, not the other way around. He saw resistance to this situation as evidence of insufficient Americanization. Insistence on maintaining Jewish practices that set Jewish soldiers apart from their compatriots and were at odds with both the structure of military life and the "necessities" of wartime offered evidence of a problem to be remedied. The provision of welfare services that actively demonstrated the harmony between Judaism and Americanism was part of the cure for such Old World intransigence.

Some of the soldiers also agreed that any insistence on the provision of kosher food was unreasonable and out of touch with the realities of camp life. A Captain Horowitz argued that in the army, "we cannot insist for instance that a 'mezuza' be fastened to the door-flap of every tent in which there is a Jew. The contents of the soldiers pack are rigidly prescribed; we cannot insist that he be allowed to make room in it for his 'talith' [prayer shawl] and 'tefillin' [phylacteries]. The prescribed ration is wholesome as well as sufficient; the prescribed components have been determined with scientific accuracy to balance the whole; we cannot in reason insist on the 'kashrith.'"[55] At times, even members of the Yiddish press expressed sympathy with the JWB's position, as in an article in *Der Morgen Zhurnal* that argued, "The Welfare Board is unjustly treated in their criticism. I understand that they want to introduce a Kosher kitchen in the camps. From the military standpoint this is inadvisable. We here can no more have a special kitchen for Jews than we can have a special kitchen for Catholics or Protestants. We ought to see that there are but few differences among the soldiers and a Kosher kitchen, in addition to being very expensive, would merely tend to separate one group of soldiers from the other."[56]

The potential for creating a separation between Jewish men and other soldiers proved to be one of most worrying aspects of the kosher food debate, for it had the potential to undermine so much of what the JWB wished to accomplish. It would not help American Jews to rise above denominational difference. In fact, it proved to be a flashpoint for religious conflict. It would not enhance the image of Judaism within the camps or make it appear as a truly American religion, such as Protestantism. If adherence to Jewish law and tradition set Jewish men apart from their fellow servicemen and made them seem different, standoffish, and unable to work as part of a team, it would be at odds with the ideals that Baker and Fosdick had identified as essentially American. The JWB could not help to build invisible armor designed to protect the morals and morale of all American soldiers if it offered un-American services that resulted in sectarian division. Colonel Cutler, persuaded of the dangers of supporting demands for kosher food, warned that doing so would prove detrimental to the soldiers themselves. In a speech to JWB field-workers given at the JWB Training School, he warned,

> There are elements who would like the Jewish Welfare Board to transplant the ghetto of the city into the camp. There are those who think . . . that the atmosphere . . . that the Jewish trooper should have should be the athus [*sic*] that he has enjoyed in this City—where I have also once lived—or in the congested center in other large cities. Of course we cannot transplant such an atmosphere. We are not dealing with a civilian situation. We are

dealing with a military condition and, of course, such things would only lead to segregation. In this connection, gentlemen, let me say to you that when the very vital question of *Kashrith* was considered and I took it up with the War Department, the Secretary of War said to me, "Colonel Cutler, go home and pray and pray hard that your people outside of the camps may not want to make martyrs of your people inside the camps." Stop to consider that, gentlemen.[57]

While no records confirm whether Cutler did, in fact, bring up the matter of kosher food directly with Secretary Baker, his comments to JWB field-workers made clear the conundrum that he and the board faced regarding the religious aspects of Jewish welfare work. As Cutler and other members of the Executive Committee saw it, Judaism had a place in the American military, but the Jewish "ghetto" of the city did not. To Orthodox Jews, dietary laws, no matter how they may have differed from the norms of Protestantism, fell clearly within the scope of Judaism and lay beyond the realm of compromise. But to the JWB, the situation seemed more ambivalent. Kosher food, they argued, might be desirable but was not worth sacrificing either the board's mission or Jewish men's ability to fit into American military life. Ultimately, however, decisions regarding the provision of kosher food, like all aspects of the JWB's program, did not rest with the board alone. Decisions of policy always relied upon the approval and support of the War Department, and the War Department eventually put an end to the debate over kosher food.

Orthodox groups continued to lobby for kosher food on military bases, while the JWB attempted to keep the needs and demands of its various constituents in balance. In its public statements, the JWB gave assurances that it was continuing to work at securing kosher food for all Jewish soldiers who wanted it. As JWB executive director Chester Teller wrote in a report to the *American Jewish Year Book*, "With the *Agudath ha Rabbonim*, the Welfare Board has been active in an inquiry as to the demand for Kosher food on the part of Jewish men in the camps, governmental sanction having been secured for the sale of Kosher nonperishable food products in the camps and cantonments wherever such supply is warranted by the demand therefore."[58] In reality, however, they soon discovered that provision of kosher food would not be possible.

Camp Upton, located on Long Island, drew many of its soldiers from the New York City area and, as a result, had one of the largest Jewish populations of any military base. Upton thus became a test case for the provision of kosher food. Military officials agreed, in theory, that there might be ways to supply kosher food to Jewish soldiers but argued that the JWB would have to demonstrate demand before any action could be taken. Demonstrating demand, however, proved difficult. Jewish men did not have to identify themselves as such to the JWB or, for that matter, to military authorities. Unlike in World War II, when a man's religion appeared on his dog tags, soldiers in World War I did not carry any religious identification.[59] JWB workers had no way of knowing the exact number of Jewish soldiers stationed at any given camp nor of identifying them. They relied upon the men to identify themselves and to seek services from the JWB.

When JWB field-worker Joseph Hyman received word from headquarters that he would have to assess the demand for kosher food among all the Jewish soldiers at Camp Upton, he replied that such a census would be physically impossible and that it "would also be a direct violation of the military system at Camp to make any attempt of this sort without official sanction."[60] When Hyman then raised the matter of a census with camp commander General Bell, the general "pointed out what he regarded as the dangers of such a step and the undesirability of permitting it here by way of a precedent for further demands elsewhere and abroad. He also was certain the Secretary of War had somewhere issued an order officially disapproving any plans for providing kosher food."[61] At the persistent urging of Mrs. Hyamson, wife of Rabbi Moses Hyamson, and a committee of Jewish ladies, Hyman pursued the matter again with General Bell and was informed that "the Secretary had written a communication, in which the War Department had determined adversely against providing Jewish food."[62]

Hyman thus found himself ordered to conduct a census because the JWB had been told by the War Department that it might be possible to provide kosher food if he could determine the number of Jewish men who wanted it, only to be informed by a Captain Crutcher, personal aide to General Bell, "that it had finally been determined not to permit this census" because the War Department opposed the provision of kosher food.[63] JWB field secretary and Orthodox rabbi David de Sola Pool

summed up the situation in a letter to Mortimer Schiff: "There is no kosher question at Camp Upton. The government *non possumus* is a hard
and stubborn fact beyond which we cannot go. The Resident Religious
Secretary . . . should try to reconcile the boys who are scrupulous as to
diet to their unfortunate situation, both by example of historic precedent
and by tactful explanation of Jewish law. Jewish law recognizes the necessity of submission to governmental *force majeure*."[64]

The debate over the provision of kosher food on military bases represented the limit of how far the JWB could stretch the meaning of
"nonsectarian." Separate food and eating facilities fell outside of the
boundaries of what the War Department defined as religion and, therefore, what it considered necessary to the proper spiritual development of
its soldiers. This made them sectarian concerns, outside the scope of the
CTCA's soldiers' welfare programs. The debate over kosher food, however, also defined the limits of the JWB's own definition of American
Judaism. JWB executives and rabbis wanted to enhance Jewish practice
and affiliation among the soldiers, but they wanted that affiliation to be
with a form of Judaism that clearly complemented the ideals of American democracy, the goals of Americanization, and the War Department's
requirements for soldiers' morale building and moral development. If
kosher food fell outside of those boundaries, then many JWB leaders
preferred to let the matter rest, not because they would necessarily have
advocated for the rejection of kosher observance in civilian life but because the demands of Americanness required a practical Judaism that
stressed the need to behave like other Americans over an adherence to
Jewish law or an embrace of Jewish separatism.

To JWB executives, concession on the issue of kosher food, a debate
they stood little chance of winning, must have seemed like a worthwhile
trade. Orthodox men and their families might complain, but thanks to
the board's unique relationship with the War Department, the JWB had
an opportunity to pursue what it saw as a far more important goal: re-
configuring the place of Judaism in American society. By successfully
arguing that Judaism served as a means of promoting good citizenship
and American values among the soldiers, the JWB had expanded official
conceptions of American religion. JWB leaders were willing to tailor the
form of Jewish religious observance in order to fit Protestant norms if
it helped them achieve this goal. The JWB succeeded in integrating Ju-

daism into the War Department's notion of moral development and in promoting a more religiously pluralistic notion of American citizenship. Convincing Jewish citizens and soldiers to embrace the JWB's vision of American pluralism, however, proved even more challenging than working with the US government.

4

American Judaism and American Jews

In his memoirs, General John Pershing, commander of the American Expeditionary Forces (AEF) in Europe, described the concerns that led him to request an expansion of the US military's Chaplains Corps. "My reason," he explained, "was that I regarded the value of religious influence among our troops during the war as of special importance. Many temptations confronted our soldiers abroad and it seemed to me that the presence, the example, and the counsel of chaplains of the right sort would exert an excellent moral effect, especially among men without experience away from home."[1] In a letter to Secretary Baker, Pershing argued that "churchmen from home" would provide the men with the sort of good influences they needed in order to live up to the standards of virtue and behavior that the military and the War Department desired. The men selected for the chaplaincy, Pershing urged, "should be of the highest character with reputations well established as sensible, practical, active ministers or workers, accustomed to dealing with young men."[2]

In earlier years, men had been selected for commissions as military chaplains largely on the basis of social connections. Since the turn of the twentieth century, the Federal Council of the Churches of Christ and the Catholic Army and Navy Chaplains' Bureau had made great strides in imposing standard requirements, but given the vital importance both Baker and Pershing saw in their work, World War I became a critical moment of reform for the military chaplaincy.[3] Pershing demanded that the number of military chaplains be expanded, that their duties be more clearly defined, and that they be organized into a Chaplains Corps with its own staff and headquarters. The War Department granted all of these requests and named military preparedness advocate, Episcopal bishop, and Pershing's friend and confidant Charles Brent as head of the new Chaplains Corps.[4] By Armistice Day in 1918, the US military chaplaincy had been dramatically restructured, and the number of chaplains in the US Army had increased from 146 to 2,230.[5]

The question of how to commission Jewish military chaplains remained as unresolved as it had been in the fall of 1916, when the Reform movement's Central Conference of American Rabbis had tried to send a representative to the Mexican border. No Jewish equivalent to the Federal Council of the Churches of Christ or the Catholic Army and Navy Chaplains' Bureau existed, and the military had no procedures through which to commission chaplains to minister to minority religious populations. With General Pershing and the War Department pushing for greater attention to religious guidance for the troops, the JWB could not allow such a situation to stand. The Chaplains Corps offered a crucial site for asserting the Americanness of Judaism. Religions represented within the Chaplains Corps carried the imprimatur of the state with them. At the start of the war, only mainline Protestantism—including African American churches—and Catholicism appeared deserving of such recognition. By the end of the war, the corps had somewhat uncomfortably expanded the definition of "Protestant" to include a chaplain from the Salvation Army, as well as a small number of Mormons and Christian Scientists.[6] The Jewish Welfare Board (JWB) took on the challenge of establishing a place for Judaism on this list of officially recognized and sanctioned American religions.

Chaplains and the staff that worked under them served a crucial function in changing perceptions of American religion. As scholar of American religion Ronit Stahl argues in her history of the military chaplaincy, "changes wrought through the chaplaincy traveled back home and permeated American life."[7] Chaplains represented their faiths in US military camps and to the soldiers they served. Soldiers carried those impressions back into civilian life after the war. Jewish chaplains would thus be in a unique position both to tangibly demonstrate what Judaism could contribute to the construction of a clean and upright military and to disprove anti-Semitic stereotypes to American society more broadly. In the nineteenth and early twentieth centuries, Jewish men were often caricatured as effeminate, shifty, and lacking in supposedly masculine virtues, such as physical stamina, honor, discipline, and sexual self-restraint.[8] Service in the military, given its association with manly virtue and Theodore Roosevelt's ideal of the "strenuous life," offered an effective means of challenging anti-Semitic slurs and asserting the manliness of Jewish men.[9] Jewish chaplains would be the most visible Jews in the military. The JWB thus sought not only to institutionalize a Jewish military chaplaincy that could represent Judaism to the military and the country but to staff it with men who could convince American soldiers and sailors, and through them the American public, that Jews lived up to American masculine ideals.

The JWB hoped, moreover, to promote these ideals among Jewish servicemen. If, as JWB executive director Chester Teller claimed, the Jewish men who served in the American Expeditionary Forces would go on to become "the prominent Jewish citizens, the upholders of our Jewish communities, the leaders and workers of our local Jewries," then they needed to be properly improved as both citizens and as Jews.[10] JWB leaders hoped to provide examples of Jewish behavior that servicemen could learn from and emulate. They envisioned their religious programs and the men who staffed them as providing a necessary component in the education of young Jewish men—men who, they hoped, would be proud of their Judaism and able to carry themselves with dignity in the non-Jewish world. Through Jewish religious services in the military, the JWB set out to further expand American definitions of religion and prepare a generation of Jewish men to take their place as fully enfranchised American citizens in the postwar world.

Military Chaplains and the Character of American Judaism

The first step in initiating this program of social and cultural change was to create a way for the military to commission Jewish chaplains. The JWB thus began lobbying Congress for legislation that would make it possible to appoint "chaplains-at-large." The commission of these men would not hinge on the religious affiliation of the majority of soldiers within a given regiment, as it had in the past, but instead within the army as a whole. At the same time, in anticipation of the passage of such legislation, the JWB began screening chaplain candidates. Cyrus Adler, a JWB founder and acting president of the Jewish Theological Seminary of America (JTS), took on the role of head of the JWB Chaplains Committee.

In making its case to Congress, the JWB turned to Congressman Isaac Siegel from the Twentieth District in New York City for assistance. Siegel, in turn, worked hard to ensure the passage of House Bill 5271 and Senate Bill 2527, which "called for the appointment of twenty chaplains at large into the Army of the United States with a rank of lieutenant at a salary of $2000 to serve during this war emergency."[11] Congress intended for these new positions to serve all religious groups not previously represented within the Chaplains Corps, including Christian Scientists, Mormons, Unitarians, the Eastern Orthodox Church, and the Salvation Army.[12] Five months after the war began, the bills passed on September 11 and September 13, 1917, respectively, and the *American Hebrew and Jewish Messenger* bragged that "it is well known that half of this number [of chaplains] would be composed of Jewish clergymen of both the orthodox and reformed congregations."[13]

Even before the passage of the new law, however, Adler's Chaplains Committee set to work searching for rabbis ready to serve in the Chaplains Corps. Adler hoped to find candidates who could embody the sort of American Jewish manhood that the JWB hoped to promote and reflect among soldiers, but his first concern lay in finding rabbis who could meet the qualifications for the chaplaincy set out by the government. The president made all appointments to the military chaplaincy, and federal law set the requirements for such an appointment. It dictated that chaplains must be "regularly ordained ministers of some religious denomination" in which they remained in good standing, and required a recommendation from an "authorized ecclesiastical body." Chaplains had to be younger than forty-five years old at the time of their commission and had to have "passed satisfactorily such examinations as to his moral, mental, and physical qualifications as may be prescribed by the President."[14]

The first requirement, that chaplains be ordained by "some religious denomination," reflected reforms made during the Civil War, when President Lincoln expanded the chaplaincy beyond its original designation of "regularly ordained ministers of some Christian denomination."[15] With this crucial change already in place, the other requirements appeared straightforward, but presented a number of challenges to the JWB Chaplains Committee. The second requirement, that candidates be "regularly ordained," necessitated ordination by a seminary or institution recognizable to the US government. This disqualified many Orthodox rabbis who had received *smicha* (rabbinical ordination) in more traditional fashion, from an individual teacher or in a *yeshiva* (seminary) unrecognized by the state.

The third requirement, which mandated that the candidate be recommended by an "authorized ecclesiastical body," also created difficulties because the Chaplains Committee represented the JWB, not an authoritative ecclesiastical body equivalent to the Federal Council of the Churches of Christ or the Catholic Army and Navy Chaplains' Bureau. Adler's correspondence reveals that someone raised questions about his qualifications to chair such a committee, as he did not have rabbinical ordination. In October 1917, Adler thus wrote with some relief to JWB chairman Colonel Harry Cutler and laid out a strategy for bolstering the ecclesiastical status of the committee while shaping the JWB's vision of American Judaism. In his letter to Cutler, Adler noted that government statutes made provision for recognizing recommendations from a body comprising "not less than five accredited ministers of said denomination." Adler therefore proposed a committee of six men, four of whom would be rabbis representing Orthodox and Reform organizations, while he and Rabbi Elias Solomon—a JTS graduate and founder of the fledgling Conservative movement's United Synagogue of America—would serve as the last two members. All established branches of American Judaism would thereby receive representation, and Adler's own non-ordained status would become a moot point.[16]

Adler's strategy saved both his own and the committee's position while setting the groundwork for creating an interdenominational, American Jewish body to select and screen candidates for the chaplaincy. Its members eventually included Adler and Solomon, William Rosenau and Louis Grossman for the Reform Central Conference of American Rabbis, Maurice H. Harris for the Eastern Council of Reform Rabbis, David de Sola Pool for the Orthodox New York Board of Jewish Ministers, Bernard Drachman for the Union of Orthodox Jewish Congregations, and M. S. Margolies for the Orthodox Agudath ha-Rabbonim.[17] Adler hoped that by choosing rabbis from all of the major Jewish denominational organizations, he had created a committee that would be able to fully represent American Jewry. Even with this plan in place, however, he encountered further challenges from government regulations.

The government's fourth requirement specified that the secretary of war would oversee the administration of mental and moral examinations of candidates as directed by the president, that only citizens of the United States could be considered as candidates, and that all candidates would be judged on the basis of their physical, educational, professional, and clerical fitness for the job of chaplain. Professional and educational qualifications would, according to the law, be assessed through written examinations on:

1. Extent of school . . . and theological education
2. Pastoral work as clergyman
3. Experience in teaching
4. Writing and spelling
5. Arithmetic . . .
6. English grammar and composition
7. Geography, particularly with reference to the United States
8. History, particularly of the United States[18]

The focus of these examinations reflected the educational responsibilities chaplains had traditionally filled within the military, but they also heavily favored men who had achieved high levels of education in the United States, particularly college graduates.[19] Indeed, in the advertisements for chaplaincy applicants that the JWB ran in both Jewish and non-Jewish newspapers, the committee recommended that the ideal candidates were "men who are graduates of a recognized Rabbinical College as well as of a secular College."[20] The requirements for age, citizenship, ordination, and education significantly limited the pool of rabbis from which the Chaplains Committee could choose. While each of the three emerging Jewish denominations had established institutions for rabbinical ordination, the Orthodox Rabbi Isaac Elchanan Theological Seminary had only recently started to consider whether to allow its students to pursue secular studies in addition to their rabbinical training, making it all but impossible to find a graduate who could meet government standards for the chaplaincy.[21] In practice, therefore, only rabbis who had earned secular college degrees while pursuing their rabbinical studies at either the Reform seminary Hebrew Union College (HUC) or the Conservative JTS could truly be viable candidates for the chaplaincy. Government regulations, therefore, helped to determine one of the defining characteristics of the type of Judaism the JWB brought to American military camps. The Judaism of the JWB did not reflect the institutions or structures of Orthodoxy.

Adler was disappointed by this situation and wrote to Congressman Siegel expressing his concerns:

> As you know there are certain differences between orthodox, conservative and reform rabbis and in making recommendations we want to consider all sections so that assurance can be given to the war and navy department and if need be to the President that the recommendations made are satisfactory to all the organizations represented in this Board whose sole purpose is to do work for the benefit of young Jewish men in the army and navy. . . . [A]s far as possible . . . I do not wish to, nor do I wish to appear to be discriminating against any school.[22]

But Adler's desire to keep all the JWB member organizations happy, to avoid the appearance of discrimination, and to serve Jewish soldiers did not mean that he had no opinion as to the appropriate training and background for Jewish chaplains. Most Orthodox men, he assumed, could not meet the qualifications set forth by the War Department, and he doubted the ability of the Reform rabbis to adequately meet the needs of more religiously traditional soldiers. As he wrote to Harry Cutler, "Reform Rabbis 'do not touch the spot,' but this is not the fault of the men, but of the reform movement, which is a little too rational and too cold. It is a condition that cannot be remedied."[23]

Adler preferred graduates of his own institution for chaplains' posts. They seemed to him most likely to be able to meet the needs of both Orthodox and Reform servicemen and to measure up to governmental requirements. As historian Hasia Diner notes in her essay on the origins of JTS, its founders, including Adler, sought to create a generation of rabbis who could, in their view, walk a middle path between "stupid Orthodoxy and insane Reform," by expressing traditional Judaism in "an American idiom." They wanted to produce graduates who "saw no inconsistency between modern America and the belief in the Torah from Sinai."[24] The Judaism represented in the newly expanded Chaplains Corps would bear the official stamp of the US government. Conservative movement leaders perceived the benefits that could accrue to both their seminary and the goals of their movement if JTS graduates were to fill a significant percentage of the chaplains-at-large commissions designated for Jews. Adler also recognized the opportunity to shape a form of Americanized traditional Judaism that would be lost if JTS graduates did not present themselves as candidates to the chaplaincy.[25] As Jewish chaplain and JTS graduate Harry Davidowitz wrote to Adler, "if the rabbis of the Jewish Theological Seminary fail to respond and join the Army as Chaplains . . . it will be the biggest set-back that the Seminary or the United Synagogue could ever get in their future influence on American Jewry, and the biggest set-back that the Jews as a religious body could get in the eyes of the American Government."[26]

Adler and Davidowitz understood that the official sanction granted to the JWB had the capacity to rub off on whichever seminary and denominational organization best helped the JWB fulfill its mission. Moreover, it could establish Conservative Judaism as the denomination deemed best suited to meet the needs of a generation of truly American young Jewish men, neither as Old World as Orthodoxy, nor as "cold" and overly "rational" as Reform. Through the Chaplains Corps, the JWB had the ability to determine what form of Judaism was most appropriate to enhancing the morals and shaping the characters of American men. The selection of chaplains was thus a weighty matter. Men chosen for the Jewish chaplaincy would have to be able to minister to all American soldiers in need of their services and would serve as Judaism's representatives to both Jews and non-Jews alike. The public nature of their role made it imperative that the right sort of man be chosen for the job—one who could meet the spiritual needs of different types of Jews and could, with equal ease, serve as a Jewish ambassador to the predominantly non-Jewish men of the American military.

The Chaplains Committee debated the sorts of qualities they sought in a candidate. The minutes of a December 1917 committee meeting record that Chairman Adler reminded his colleagues "that for the first time since the Civil War, Jewish chaplains are being placed in the United States Army, and will be thrown together with chaplains of other denominations, It was, therefore his opinion that they should have a good knowledge of Jewish history, literature and theology, so that if a question is asked them, or if their colleagues wish to discuss theology with them, they are able to do so intelligently."[27] Rabbi Bernard Drachman, representative of the Union of Orthodox Jewish Congregations, added that he "thought that it was desirable to have a man who . . . has a good knowledge of Hebrew, Judaism, Jewish literature, Jewish thought, etc. . . .

If he did not have good Hebrew knowledge, he would be disqualified. In addition, good presence, culture, manners, preferably single, good breeding, good English, accent, tact, and character are very essential."[28]

Committee members also had to meet external standards as they searched for their contributions to the enlarged Chaplains Corps. The *New York Times* wrote that "army and navy Chaplains ... have to be two-fisted, meat-fed, red-blooded men to win and hold the admiration and respect of their charges."[29] General Pershing urged the various ecclesiastical bodies to come up with candidates but reminded them that "men selected should be in vigorous health, as their services will be needed under most trying circumstances."[30] The War Department's adjutant general, moreover, urged the committee members to "bear in mind the fact that the candidate should be one who is accustomed to outdoor life, interested in athletics, and able to ride a horse."[31]

The search for a pool of well-bred, well-spoken, thoroughly educated, horse-riding rabbis who were under the age of forty-five and willing to volunteer for military service proved tough going—particularly as the Chaplains Committee further narrowed the field through its wariness of nominating naturalized citizens from enemy countries, such as Germany, Austria, and Hungary.[32] One hundred and forty-nine rabbis applied to the JWB for positions as military chaplains. The Chaplains Committee passed the names of thirty-four men on to the War Department for consideration. Twenty-five eventually received commissions, and the vast majority of them, in spite of Adler's reservations, were graduates of the Reform HUC. Twelve of the chaplains—Israel Bettan, Harry S. Davidowitz, Louis I. Egelson, Solomon B. Freehof, Benjamin Friedman, James G. Heller, Jacob Krohngold, Lee Levinger, Elias N. Rabinowitz, Harry Richmond, David Tannenbaum, and Elkan Voorsanger—served with the AEF in Europe. An additional thirteen rabbis—Nathan E. Barasch, Harry W. Etteleson, Max Felshin, Samuel Fredman, Raphael Goldenstein, Abram Hirschberg, Morris S. Lazaron, Emil W. Leipziger, Julius A. Liebert, Abraham Nowak, Jerome Rosen, Leonard W. Rothstein, and Israel I. Sarasohn—received commissions too late to be sent overseas and served on military bases in the United States.[33] One additional chaplain, David Goldberg, an HUC graduate from Corsicana, Texas, bypassed the JWB and applied directly to the Department of the Navy for a commission. He received his commission on November 5, 1917, and became the first Jewish chaplain to serve in the US Navy and the only one to serve there during World War I.[34]

Judaism in the AEF: "Star of David Men"

This carefully vetted group of chaplains received assistance in their religious work from JWB "camp rabbis." These men were usually rabbis based at congregations located near military bases who volunteered to serve as noncommissioned, unofficial chaplains to Jewish soldiers. There were also JWB field-workers, whom the JWB hired to oversee the provision of welfare services on American camps and bases. Nominally, the official chaplains had charge of all Jewish religious services. In practice, however, the relatively small number of Jewish chaplains could not possibly oversee all the programs provided by the approximately 30 camp rabbis and 325 field-workers in 193 military camps and bases throughout the country.[35] Therefore, field-workers, known as "Star of David men," and local rabbis led the majority of the religious and social services provided by the JWB.

As in its campaign to find candidates for the Jewish chaplaincy, the JWB ran newspaper advertisements seeking men ready to serve as field-workers. These notices stressed the importance of the job and of the education, tact, fitness, and skill of the men needed for such positions. The actual qualifications of the men who became JWB field-workers, however, varied significantly. Some were rabbis too old for the draft or the Chaplains Corps but who had extensive congregational experience and a desire to do their bit for the war effort and the men. Others were young men deemed unfit for the draft or looking for ways to avoid the draft altogether—although the JWB, always concerned about the image of Jewish men it projected, took care to ensure that it did not employ shirkers.

Some field-workers brought significant Jewish education and training to their job; others did not. The JWB, under pressure to get its programs off the ground as quickly as possible, did not always have time to wait for ideal candidates to present themselves. As Colonel Cutler wrote to executive director Chester Teller, "The only qualification is and should be that these men be capable of imparting a message, either in their sermon or their address, of a character to interest non-Jews, as well as soldiers of our faith." Beyond this, he argued, "the man—rabbi or layman—who goes into a camp as our representative must be beyond reproach as to his avowed Americanism."[36]

The JWB preferred men with a solid Jewish background, as well as "avowed Americanism," but as it did not require a particular degree of Jewish education, it decided it was necessary to provide representatives with some guidance as to the proper structure of Jewish religious services in the camps. Field representatives received explanations of the various Jewish holidays, as well as suggestions for how those holidays should be celebrated.[37] The JWB also sent suggestions for Shabbat sermons connecting the stories of the Old Testament with American history and American values. One memo from JWB headquarters, for example, suggested a quotation from Abraham Lincoln on the need for patience and faith in achieving the "rightful result" to help tie the Torah portion *Chayye Sarah* to the themes of duty and national idealism.[38] Another paralleled Abraham's migration from the land of his fathers to the story of Roger Williams's founding of Rhode Island and compared the sacrifice of Isaac, dubbed "Abraham's Quest of Pure Worship," to both the "implicit obedience" of the soldier and efforts to abolish child labor.[39]

A sermon outline provided for the Torah portion *Toledoth* interpreted the conflict between Jacob and Esau as a useful device for explaining the global conflict in which the country fought, while reinforcing the Jew's commitment to American democratic ideals:

> Esau represents the element that craves for worldly power and domination, wielding the sword to attain it . . . the very thing that the Teuton has typified with all the menace that that constitutes for the world, human liberty and civilization. Jacob on the other hand, stands for the ideals that the Allied nations have made their own, the love of truth and justice, the securing of peace for all the world, the extending of the blessings of freedom to all nations. These are the very ideals to which the Jew has always been committed. . . . The Kaiser-ridden Prussian hordes have not availed against the idealism, the love of freedom, reverence for moral standards, respect for the rights and liberties of mankind, which animate altruistic humanitarian, noble America and her Allies.[40]

In each of these suggestions, the JWB sought not only to assist its less experienced field-workers in providing religious services but also to shape the type of Judaism that they would present in the camps. Even if it could not always exert perfect control over who would represent American Judaism, the JWB could still attempt to dictate the values reflected in the religious services and programs held in the military. The connection between Judaism, patriotism, and American democracy remained central to this effort. In addition to sermon suggestions that linked Judaism to Americanism and American history, the JWB also distributed pamphlets for soldiers that reinforced this connection and argued that Judaism provided the model for American democracy. The pamphlet entitled *"Golden Rule" Hillel* paralleled the life of the Jewish sage Rabbi Hillel with that of Abraham Lincoln and drew a connection between Hillel's *halakhic*, or Jewish legal, rulings and the development of American law and democracy:

> Poor and proud, Hillel supported himself by manual labor while he was securing his education. Like Abraham Lincoln, he was a woodchopper. . . . Hillel's career is a shining example of the democratic principle which has always prevailed in Jewish life, of the opportunity open to all men of talents, however humble their origin, to achieve position in the republic of Jewish learning. . . . Some of his innovations anticipate in a striking way the developments under similar circumstances of the common law of England and the United States many centuries later.[41]

Through the selection of Jewish chaplains, camp rabbis, and JWB field-workers, as well as in the structuring of its religious programs, the JWB sought to realize the connection it had drawn between Judaism and Americanism. It looked for representatives who could put a polished, educated, unaccented, American face on the Judaism found in American military camps. It worked to configure a mode of Jewish worship, practice, and belief in keeping both with the American ideals it espoused and the War Department's desire to use its welfare programs to build better citizens. While doing so, however, the JWB remained vigilant in its struggles to protect Jewish men from the proselytizing of the Young Men's Christian Association (YMCA) and to enhance the soldier's commitment to Judaism. It worked under the constraints of the Commission on Training Camp Activities (CTCA) and against the allure of the YMCA to express a form of distinctly American Judaism that would be attractive and welcoming to Jewish soldiers without alienating them from their non-Jewish compatriots. And because of the need to have all programs and events adhere to the rhetoric of nonsectarianism, the JWB strove to project a form of Judaism that would make non-Jewish men feel welcome, confident that Jewish values closely resembled their own, and certain that Jewish soldiers could be trusted as fellow Americans and as comrades in arms.

Shaping the Character of American Jews

The JWB envisioned the ideal Jewish soldier as a man who could dispel anti-Jewish stereotypes and embrace the best of being an American while remaining loyal to his distinctive Jewish heritage. Secretary Baker and Chairman Fosdick hoped that, through the programs of the CTCA, they might improve the characters, loyalties, and cultural standards of all American men. The JWB also hoped to use soldiers' welfare work to create a generation of proud Jewish men who lived up to American standards of masculine behavior and felt perfectly at home among their non-Jewish compatriots.

Like other civilian CTCA agencies, the JWB focused on the charge to use its religious, educational, athletic, and recreational programs to instill high moral standards in the men under its care, raise their morale, and build their character. It encouraged unambiguous expressions of patriotism from all American soldiers and urged them to remember their obligations to behave honorably even as they trained for the trenches. The first issue of the *Welfare Board Sentinel*, a magazine published and distributed in US military camps by the JWB, included Rabbi William Rosenau's "Ten Commandments for the Soldier," which urged readers to remember that these commandments "were well worth memorizing by every Welfare Board worker, as well as by every soldier":

> First Commandment: I am America, thy country, which brought thee
>   out of bondage to liberty.
> Second Commandment: Thou shalt have no other country besides me.

Third Commandment: Thou shalt not take the name of America, thy country, in vain.

Fourth Commandment: Remember the Declaration of Independence, and keep it holy.

Fifth Commandment: Honor thy Superior Officers.

Sixth Commandment: Thou shalt not despoil.

Seventh Commandment: Thou shalt not ravish.

Eighth Commandment: Thou shalt not loot.

Ninth Commandment: Thou shalt not betray.

Tenth Commandment: Thou shalt not annex.[42]

In these new commandments, the United States assumed divine status, displacing God and sacred texts as the ultimate source of freedom and righteous behavior. Nothing about these ten commandments differentiated Jewish men from their compatriots. All were admonished to put country first and to behave in accordance with the very highest standards of American manhood. Indeed, the commandments reminded soldiers of President Wilson's claim that the United States' war was not being fought for mere conquest but as part of a mission to spread American-style democracy throughout the world. As American servicemen, their primary responsibility lay in upholding their country's goals and standards, rather than in any separate religious tradition or community. This position resonated with the JWB's insistence that Judaism and Christianity equally supported the ideals of American democracy. The commandments conveyed standards of loyalty and behavior expected of all American men, but they also revealed anxieties about areas where JWB officials feared that soldiers needed to be reminded of what honor and duty demanded of them.

The first commandments surely spoke to concerns about the 18 percent of all American soldiers—and possibly as many as one-third of all Jewish soldiers—born in other countries. With anti-immigrant hostility and suspicion on the rise, the JWB commandments instructed men to be sure that they put the United States first and treated their country and its founding tenets with reverence.[43] Other commandments focused on personal behavior and echoed the sentiments of official publications such as Frank Allen's *Keeping Our Fighters Fit for War and After*, which promised that the war would produce a generation of men schooled in "the meaning of concerted effort, obedience, loyalty, cheerfulness, courage and generosity."[44] In keeping with Progressive Era ideas about ideal manhood, the JWB's commandments stressed the need for honesty, loyalty, self-control, discipline, and particularly sexual restraint. Reminders to avoid acts of violence against civilians, such as looting, ravishing, and despoiling, indicated both the era's assumption that men's nature drew them to such acts and an admonition to remember that all civilized American men mastered and resisted such urges.[45]

While these commandments presumed to set standards of behavior applicable to all servicemen, many other JWB speeches and publications focused on Jewish men in particular. They promised that the honorable behavior of each Jewish soldier would reflect well on American Jews as a whole, which made the good behavior of all Jewish soldiers vitally important. The JWB insisted that through adherence to Judaism, Jewish men became good Americans.[46] But this insistence meant that any failure to live up to ideal American standards might indicate that Judaism could not contribute to the moral welfare of either the military or the country as effectively as the JWB claimed. JWB workers and representatives, therefore, had to persuade Jewish soldiers to behave themselves in accord with ideal American norms. In a letter distributed to its camp workers, the JWB advised, "He [the camp worker] should try to influence the men by tactful talks to live clean lives and keep morally straight. . . . The worker should keep in friendly touch with the officers so as to create sympathetic interest in the welfare work and a fair attitude toward the Jewish men. The worker should also aim to further and emphasize good will between the Jewish units and their non-Jewish confreres."[47] The JWB expected its workers to be diligent promoters of goodwill between Jewish and non-Jewish men, working preemptively to dispel stereotypes and promote fair attitudes and encouraging harmony between Jews and Christians. Friendships and relationships of mutual respect would offer proof of Jews' and Christians' common ideals and commitment to Americanism; tension between them would undercut this message. Worried about building good relationships between Jewish and non-Jewish soldiers, the JWB urged its workers to remind the men of their responsibilities to themselves, to their country, and to the protection of Jewish honor.

Fearing that not all Jews would live up to American masculine ideals, however, JWB headquarters urged its workers to encourage upstanding conduct even among Jews living near military camps, lest their behavior reinforce anti-Semitic stereotypes and reflect badly on American Jewry as a whole. In one circular, the JWB argued, "The worker should by a judicious word to the Jews who are the retailers in the environs of the camp, try to keep these dealers fair so as to keep the Jewish reputation and name unsullied. Whenever prudently necessary impress upon the men the thought that they are no less Americans and no less soldiers when living up to Jewish ideals, which teaches duty to our country in the fullest measure."[48] In another memo, JWB field-workers were told, "There are some cases in which Jewish merchants attempt to mulct the soldiers. While this practice is by no means confined to Jewish merchants—you will find it necessary in the name of our people to take this matter up with the merchants directly. This is another matter that should be handled with the utmost tact. It is a matter that should be handled without the assistance of the military authorities."[49]

The JWB saw its workers as guardians of the good name of the Jewish people and sent them to monitor and improve the behavior of soldiers and civilians alike, handling incidents of Jewish misbehavior quickly, with tact and discretion, and smoothing the path to a future in which Jews and Christians could embrace each other as fellow Americans. Careful consideration, therefore, had to be given to the type of man chosen for positions as JWB workers. They had not only to do the job of running JWB educational, recreational, and religious services but also to make the right impression among the men, in the broader Jewish community, and, crucially, on the non-Jewish soldiers and civilians they encountered.

The JWB preferred to hire men who were born in the United States, who spoke unaccented English, and who reflected the type of masculine identity that it wished to project and promote for all Jewish men. In personal correspondence, board members carefully discussed their concerns about the appearances and accents of their field-workers. In letters to Chairman Cutler, Cyrus Adler took careful note of the type of impression certain applicants created. "David Aronson, who is a student at the seminary," Adler wrote of one applicant, who went on to a successful career as a Conservative rabbi and president of the Conservative Rabbinical Assembly, "Mr. Teller tells me does not in his opinion quite measure up physically and in some other ways for the work. He may be right about this as Aronson is a rather unhappy looking individual."[50] "With regard to Spitz," he wrote about another, "I would say that Mr. Brickner's memorandum . . . that he has a lisp and foreign accent are correct. . . . He is not the type of man that I would pick for camp work but he is better than some of the men we have picked out. However, that is no argument on his behalf."[51]

The selection of JWB field-workers depended on a variety of factors. The board valued Jewish education and experience in working with young men. Personal connections and recommendations also played a role in the selection process, but evaluations of workers suggest that good looks, physical prowess, and an appearance and accent that fell in line with American ideals of masculinity mattered a great deal. Without these qualities, the JWB worried, the worker would fail to embody the harmony between Americanism and Judaism it touted and, as a result, would fail to serve as the sort of model for Jewish masculinity that it wanted to display to both Jewish and non-Jewish soldiers.

JWB efforts in Montgomery, Alabama, were spearheaded by Rabbi Bernard Calonius Ehrenreich, a founder of the ZBT Jewish fraternity and of Camp Kawaga in Minocqua, Wisconsin, which was dedicated to helping Jewish boys develop "meaningfully into manhood" through athletic training, outdoorsmanship, and Ehrenreich's own interpretation of Native American traditions.[52] In a letter to JWB national headquarters, Ehrenreich expressed in strong terms his concerns about camp workers and their appearance and bearing:

> Another matter that is confidential and I do not wish divulged: Mr. Gordon who represents the Jewish Chronicle was here this week. . . . He is very anxious to come to Montgomery as my assistant a few weeks before I leave for my boys camp in Wisconsin, and then to remain here during my absence over the summer months. I regard him very highly, but as his external appearance, his manner and methods are not what I would expect in a man working among military men, I want you therefore to stay him off from Montgomery should he make application for the same. You will have to send somebody here in the middle of May and when you do so, I want an American, of college breeding, with pep, tact and willingness to work, regardless of the hours. You know what I mean. "No others need apply." This is between you and me, and mum's the word.[53]

Ehrenreich realized the delicacy of his request when he asked that his assessment of Mr. Gordon's appearance be kept mum, but his concerns found a ready audience at the JWB, where board members desired that their organization and American Jewry as whole be represented by workers who looked the part of the well-bred, well-spoken American man. Captain Horowitz, a soldier involved with the Young Men's Hebrew Association, wrote to the JWB to advise it of the qualities to look for in its workers:

> The man in charge of this work, call him Rabbi, Chaplain or Secretary, what you will, must be carefully chosen. He should possess the following qualifications:
>
> He must be a man of infinite tact and patience.
>
> He must be an optimist; but his optimism should not blind him so much that he cannot size up the value and progress of his work at all times.
>
> He should be a practical man, able to utilize any opportunities that may present themselves to him, and to do so on the instant.
>
> He must be a good mixer and a good student of human nature.
>
> He must be broad enough to treat every case on its merits.
>
> He must know the world enough to sense the real truth that may lie beneath the gloss of a man's tale.
>
> It is not essential that he be familiar with military procedure, for it he possesses the above qualifications, he will soon learn.
>
> He should be young, active and athletic.
>
> He should be a good practical Jew.[54]

The JWB's representatives should, in Horowitz's assessment, be first and foremost men who could command the respect of other men, regardless of their religion. Judaism, defined by practicality, was not excluded from consideration but came last on his list. In addition to these qualifications, Chaplain Elkan Voorsanger advised that workers should be "men of force and character," "sympathetic and impressive, but not too 'Goody Good.'"[55] JWB field representative Cyrus Janover wrote to advise that "the worker must always dress neatly, wear a uniform with the 'Star of David' and be as careful about his appearance as an officer. He must fraternize with the officers so that when a Jewish problem arises they may call upon him for guidance."[56] And Cyrus Adler wrote the following in a memorandum sent out to all JWB workers:

> The Welfare worker must establish some position of authority. He should be very particular about his person. His uniform should be clean and in good condition, He should as an example to the men, salute and obey all military regulations, Good manners and dignity are of extreme importance in the relationship of welfare workers. . . . Avoid impatience and bad manners. . . .
>
> Each worker must feel that he has a solemn responsibility at once as a representative of the United States and of the Jewish people in America. He must all times conduct himself in such a way as will shed luster upon these two ideas. To many people—American and French—his conduct will create a lasting impression for good or ill of Americanism and Judaism.[57]

These lists of qualifications for JWB workers can surely be read as the JWB's description of the ideal American Jewish man. He should be athletic and good looking, dignified in his bearing, personable, open, liked by all, and possessed of intuitive good sense and pride in his Judaism, but not overly punctilious about religious observance. And although JWB representatives would take the lead in providing Jewish religious services in the military, there is no mention of piety or religious learning in any of these descriptions. Instead, the JWB sought men who could live up to the highest standards of Jewish manhood and reflect the type of thoroughly American Jewishness it sought to model in the camps and encourage among the soldiers.

Finding a full staff of such men proved difficult, and the JWB had little choice at times but to compromise. For example, Rabbi Spitz, whom Cyrus Adler described as "not the type of man that I would pick for camp work but he is better than some," received a post as the JWB's "Star of David man" at Camp Upton on Long Island, in spite of Adler's reservations.[58] Indeed, the fact the Adler felt the need to write a memo spelling out details such as the need to wear a clean uniform and obey military regulations indicates that he feared that some field-workers, like the soldiers in their care, might need reminding of the example the board expected them to set.

"The Fighting Rabbi"

The reality that not every field-worker could have measured up to the JWB's ideals perhaps explains the enthusiasm generated by Elkan Voorsanger, the JWB's first Jewish military chaplain in France. Dubbed "the Fighting Rabbi," the JWB celebrated Voorsanger as an ideal representative of American Jews and American Judaism. Elkan Voorsanger was the son of prominent San Francisco rabbi Jacob Voorsanger. He had earned a bachelor's degree at the University of Cincinnati in 1913 and was ordained at HUC, the Reform seminary, in 1914. When the United States entered the war, he gave up his clergy exemption and resigned his position as assistant rabbi at Congregation Shaare Emeth in Saint Louis to enter the army as an enlisted man. The *St. Louis Star* reported that although Voorsanger opposed the war, he enlisted in order to alleviate the suffering of the soldiers and because "we are fighting for democracy and against autocracy." He had socialistic tendencies, the *Star* reported, but not internationalist ones "because," Voorsanger exclaimed, "I have a country and that country is the United States." Voorsanger told the reporter that the war "would be followed by a millennium of education in which the world would be brought to realize the futility of killing" and that "this will be the last great war." The *Star* noted that Voorsanger had turned down a well-paying job as a JWB worker at a salary of $300 a month because he feared that welfare work would not take him to the front. Instead, he enlisted in a hospital unit and accepted an enlisted man's salary of $21 a month. He went to France with his unit, but after Congress authorized the appointment of Jewish chaplains, Voorsanger became the first rabbi to receive such a commission. He was eventually promoted to senior captain of the Seventy-Seventh Division and earned a French Croix de Guerre and a Purple Heart during his service.[59]

In an article published after the war, the *American Hebrew and Jewish Messenger* described Voorsanger, "the Fighting Rabbi," as

> living in the trenches, sharing their hard-tack and bully beef, "over the top" with his men at dawn he was "one of the boys" in every sense of the word. A figure of powerful physique, forceful personality, military bearing and yet, in his intercourse with the men, one of a dominant spiri-

tuality, calling forth an evident response wherever a kindred feeling was innermost hidden—that was the figure, in the sand-colored Ford, which rode up the lines where shells whizzed most often and made its owner known and loved by every doughboy in the vicinity.[60]

The depiction of Voorsanger in both the *St. Louis Star* and the *American Hebrew and Jewish Messenger* reflected the image the JWB hoped to project. The first showed him as a man opposed to the senseless killing of war but willing to fight for his country. Uninterested in personal gain or in finding the easy way out, he was depicted as someone motivated only by principles and patriotism. The second piece characterized him as strong, dignified, unafraid, "one of the boys," able to connect with all soldiers. His "dominant spirituality" allowed him to draw forth the hidden feelings of the men but did not set him apart from them. His title of rabbi served as proof of his pride in being Jewish but did not interfere with his ability to connect meaningfully with *all* the men in his charge. Rather than speak of him as a rabbi possessed of piety or learning, the *American Hebrew and Jewish Messenger* portrayed him as a man possessing the manners, tact, and common touch that made him a real American. He apparently possessed a sense of Jewishness of the "good practical" type that the JWB sought, although it came second to his physique, personality, and nonsectarian spirituality.

The images of Voorsanger that appeared in the media modeled the distinctly American Jewish manhood that the JWB hoped both to project and to inspire, and JWB leaders promoted the belief that only the benefits of American democracy had allowed this new Jewish man to emerge. As Reform rabbi Hyman Enelow explained,

No longer can it be said, as they were wont to say of old, that the Jew is nothing but a usurer or a trader. In America hundreds of thousands of Jews work with their hands. . . . What America has done for the material progress of millions of Jews is one of the marvels of history—a marvel augmented by the moral transformation which has accompanied the process. Men, who for generations had been hounded and haunted by persecution, who had been engrafted with all the moral evils of persecution, who had been humiliated and all but crushed—millions of such men by the liberty and humanity of America have been freed from the old chains, purged of the old stains, turned into free, strong, courageous, self-reliant, and self-respecting human beings.[61]

The JWB saw its role as helping to ease and assure the transformation of men haunted, hounded, and afflicted by moral evils into self-respecting American Jews of the type modeled by Chaplain Voorsanger and, it hoped, by its field-workers more generally. In some cases, this meant guiding the Americanization of immigrants. In others, it meant working to improve the character and taste of native born men. In all cases, it meant helping to foster the sort of mutual respect between Jewish and non-Jewish soldiers that could advance a religiously pluralist vision of American democracy and promote a better Jewish future.

Government authority helped the JWB in this task. It allowed the JWB to control Jewish religious services, to use its field-workers in an attempt to model and regulate appropriate Jewish behavior, and to determine which sorts of recreational and educational programs and activities it deemed conducive to the improvement of American servicemen. But the CTCA and the JWB could not compel Jewish servicemen to attend their events and programs, nor could the JWB make them accept its conception of Judaism, its ideals of Jewish manhood, or its vision of the Jewish American future. The men in the camps often had quite different ideas about their Jewishness and about the possibilities for building a society in which self-respecting men saw one another as Americans first and as Christians or Jews second.

"Real Jews," "Poor Jehudas," and Resistance to the JWB's Agenda

In 1917, Jacob Rader Marcus, a young rabbinical student, defied the wishes of his family, ignored the exemptions open to seminary students, and enlisted in the army. He served as a company clerk, first on a base near Cincinnati, then at Camp Sheridan in Montgomery, Alabama, and finally in France. Marcus went on to an illustrious career as a Reform rabbi and an eminent scholar of Jewish history. He founded the American Jewish Archives on the Cincinnati campus of Hebrew Union College (HUC), where he taught for many years, and he served as president of both the Reform movement's Central Conference of American Rabbis and of the American Jewish Historical Society.[1] Marcus kept a diary during his time in the service and periodically published his reflections in Jewish newspapers and journals, including that of his alma mater, the *Hebrew Union College Monthly*.[2]

Marcus had not yet received rabbinical ordination when he entered the army, so he could not qualify for a commission as a chaplain, and as he was an enlisted man rather than a civilian, he could not work directly for the Jewish Welfare Board (JWB). But as a rabbinical student, he maintained connections with local JWB representatives, led informal religious services, and consulted with the JWB on matters pertaining to Jewish soldiers.[3] Through his position as a sort of semiofficial Jewish religious worker, Marcus often heard about the experiences of other Jewish soldiers, and his diary entries show that he took an active interest in the status of Jewish men in military camps and in the dynamics of Judaism and Jewish life in the WWI American military.

Marcus agreed with the JWB that the behavior of each individual Jewish soldier reflected on all Jewish soldiers. He believed that every Jewish man bore a responsibility to maintain high standards of conduct in order to protect the reputation of his fellow Jews, but while the JWB argued that honorable behavior could not fail to enhance non-Jewish opinions of both Judaism and Jewish soldiers, Marcus took a less optimistic position. In an essay entitled "The Jewish Soldier" for the *Hebrew Union College Monthly*, Marcus wrote,

> The Jew, manifestly even in the army, stands out as a distinct group, and to the American nation as a whole becomes the representative par excellence of American Jewry, whether they will or no. A Jewish deserter, a Jewish coward, a Jewish scoundrel reflects not only upon himself but upon the entire Jewish following. Jews are constantly under fire; to deny this would be foolish; consequently, it is incumbent upon the group to help every individual member thereof to attain a high degree of moral pride.[4]

Where the JWB aspired to a new era of friendships and mutual respect between Jews and non-Jews, Marcus believed that Jews in the military faced constant fire from their compatriots. Where the JWB depicted ideal Jewish men engaged in the shaping of a better Jewish future, Marcus focused on men who needed awakening to the fact that, as Jews, they could not make it in the army without one another's help. To Marcus, the differences between Jews and non-Jews seemed obvious and unlikely to fade away. Even in situations in which non-Jewish soldiers accepted a Jewish man among them, Marcus speculated that such relationships did not indicate greater acceptance of Jews more broadly but rather an assumption that the man in question was not "really Jewish." Analyzing why he himself managed to get along with his non-Jewish comrades while other Jewish soldiers did not, Marcus wrote,

> Sgt. told me in a whisper that the whole Supply Co. raised Hell when they heard a Jew (Aaronsohn) was going to come into their outfit but they soon found that he was a good kid. Traeger they also say is a fine boy. No commentary needed. Jew, no good, pariah—know him, find he's honorable and true and capable. I wonder what they think of me. They tell me these things. Maybe I'm one of those Jews who are not really Jews.[5]

Marcus did, in fact, differ in significant ways from many American Jewish soldiers. American born and educated, he was affiliated with the Reform movement and saw himself as thoroughly American. Indeed, Marcus came close to embodying just the sort of ideals the JWB hoped all Jewish soldiers would live up to. He had volunteered for the military and served honorably. He won the trust and confidence of his non-Jewish officers and comrades while remaining unashamed and outspoken about being Jewish. But any man who had filed his first papers for citizenship qualified for the draft, and many Jewish soldiers in the American Expeditionary Forces (AEF) had immigrated to the United States only a few years or even a few months before entering the service. Foreign-born men may have composed almost one-third of the Jewish soldier population, nearly twice the percentage of foreign-born men in the AEF as a whole.[6] Yiddish speakers—newly arrived from eastern and east-central Europe, Orthodox in their religious practice or leftist in their political leanings—were much more likely than Marcus or his friend and HUC classmate Aaronsohn to be seen as "really Jewish" rather than "100 percent American."[7]

On the one hand, Marcus's comments offered support for the JWB's hope that through military service, non-Jewish soldiers could come to see individual Jewish men as "honorable and true and capable." But they also emphasized the challenge of transcending not just the religious differences between Americans but the cultural, political, and linguistic differences that set some Jews apart from their fellow soldiers. In asking whether or not he was "one of those Jews who are not really Jews," Marcus pointed out that Jews did not constitute a uniform or unified community and that Jewish soldiers did not necessarily understand their identities in the same ways as one another or as the JWB representatives who were there, ostensibly, to serve them. Many Jewish soldiers had no interest in redefining themselves in light of what the JWB deemed to be appropriate, and even more felt highly skeptical of the possibility of true camaraderie between Jews and Christians. Marcus noted that non-Jewish soldiers confided in him, but he suspected that they would not have done so if they saw him as "really Jewish." Marcus did not attempt to pass himself off as a non-Jew but suggested that ambiguity about his Jewishness allowed him to integrate into his outfit in ways that "real Jews" could not. He worried that, rather than leading non-Jewish soldiers to look beyond their prejudices and see what they shared with Jewish men, his acceptance merely drew attention to the fact that while some Jews resembled Christian Americans, many did not.

JWB officials remained convinced that they could use the war as a chance to craft a cohesive and appropriately American Jewish identity that reinforced the essential equality between American men— Protestants, Catholics, and Jews. Jewish soldiers and their communities, however, were often reluctant to embrace this vision and vocal about their dissatisfaction. Letters chronicling the complaints of Jewish soldiers and their families rained down upon the heads of JWB fieldworkers and poured into JWB offices. Orthodox Jews complained that the JWB was forcing Reform Judaism down the throats of their defenseless sons. Reform Jews expressed anger over the uncompromising and un-American demands of their more traditional coreligionists. Other Jews, particularly more recent immigrants, rejected the notion that differences between Christians and Jews had ceased to have significance in the military. The attempt to use the soldiers' welfare work in order to shape a unified American Jewish identity faced resistance from across different factions of a diverse Jewish civilian and soldier population. The JWB had secured a unique position from which to advance its vision of American Jewish manhood and American Judaism. Getting Jews to comply with that vision, however, proved no easy feat.

Orthodox Complaints

While the JWB had managed to successfully advocate for the practice of Judaism in the military, the nature of that practice remained a highly contentious issue. In the debate over the provision of kosher food, the JWB demonstrated both a willingness to comply with the requirements of the War Department and a desire to find a middle path between Orthodox and Reform Judaism. The Jewish public, soldiers, and even some Jewish chaplains apparently did not share this desire and were vocal in their objections. Orthodox rabbi Nachman Heller, who had evidently been turned down for a position in the chaplaincy, wrote to JWB chairman Colonel Harry Cutler to voice his anger about the type of Judaism the JWB seemed to be promoting in the US military. Filled with frustration, he concluded that his refusal for a commission

> strengthens the proof that your subordinates taboo the Orthodox, justifying this wise the numerous accusations and the multifarious indictments

that the Yiddish press arraigned against the Jewish Welfare Board and its
one-sided activity, being an adjunct to the reform propaganda and forc-
ibly imposing reform notions upon innocent and devoted Jewish soldiers
of Orthodox and conservative parentage. Every Tom, Dick and Harry
of the Reform Rabbinate gets commissions at the expense of the poor
soldiers, and when some of the latter wished to hear an orthodox sermon
or a Yiddish address there is none to make it, notwithstanding the fact
the many Orthodox Rabbis offered their services for the Jewish Welfare.
Pardon my remarks, but they are true just the same.[8]

Letters from Orthodox rabbis, parents, and soldiers complained that
JWB workers lacked the experience to lead even Reform services and
had "insufficient knowledge of Hebrew to conduct orthodox service."[9]
Others writers argued that workers' lack of knowledge alone did not create the problem but rather that the seemingly anti-Orthodox bias of the
JWB made its workers unacceptable to many soldiers. JWB headquarters received reports from soldiers complaining about the seemingly reformist agendas of the rabbis it employed. Lieutenant M. E. Gross wrote
at length to angrily describe the attitude and conduct of Dr. Newfeld, the
camp rabbi at his base, Camp McClellan in Alabama:

Dr. Newfeld opened the service by saying "Gentlemen, kindly remove
your hats, but of course, those that don't care to, need't [sic]; for you see I
pray without a hat, and my prayers are just as well accepted; and besides
I do things here, just the same as I have been doing home in my house.
So do as you please.["]
    I noticed several of the men looking around trying to see just what the
others would do. [Some "young men of the good Jewish type" covered
their heads] but others kept their heads bare, because they had faith in
the Rabbi, and they thought that anything he does ought to be right. Then
he remarked, "You know gentlemen, in my temple where I was Chaplain,
I have the richest and best type of men, and they all pray without their
hats, so you therefore can do as you see fit." He then started the evening
services and night, starting with "Mayariv" leaving out the Le Chi Dode,
etc. The reason for same he stated was that the books did not contain
them, and besides, were not so important.

[After the service was finished] . . . he bid us to sit down, and continued our previous discussion. In the meantime, he takes out from his desk a nice big cigar, and strikes a match, lighting it and continues to smoke. The men were very much astounded at this. . . . The men at first held back, but some of them seemed to say, "If our Rabbi can smoke on Sabbath why can't we?" Immediately the boys started asking each other for smokes, and finally lighted up their cigarettes, and puffed away to the delight of the Rabbi.

He then explained that there are various things that he considers fanatic, and he mentioned several amongst which he enumerated, the "Prayer of the Havdulah" on Saturday nights, praying [with] a hat, not doing this and that on Sabbath and the many restrictions etc. He practically proclaimed himself a reformed Jew and stated that he did not believe in this and that. . . .

As far as I am concerned, I decided the best place for me to pray is right in my own quarters, and in the good old way, and not to be beguiled by this reformist. Just imagine before the men left the tent, he announces there are no services tomorrow (Shabes), but there will be Sunday morning. Can you imagine the effect it is taking upon these young men, some of whom come to the tent to try to learn what is right, and some to continue their services as they have done in the past. Davening with Tfillen or a Tallus [praying with phylacteries or a prayer shawl], is an unheard of thing here.[10]

Lieutenant Gross described multiple violations of traditional Jewish law committed by Rabbi Newfeld: praying without a head covering, eliminating prayers from the liturgy, lighting a flame and smoking on the Sabbath, and disregarding the Sabbath day services altogether. According to Gross, he found Rabbi Newfeld's transgressions disturbing, but even more egregious, Newfeld appeared to be using his position as the JWB's representative on the base as an opportunity to lead Jewish soldiers away from traditional practice and into the camp of the Reform, and Gross feared for the souls of the more naïve and susceptible Jewish men around him.

Harry G. Fromberg, president of the Orthodox Young Israel Synagogue in New York City, had heard reports similar to that of Lieutenant

Gross from soldiers affiliated with his own congregation. Outraged by the religious conduct and practice of JWB field-workers, he wrote to Colonel Cutler to demand change:

> In some cases, your representatives do not know the first thing about Judaism, or Jewish customs. In almost all cases, your representatives openly violate and desecrate the Sabbath by smoking, and permitting smoking on Friday night and Saturday, and even ridiculing the idea of those who feel differently, and whose feeling they have hurt. In one case in a Southern Camp, a young man approached one of our members in service, and stated that that day was his "Jahrzeit" [anniversary of a death, presumably one of his parents] and asked if a "minion" [quorum of ten men] could be gathered, to enable him to say the "KADDISH," [prayer recited by mourners] our member accompanied this young man to "your representative," and informed him of the facts and peculiarly enough, the gentlemen in charge of the Jewish Welfare work asked, "what is a minion"?[11]

Fromberg further warned that "Young Israel Synagogue is determined to take every possible means to remedy these evils. I hope it will not have to go any further than the sending of this communication."[12] Even the JWB field representative and Orthodox rabbi David de Sola Pool, who traveled around the country assessing conditions in military camps, admitted that the religious services provided did not always suit the soldiers. In one camp, he reported that even though "the boys who come for the services and Jewish talks are about 90% of old fashioned Jewish upbringing with a Yiddish orthodox background . . . [t]he service was so thoroughly Americanized that no one of the boys could join in with the Kaddish even when the Kaddish was announced. They did not recognize that the opportunity for saying Kaddish had arrived."[13]

JWB chairman Harry Cutler and Chaplains Committee chairman Cyrus Adler sympathized with the demands of traditional Jews, both soldiers and civilians, for Orthodox religious services in the camps. Indeed, Adler still considered himself and the seminary he led as part of the Orthodox "wing" of Judaism.[14] The JWB, however, remained bound by the regulations of the War Department and by the JWB's desire to transcend denominational differences and prove that Judaism was no barrier to Americanness. Both Cutler and Adler were thus reluctant to advocate strongly for Jewish practices such as dietary laws or Sabbath observances, which deviated too far from the norms set by the Protestant Young Men's Christian Association (YMCA).

The JWB also faced significant logistical challenges to providing traditional Jewish religious services. HUC-trained Reform Jewish men represented by far the largest group of rabbis in the Chaplains Corps, and given the obstacles set up by both the War Department and the JWB itself to the appointment of Orthodox Jews either as chaplains or fieldworkers, the JWB often had to rely upon the voluntary services of local rabbis to meet the religious demands of tradition-minded soldiers. Even in the New York City area, with its large Jewish population, finding sufficient numbers of Orthodox rabbis with the necessary qualifications and the willingness to volunteer their services proved difficult.[15]

David de Sola Pool, reporting on conditions at Camp Upton in Yaphank, New York, on eastern Long Island, wrote that despite the large population of traditional Jews at the camp, JWB representatives struggled to find a rabbi willing to travel there in order to lead Sabbath services: "Only a few Rabbis can be spared, or believe they can be spared, over the Sabbath. Going to Camp Upton to conduct services on Friday evening involves leaving town on Friday morning at 10 o'clock and not getting back to town until Saturday evening at 8 or 9 o'clock."[16] Moreover, these rabbis would still be required to function within the Commission on Training Camp Activities (CTCA) requirement that welfare services be open to all interested soldiers, which meant that the rabbis had to speak English. According to de Sola Pool, "The English speaking orthodox Rabbis who can be called upon for this service are few in number," making the task of finding one willing to spend his Shabbat in Yaphank all the more challenging.[17] Joseph Hyman, a JWB field-worker at Camp Upton, made the point even more strongly:

> May I point out, that although the majority of the boys here are orthodox, it has been difficult for me to get an orthodox Rabbi to conduct our services, for the reason that few orthodox rabbis will ride on the Sabbath. Consequently they must come up before sunset, sleep over-night, stay all day Saturday, and return Saturday after sunset. To do this, we must have a place for them to sleep and must make some arrangements for kosher food. I have the facilities neither for the one, nor for the other.[18]

Beyond the problem of finding rabbis willing to volunteer, however, military regulations often interfered with adherence to traditional religious practice. The camp rabbi whom Lieutenant Gross complained about may have purposefully chosen to replace traditional Saturday morning Sabbath worship with a Sunday service instead, but he may also have had little choice in the matter. When Colonel Cutler questioned US Navy chaplain David Goldberg about his decision not to hold Shabbat services on Saturday mornings, Goldberg explained, with some exasperation, that Saturday mornings are "devoted to inspection of men and barracks." He held Friday evening, Saturday afternoon, and Sunday morning services because the men were free to attend at those times.[19]

Far from finding an acceptable and unifying middle path toward shaping an American Judaism, the JWB found that military regulations, CTCA priorities, and logistical limitations left its programs open to charges that the board sought to be an agent of religious reform. To make matters worse, Reform Jewish rabbis and soldiers also found much to dislike in the JWB's programs and attempts to establish common ground.

Reform Complaints

Chaplain Goldberg, a Reform rabbi, had his own complaints about the JWB's religious programs and its attempts to create a unified American Judaism. In his opinion, the JWB opted to pander to an Orthodox civilian population without considering the needs of the men or the realities of military life. In particular, he objected to the JWB's attempts to create a standardized liturgy for Jewish soldiers. The JWB put a great deal of effort into the preparation of an *Abridged Prayer Book for Jews in the Army and Navy of the United States*, published by the Jewish Publication Society and distributed to all Jewish soldiers, chaplains, camp rabbis, and field-workers.[20] Orthodox, Conservative, and Reform rabbis worked together to determine its composition, but Goldberg refused to use it. Instead, he designed his own "service folder, appropriate for communal prayer." When challenged by Cutler on this deviation from JWB policy, Goldberg replied that he found the JWB's prayer book, with its attempts to reconcile the needs of traditional and Reform Jews, utterly useless. He stated that regardless of the background of the men under his care, "less that fifty percent of [them], according to actual census taken, understand how to read the Hebrew, and of those that understand to read it, only about three percent could give the meaning of what they read, hence most of the service must be conducted in English." Moreover, he added, "the committee will also readily understand that a well conducted, disciplined and dignified service for men in uniform must necessarily culminate in the singing of the National Anthem, and in a prayer for the government," a prayer that the JWB had evidently not seen fit to include.[21]

In a two-part article for the *Reform Advocate* entitled "A Chaplain's Arraignment of the Army Prayer Book," Goldberg made his case:

> From cover to cover it completely ignores the needs of both soldier and sailor in that it provides nothing that would be expressive of the spirit that animates, or ought to animate the man in uniform. It is simply an abridged book for the civilian Orthodox Jew. The book is inadmissible because of the very alien spirit in which it was conceived. Throughout the prayers, daily or Sabbath, the *goluth* [diasporic] sentiment alone reigns supreme, while there is nothing in keeping with the spirit of the brave American soldier who has joined the colors of our great commonwealth to fight the battle of democracy. . . .
>
> Now, no one, unless he wishes to shut his eyes to existing conditions, could reasonably expect the Jewish soldier or sailor to lay his *Tephillin* [phylacteries], to robe himself with his *Talith* [prayer shawl] and to keep up with the "silent" *Modim* while the reader recites the "loud" one. Nor could anyone believe the men in uniform to have the time for such a lengthy after-meal grace. . . . And it is necessary to point out the utter incongruity of the "*Shelo Asanu*" prayer—one of a type that bids the *goluth* Jew to utter praise for not having created him a woman, a slave and a Goy—during a service at which, it is inevitable, that there should be as many non-Jews present as there may be Jews?[22]

> [T]he Book . . . is wholly inadequate, certainly for our men in the naval service who are mostly American born, and all so decidedly American that fixed formulae and *goluth* sentiment hold no appeal to them.[23]

To Goldberg, the JWB's attempts to serve the needs of all Jews left it kowtowing to Old World tradition and out of touch with the attitudes of American men who felt themselves to be at home in America and enfranchised as American citizens.

Company clerk and future Reform rabbi Jacob Rader Marcus agreed that the JWB's attempt to create a liturgy acceptable to all Jews had failed miserably. Unlike Goldberg, however, Marcus did not concern himself with the American spirit of the men. Rather he objected to the attempt to use the war to force Jewish religious unity. He wrote in his diary that "the Welfare prayer book is looked upon with disgust by the orthodox boys."[24] He later wrote an article for the *American Hebrew and Jewish Messenger* in which he declared,

> The Soldier's Prayer Book is a Nightmare. . . . This prayer book is a serious error. You would feel quite dejected if you saw a group of American soldiers trying to conduct a religious service with a set of them. The young man who has been accustomed to pray with the aid of the reform Liturgy finds it bewildering, and after aimlessly turning a page or two, stops reading altogether. The Orthodox boy takes a look at it, reads whatever is there of the Hebrew prayers and supplies the remainder from memory. . . . Leaders among Jewish groups should rid themselves of the false notion that they can legislate Judaism for the Jew. The mere fact that the representatives of all the important Jewish groups determined on a literary error does not mean that the Jewish soldier will bow in reverence to it.[25]

To Marcus the idea of "legislating" Judaism to the Jews seemed at best foolish and at worst an expression of the paternalism that the "important" and Americanized Jewish leaders at the helm of the JWB felt toward common soldiers. In many ways, however, this act of trying to determine and enforce a cohesive form of American Judaism and American Jewish identity was central to the JWB's self-assigned mission. Just as it expected its rabbis and field representatives to create models of Jewish masculinity, JWB officials hoped to legislate Judaism to the Jews—or at least to provide a cohesive, American version of Judaism that all Jewish soldiers would be willing to embrace as their own. The opportunity that the war and the War Department created for bridging denominational differences—as well as building a unified community with an identity centered on religious observances that reflected American values, citizenship, and democracy—lay at the heart of what the JWB sought to accomplish in taking on its role as the provider of Jewish soldiers' welfare services. Much to its chagrin, however, Jewish soldiers, while a captive audience, were not a passive one. Chaplains Committee chairman Cyrus Adler sought to build genuine consensus among the different denominational and organizational leaders on his committees, but consensus at the top did not necessarily translate to agreement among the men.

The JWB argued that it had no particular agenda beyond serving what it saw as the best interests of the men. "The type of service must be that desired by the men, irrespective of the personal view of the Rabbi or Field representative conducting the service," JWB headquarters wrote to field-workers, camp rabbis, and chaplains. "The JWB cannot countenance anything in the way of propaganda for any one branch or section of the Jewish people. The democratic standard is the one which should be adhered to."[26] But imposition of this democratic standard asserted the value both of adapting Jewish cultural practices in order to find middle ground between diverse Jewish needs and, occasionally, of placing the requirements of the military and the government above those of tradition. Jews advocating for Yiddish cultural identity, Zionism, Orthodoxy, or Reform Judaism did not necessarily agree with the value of compromise, nor did they always accept that the dictates of the War Department should be allowed to interfere with their understanding of either Judaism or Jewish identity. The JWB's attempts to impose democracy on American Judaism fell far short of expectations: JWB executives eventually decided that *The Abridged Prayer Book for Jews in the Army and Navy of the United States* would be reserved for overseas use, while "both the [Orthodox] Singer Prayer book and the [Reform] Union Prayer book should be supplied in accordance with demand" on US military camps and bases. The JWB had also intended to put out a songbook for Jewish soldiers and sailors, but the selection of appropriate songs proved too contentious to bring the project to fruition.[27]

The Jewish Press

Writers in the Yiddish press also joined in the chorus of criticism leveled at the JWB. Like some Orthodox critics, authors from across the spectrum of opinion accused the JWB of promoting assimilation, but many of their concerns focused less on the sacrifices of religious stricture than on threats to Jewish cultural distinctiveness. Articles and editorials depicted the JWB as an agency of the "Jehudim"—of snobby central European Jews—who sought to use the war to force a program of social and religious reform on their eastern European brethren and compel them to Americanize. In *Dos Yiddishe Folk*, a Yiddish-language Zionist publication, author Isaac First railed against the JWB, claiming that "faithful to the Jehudic assimilitative traditions, it has from the very outset cancelled every thing that was genuinely Jewish from its program. . . . '[D]ie Herren' of the Board sought to obliterate the home influence from the soldier's memory, to wean him from his Jewish rites and customs, and in general, to 'make a man of him.'"[28]

In the Orthodox-leaning *Yiddishes Tageblatt*, an editorial also took umbrage with the suggestion that the Jewish men of the East Side were not manly enough already and required instruction from the JWB to be remade as real Americans:

> The aim of the Jewish Welfare Board . . . is to make better Americans of the . . . Jewish soldiers in the American army. This . . . cannot be the aim of welfare, for the simple reason that the Jewish soldiers are Americans of the best type, and it is impossible to have better Americans than they are. . . . It is the biggest insult for the Jewish soldiers to be told that their Americanism needs improvement, as if there were any doubt of their loyalty and appreciation of America. . . . A few weeks ago we stated in the same column that the Jewish Welfare Board takes the same played out stand, taken by the little group of rich Jewish aristocrats who send their hirelings to "uplift" the East Side, as if the East Side or the other Jewish immigrants in general are in need of anyone to lead them on the straight path. The Jewish Welfare Board is of the opinion that that it must send to the camps "chinovnikes," (officials) who are to teach the Jewish young men a lesson in Americanism. The Jewish soldiers have nothing to learn of the Welfare Board, its leaders and employees. It is the duty of the Jewish Welfare Board to send to the camps men who understand the religious and social needs of the Jewish soldiers.[29]

Likewise, an editorial in the socialist-leaning *Forverts* argued that the JWB was completely out of touch with the men's real needs. The board's workers tried to satisfy the soldiers with Americanized Judaism but missed the essence of what the men required: "The Jewish soldiers have not the spiritual food, the spiritual satisfaction which they require, and without which they cannot possibly get along. This is the trouble. The soldiers have no Yiddish books to read, they get no Yiddish entertainments, theatrical performances, concerts and the like. . . . The German Yehudim have built a small house for the Jewish soldiers and all of the Jewish young men assemble there every evening, but there is nothing for them to do. The only Jewish book which is there provided is the Pentateuch."[30]

In the Hebrew-language paper *Ha'ivri*, editors commented that "recently, one hears many complaints about the work of the Jewish Welfare Board. Many of the soldiers themselves complain regarding the Board because of the fact that it is not interested in the Jewish soldier and does not take into consideration his feelings and his moral needs."[31] And the radical newspaper, *Die Warheit*, which had been critical of the JWB since its founding, doubled down on claims that the JWB was an institution characterized by German Jewish high-handedness, hostility to, and ignorance of authentic Jewish culture, going so far as to suggest that the JWB was attempting to Christianize the men in order to make them fit better into American society. In an editorial entitled "Verboten," the author complained that the JWB actively undermined the type of welfare work that the men truly wanted and that *Die Warheit* was trying to provide:

> The work undertaken by the "Warheit" to ease the moral and spiritual condition of the Jewish soldiers in the camps and to give them the thing which they need so badly while they are preparing to offer themselves for America and for the Jewish name, was suddenly stopped by the Jewish Welfare Board without warning.
>
> The infamous Junker "Verboten" the poison which kills the spirit and brains, was spread by a brutal hand among the Jewish soldiers in Camp Upton, and put an end to all hopes and expectations of the thousands of our boys who are aching for a Jewish word, a Jewish folk song, a Jewish performance. . . . The "Warheit" decide to help the Jewish soldiers . . . and it arranged a number of first class concerts which would appeal to the Jewish soldier in camp. . . . This caused great panic among the Yehudim.

It was too much Yiddish. The Warheit interferes with their program of driving the Jewish soldiers to spiritual conversion to Christianity.[32]

Through its connection to the War Department, the JWB had the power to keep *Die Warheit* and other Jewish organizations, particularly those with different political views, off of military bases and even to silence complaints in the press. However, the broad base of these critiques, across religious and ideological perspectives, indicated mistrust that was too widespread to be easily squashed. Eastern European Jews feared that the JWB was working against the real interests and needs of Jewish soldiers, which they understood as based on cultural distinctiveness rather than shared American identity. Eastern European journalists and editors additionally resented the condescension they perceived in the action and attitudes of the wealthier, more Americanized men who led and worked for the JWB, but even acculturated Jewish critics raised objections to the JWB's programs. Writing in the English-language newspaper, the *American Jewish Chronicle*, philosopher and advocate of Zionism and Jewish cultural distinctiveness Horace Kallen lambasted the JWB:

> We do not know what the Jewish Welfare Board is doing, anyhow. We only know that it is composed of a promiscuous lot of philanthropic Jews, most of them considerably beyond middle age, with the rabbinic or near rabbinic element dominating. We know that it has started with certain assumptions concerning the needs of Jewish soldiers which a Jewish Welfare Board might serve. . . . [But b]ecause the purposes of the Welfare Board seem to have nothing to do with the needs of the solider . . . its aim appears to be to satisfy itself, not to serve the soldier.[33]

For Kallen, as for many of the writers in the Yiddish press, support for an Americanized form of Judaism, under the influence of rabbis or "near rabbis" and bolstered by access to copies of "the Pentateuch," was a laughable substitute for the Jewish culture needed to support the social and spiritual needs of "soldiers of Jewish blood."[34] These needs, according to Kallen and others, went unmet and misunderstood by the JWB as it attempted to prove that Jews were just like their Christian compatriots.[35] The young Jacob Rader Marcus feared that the real Jews among the troops could not easily fit in. Critics in the Jewish press argued that they did not—and should not want to.

Real Americans and "Poor Jehudas"

True to the accusations raised in the Jewish press, the idea of improving Jewish soldiers who failed to live up to American standards did play a crucial part in the JWB's wartime agenda. Just as the War Department sought to use soldiers' welfare programs to create better American citizens, the JWB hoped to use its own programs to create better American Jews. The debate over the extent to which Jewish ritual practices on military bases could or should tilt toward either Reform or Orthodox Judaism was part of a larger discussion about Americanization and the identity of American Jewish men. Adler hoped to find an acceptable middle ground upon which to base Jewish religious practice in the military in order to help reform traditionally minded immigrant Jewish men among the troops while still encouraging them to remain committed to Judaism. JWB leaders hoped that time in the military would teach Jewish soldiers how to comport themselves as American men and prepare them to take their places as Jewish American citizens at the end of the war.

Company clerk Jacob Rader Marcus, a skeptical observer of Jewish life in the camps, doubted whether such a rapid transformation was possible. On the one hand, he had no sympathy for Jewish soldiers who tried "to deny themselves" and pass for Christians, but he saw those Jews who could not or would not live up to the standards of Americanness as damaging to the position of all Jewish soldiers in the military.[36] "It seems," he wrote, that "there is bound to be prejudice all the time" between Jews and non-Jews.[37] Yet sometimes, he claimed, those "poor Jehudas" brought it upon themselves by behaving in ways that seemed strange to the other men, by making it appear that Jews were conspiring to help one another, or simply by appearing weak. About one such Jew, Marcus wrote, "That egg, Baumgarten is a might poor Jehuda he is always around when there are privileges for Jews especially passes. You'll often find men of his type. He talks too much that fellow does. . . . When the Lt. is a Jew, and the Top Kick and the Company Clerk are Jews then rest assured that you will find prejudice."[38]

On another occasion, Marcus commented, "I got the boys talking on Anti-Semitism just to try them out and find out their experiences, I find that the boys who stick up for their rights have little trouble tho' they meet the A.S. invariably. Others, weaker members, suffer a great deal. Even in the fighting divisions right on the lines the Jewish boys had trouble. It exists at all times and under all circumstances."[39] In one entry, Marcus complained that Jewish "whore mongers" provided a veritable "sermon" on the sinful Jews versus "the clean-cut . . . Christian."[40] Another day, he noted that "Jews are not popular and furthermore they have trouble with their commanders because of their individualism. C.C.'s find trouble with Jews because they approach them with suspicion."[41]

Marcus claimed that anti-Semitism existed regardless of the behavior of Jewish soldiers or even the presence of Jews, but he held those men who did not conform to American military norms as partially responsible for the prejudice that existed. Some among his friends blamed these "really Jewish" Jews for their Orthodoxy, their Zionism, and their inability to speak English properly.[42] Marcus had more sympathy for them but argued that these men had no chance of fitting in and that this inability was often the cause of attacks against them. Just after the war's end, while still stationed in France, Marcus wrote,

> I have found something that has been crystalizing in my mind in regard to prejudice as we understand it. It is this: The orthodox, the foreign born for the most part have trouble. Americans who are intelligent do not experience much. Just the ordinary attack that one hears and has almost learned to expect. The common Jew, the foreigners however suffer indescribably, because they cannot accustom themselves to American ways. Other Jews say they bring it on themselves. They do at times but they are not to be blamed. Their environment is. What can a poor foreigner, with a limited education who has suffered Hellish persecution in Russia from the Military know of American patriotism? Often they have come to this army after escaping the Russian army. From one to another. For a native American patriotism is no virtue. It is natural with us. Yet they expect it of these poor creatures who have never been taught the virtue and to whom it can have no significance by virtue of the fact they lived under tyranny.[43]

To JWB leaders, the military provided the ideal environment in which to teach those "poor foreigners" about American patriotism, virtues, and standards. In an American military camp, soldiers would be exposed to real Americans—Jewish and Christian. They believed that this exposure would lead to feelings of friendship between the men, and they were equally convinced that by socializing together, un-Americanized Jews would come to embrace American norms.

The space in which this socialization was to occur was the soldiers' welfare hut. Huts served as headquarters for all welfare activities in camp and often served as the office and sleeping and living quarters for camp welfare workers. While the welfare organizations paid for the huts themselves, permission to build one had to be obtained from the CTCA, and the JWB did not receive that permission immediately.[44] Instead, the CTCA decided that it would be preferable for JWB workers to simply borrow space from the larger, better funded, and better connected YMCA.[45]

Some members of the JWB Executive Committee agreed with the CTCA's decision to have JWB-sponsored activities take place in YMCA buildings, rather than in separate Jewish ones. If they planned to use welfare services to shape a generation of men who embraced their Jewishness while socializing and interacting easily with non-Jews, then providing separate spaces for Jewish soldiers to relax, read, or attend classes, lectures, or sing-alongs could only prove unnecessary or even counterproductive. Insistence on separate Jewish huts, moreover, ran the risk of running afoul of the CTCA's demands for nonsectarianism. The JWB made its case for the need for separate religious services, but recreational huts seemed hard to justify on that basis. The erection of separate huts could, moreover, provoke suspicion that Jewish men did not want to socialize with other soldiers or that they received special treatment. "A separate Jewish 'Hut' a separate Jewish Hostess House, even a separate Jewish auditorium," warned Eustace Seligman of the Judge Advocate's Office at Camp Upton, "would have that undesirable effect [of creating sectarian discrimination]."[46] Jewish chaplain Lee Levinger also feared that separate Jewish huts would do more harm than good. He wrote to JWB headquarters from a camp in Illinois to attest, "I do not believe in our erecting recreation huts in a camp such as this one. . . . I have found no demand from the Jewish men for recreation huts. . . . My opinion is that our buildings should always be planned so as to help the general needs and not at all for the specific needs of the Jewish men."[47]

Levinger offered no evidence from soldiers regarding their opinions on recreation huts, but his assessment of what the soldiers wanted and what would prove best both for them and for the JWB's plans received powerful support from the financiers Jacob and Mortimer Schiff. The Schiffs, both of whom played significant roles in the founding and funding of the JWB, wrote to Chairman Cutler to express their disapproval of any suggestion of creating separate Jewish buildings. The elder Schiff wrote:

> I am firmly of the opinion that your Board should make no appropriation for buildings and should in every instance arrange with the YMCA for the use of their buildings in every camp, for religious services and perhaps some special lectures.
>
> I think it would for obvious reasons be a grave mistake if beyond this, Jewish soldiers and sailors were segregated from their comrades, and would likely lead to prejudice and other consequences which would be very much deplored.[48]

The younger Schiff agreed with his father. After the erection of a building at one camp for use by JWB workers, Mortimer Schiff received word from a Mrs. Levi, who had recently visited the camp, that soldiers used the building like a recreational hut.[49] Schiff immediately wrote to Cutler to object, explaining that

> according to her description, our building is being used as a social and recreational center—in fact, as a Jewish club—which is, of course, exactly what we did not want to happen. In addition, it appears to be used as a hostess house and Mrs. Levi told me that when she was there, the boys were using it to receive their women friends and relatives.[50] It appears that this is just the kind of segregation we have been trying to avoid and that it is not being sufficiently impressed upon the boys that the [Young Women's Christian Association] hostess houses are there to receive their friends, and the YMCA buildings for their own recreational and social purposes.[51]

David de Sola Pool wrote to Mortimer Schiff to agree that separate JWB huts could only prove detrimental to the men and to the goals of the JWB. In a memo about conditions at Camp Upton, de Sola Pool explained to Schiff, "The policy of not putting up special buildings for Jewish men is unquestionably sound. The Knights of Columbus, in erecting their own buildings for Catholics, have created much frictional feeling. In fact, there is a better relationship and far more cooperation between the Jews and the Protestants, than between the Protestants and the Catholics."[52]

Just as the question of whether or not to provide kosher food pressed the limits of what the JWB could define as nonsectarian within the rhetorical framework created by the CTCA, the question of whether or not the JWB should build separate Jewish huts put the issue of Jewish difference to the test. The JWB insisted upon the importance of preserving a sense of Jewish religious difference and argued that by drawing on the best of Jewish tradition, Jewish men would become better Americans. The best in American democracy, the JWB argued, not only allowed but even demanded that Jews maintain their religious distinctiveness. But the prospect of separate Jewish soldiers' welfare huts threatened to cross the line from drawing strength and pride from one's tradition to outright advocacy of segregation. This, argued men such as the Schiffs, Levinger, and de Sola Pool, went too far. Besides, de Sola Pool added, building Jewish huts created the risk of hindering exactly the sort of social and cultural improvement that the JWB saw as part of its mandate. Providing Jewish soldiers with separate spaces would indicate a willingness to cater not to the essentials of Jewish tradition but to those elements that encouraged the "really Jewish" Jews—the sort who could not adapt appropriately to their American environment, provoked anti-Semitic attack, and made other Jews look bad. As de Sola Pool wrote to Mortimer Schiff,

> I see no call for us to do special educational work. The teaching of English to Yiddish speaking men is a pressing necessity. But it is no different from the teaching of English to Italian speaking men. Americanism does not necessitate the erection of a Ghetto through which to work. . . .
>
> The Yiddish speaking element at Camp Upton is surprisingly large. Nevertheless, I feel that Yiddish lectures, whether sermons or educational, are hardly called for. In these respects Americanization and Judaisation are required, not 'Yiddishisation." . . . Yiddish entertainments should not be encouraged [as they are] apt to be uncouth."[53]

Cyrus Janover, a field representative reporting from Camp Dix in New Jersey, supported de Sola Pool's observations and conclusions:

> A good many of the men have always lived in ghettos and are clannish. The circle of their acquaintance at home was always Jewish and they cannot all of a sudden change their habits of life. They want to be among Jews all the time when they are off duty in the camp. When they are in their barracks they group together and speak Yiddish to one another. When they speak to the representative who visits them in the barracks they often lapse into Yiddish. That practice incurs the wrath of the "Goyim" because they feel that they are talking about them when they do speak Yiddish. Some have said so. A man in the army cannot act in that manner. All must be friendly and mix well to enhance the esprit de corps. This condition of clannishness exists among the men upon entering a national army camp. It will wear off as they get accustomed to the service and get acclimated so to speak.[54]

To these JWB executives and informants, the risks involved in requesting permission to erect separate JWB huts seemed clear: They would provoke resentment from non-Jewish soldiers and slow the integration of Jewish ones. Rather than foster those aspects of Jewish tradition that complemented and supported Americanism, they would nurture those qualities that kept Jewish men separate from their compatriots and encourage attitudes out of keeping with American values. In de Sola Pool's words, Jewish huts would foster "Yiddishisation," which he associated with uncouth behavior, poor English, and unnecessary separation from other soldiers. They would be little more than Jewish "ghettos" within the camps, and nothing could be more undemocratic or further from the JWB's vision of America as a place where Jewish and Christian soldiers saw one another as brothers in arms. Better by far, these men agreed, that Jewish soldiers shake off their "clannishness" as soon as possible and embrace an American esprit de corps.

"Why in Heaven's Name Expect Us to Mingle with the Christians?"

Despite the confidence with which Janover predicted that Jewish and non-Jewish soldiers would learn to mix and socialize with one another, reports of Jewish soldiers' and field-workers' unhappiness at having to use YMCA buildings soon arrived at JWB headquarters. It seemed that some of the men, no matter how accustomed they may have become to the military or to American norms, felt uncomfortable in the huts provided by the YMCA and did not wish to use them.

Part of this discomfort resulted from the policies of the YMCA. While the JWB issued official statements praising the cooperativeness of the YMCA, field representatives complained in internal reports that YMCA secretaries, struggling to meet the demands of their own soldiers' welfare programs, accommodated the JWB only begrudgingly.[55] And while the YMCA insisted that its facilities remained open to all, sources of tension and irritation emerged between the two agencies. For example, YMCA chairman John Mott readily agreed that "the JWB is allowed to use the YMCA buildings when possible, and to have a representative stationed there," but felt compelled to add that "they are also allowed to distribute JWB stationery, but it is not to be left about on the various tables and desks."[56]

The distribution of stationery may seem like a small matter, but clearly Mott perceived it as important enough to banish JWB stationery from public view in YMCA buildings. And the JWB showed equal concern over the question of how to get the proper letterhead to Jewish and Christian soldiers. Distressed over the stationery situation, camp rabbi Bernard Ehrenreich wrote to JWB headquarters to warn that if a remedy could not be found, "the Jewish boy will write home on YMCA paper and the Gentile boy on Jewish Welfare paper."[57] Ehrenreich did not explain exactly what he feared would result from such a mix up, but certainly every letter sent by a Jewish soldier on YMCA paper represented a missed opportunity to advertise the good works of the JWB to the folks back home. The JWB must have agreed that the matter required attention because they wrote to all of their camp workers to stress the importance of the proper distribution of letterhead. The board's second general circular firmly told all field representative to "urge the men to write home on *our* stationery. Hand it to them, if necessary!"[58]

The demand that the JWB share the YMCA's buildings transformed the seemingly small matter of distributing stationery into a problem that required planning and strategy to resolve. Larger issues, such as how the JWB would be able to staff a camp if the YMCA deemed it impossible to have one of its men stationed in a YMCA building, proved far more intractable, as did questions concerning the content of YMCA programs. While, from their offices in New York, the Schiffs and some of the more highly placed JWB board and staff members may have seen the sharing of space with the YMCA as a golden opportunity to build trust and friendship between Jewish and non-Jewish men, many soldiers and JWB camp workers insisted that the YMCA used its huts not in the interest of religious pluralism but in order to pursue its evangelical work.

Soldiers, camp workers, and local rabbis sent letters to JWB headquarters complaining about the programs of the YMCA. One soldier wrote to his rabbi,

> Last night we marched into the YMCA and after witnessing some movies and listening to some singing, an army chaplain got up and spoke about Jesus Christ. Can you beat that for nerve when you stop to consider that every religion in the world was represented at the gathering? And at the close, he cried, "Who will stand up and pledge allegiance to his flag and Jesus Christ." Can you see his trick in trying to get us to stand up for Jesus Christ? I think it was a dirty, contemptible trick and it should be reported to the proper authorities.[59]

The rabbi, asking what the JWB planned to do about such "contemptible tricks," added that he had also heard that the YMCA at Fort Slocum near New York City had been distributing Yiddish translations of the New Testament.[60]

Some soldiers and camp workers noted that even when no overt evangelizing work was being done by the YMCA secretaries, it remained impossible to ignore that a YMCA building or a YMCA event was a distinctly Christian environment. Adolph Shirpser, a JWB camp worker stationed at Camp Fremont near Palo Alto, California, explained,

The YMCA as stated by their General Sec. J.R. Mott "is essentially and pre-eminently a Christian movement." The YMCA does not deny this [n] or in their work do they forget this. In their statistics of their buildings they register the number of "Christian" talks they have each day. Only today I was on a "retreat" with the Y Secretaries and if some of our doubting friends were along I feel assured they would have a decided change of mind on their return. The hymns, the talks, everything was decidedly Christian. They discussed the intercourse with the soldiers and were instructed how to act and what to do in a Christian way. I am not condemning them for it, in fact it is their duty and they are doing it.[61]

Shirpser did not blame the YMCA for pursuing their "decidedly Christian" goals and agendas, but he did wish to awaken his "doubting friends" at JWB headquarters to the fact that the YMCA used its buildings to further these goals, not merely to provide spaces for recreation. Other JWB representatives complained that using YMCA buildings made it difficult for them to fulfill their own mission to the soldiers. The JWB charged them with providing for the spiritual development of the men, but they found it impossible to hold Jewish religious services in YMCA buildings. The YMCA did not forbid them from holding services, but YMCA programs took precedence and often sapped Jewish services of their desired impact and influence. Joseph Hyman reported from Camp Upton,

The Friday night program of the YMCA includes boxing. It follows, therefore, that a great mass of soldier swarm into the building for the purpose of getting good seats for the boxing, and therefore stay through the Jewish services. Needless to say, the sort of crowd which is attracted by the boxing bout is not at all in keeping with the reverence and decorum due a prayer meeting.[62]

George Cohen reported from Camp Devens in Ayer, Massachusetts,

At one of the large YMCA hall[s] there are seated about 100 Jewish soldiers with prayer books in their hands. Along the sides of the room, Gentile soldiers are writing letters, smoking, chewing and conversing among themselves. Behind the Jews there are seated or standing several hundred

other Gentile soldiers who are either exchanging stories, smoking or star-
ing in wild-eyed wonder at the strange sight of a Jew leading the prayer
as he stands with a shawl thrown over his shoulders. Many snicker and
grin, as they hear a Hebrew word, or as they see the Jews rise and sit again
and again. In this environment a Jewish soldier is expected to say Kaddish!!! And to crown all this, a moving picture show is always scheduled
to take place in the same hall just as soon as the Jewish services are ended.
Imagine sir, the impatience of the other soldiers, and whether or not this
impatience is likely to show itself concretely.[63]

JWB workers declared that sharing quarters with the YMCA made
their job all but impossible. It made their programs and services entirely
dependent on the good will of the local YMCA secretary. It exposed the
men to exactly the sort of evangelizing activity that the JWB meant to
prevent, and it made conducting Jewish religious services awkward and
embarrassing. Upon discovering the conditions under which religious
services took place, Cohen noted, many of the soldiers became "too
timid or too disgusted to pray in such an environment" and opted to
pray on their own or to refrain from prayer altogether.[64] In either case,
the men's refusal to attend JWB religious services in YMCA buildings
threatened the JWB's project at a number of different levels. It undercut
the JWB's ability to determine the nature of Jewish religious practice in
the military, and it meant that at least some of the men would not benefit from the moral and spiritual guidance the JWB argued that Judaism
had to offer. Worse still, conducting Jewish religious services in YMCA
buildings did not promote religious pluralism or greater recognition of
Judaism's inherent affinity with Americanism. Instead, it enhanced the
sense of distance between the men and pointed out the differences between their religious traditions, leaving Jewish soldiers feeling embar-
rassed or ashamed and their non-Jewish compatriots "wild eyed" over
the bizarre rituals of Judaism.

As for the argument that separate Jewish huts would provoke anti-
Semitism and promote suspicion of Jewish separatism, several JWB
workers argued that both hostile feelings and separatism already existed, regardless of the policy on huts. JWB workers at Camp Devens,
Camp Upton, and Camp Dix pointed out that many of the Jewish soldiers could speak and read only in Yiddish and that forcing them to

spend their leisure time in a YMCA hut only made them uncomfortable and certainly did not help them form friendships.[65] These camp workers argued that the Jewish men first needed to learn English and familiarize themselves with American norms before they could benefit from shared social spaces. Until then, many of the Jewish soldiers simply did not want to socialize with non-Jewish soldiers. Some of the JWB workers lamented this fact but noted it nonetheless and urged the board to amend its plans in the face of resistance from the men. Coleman Silbert wrote from Camp Devens,

> 90% of the men here are of the orthodox type. Many, if not illiterate speak broken English. Few have more than a common school education. Many have immigrated within the last five to ten years. . . . These men with their distinctive features must have a haven. . . . Those opposed to such a building as I was at the beginning say that it runs counter to developing true Americans among the men. . . . We are dealing with realities and not theory. Donning a uniform has not transformed the man over night. He has not lost his old feelings and prejudices. Although it would be a pity if the war should accomplish no good, the millennium has not yet come.[66]

Reports from other camps struck a similar note. At Camp Upton, Joseph Hyman noted regretfully, "A great mass of the boys from the lower east side and in particular the Yiddish speaking and reading Russian Jewish boys, many merely declarants, cannot be brought to a sense of immediate communion socially with the Protestant American and the Catholic Irishmen up here; nor can they be educated over night in this respect."[67] And expressions of unwillingness to socialize with non-Jewish soldiers did not come only from Yiddish-speaking immigrants. Even Jacob Rader Marcus—who spoke English, got along well with the non-Jewish men in his unit, and expected Jews to adopt American military norms—lacked interest in socializing with non-Jews. While still based near Cincinnati, Marcus planned a social event with some of the Jewish men in his company. When one of the other men present suggested that they include non-Jewish soldiers among their guests, Marcus objected:

> He wants to pull some Goim [non-Jewish men] into the Hop. One of the[m] has referred to it as the Kike Ball. I'd like to have a talk with that

chile [*sic*]. He comes to our ball and then makes such insinuations. He'll not come at all if I have anything to say. O, No Boy. This is a Jewish ball, not a mixed affair. When Goim come they do you a favor; they condescend to honor you. I refuse to be honored. I try to be half-decent. Thank God I'm not a sniveling sycophant.[68]

In his more formal essay "The Jewish Soldier," Marcus used more delicate phrasing but still insisted that self-respecting Jewish men had no desire to mix with non-Jews socially. "Despite the fact that they all wear the khaki," he wrote, "they are still Catholics and Protestants and Jews, yes, Baptists and Presbyterians and Methodists, North and South. Miracles have not yet happened."[69]

Without miracles, Marcus and many camp workers argued, Jewish soldiers wanted separate Jewish spaces in which to socialize and relax, and if the JWB would not provide them, they would take matters into their hands. Coleman Silbert at Camp Devens warned that if it did not respond to the soldiers' demands for a separate Jewish hut, the JWB ran the risk of losing control over Jewish welfare activities in the area. The JWB could prevent other Jewish agencies from entering military camps, but it could not compel the men to attend its activities, nor could it keep them from seeking other Jewish resources when they had leave to venture outside of the camp or from forming their own organizations inside the camp. "The YMHA is exceedingly strong in New England," Silbert wrote, "it will be only a short time before the boys form one, unless we do something. It is far PREFERABLE that they meet in PROPER SURROUNDINGS UNDER PROPER GUIDANCE."[70] From Camp Upton and Camp Dix, the same refrain was heard: "The Protestants have the YMCA, the Catholics have the Knights of Columbus, we want ours."[71] Marcus proclaimed, "You must build Jewish shacks because the men in the ranks want them. Tell them that their request is horribly out of place, that it is un-American, that it smacks of separativeness, and they will look at you in unfeigned astonishment, in disgust."[72] Coleman Silbert, however, summed up the situation most clearly:

If at least we saw a non-sectarian building, we might pause and consider. But we see a building whose counters [display] certain distinctly Christian literature, where Christian songs are sung and played even when

there are no services, where the very air is Christian, whose whole movement is Christian. . . . The YMCA is not non-sectarian unless it be for all
shades of Protestantism. The YMCA claims it, no man thinks so except
the Jew. It is laughable if not ridiculous. . . . WHY IN HEAVEN'S NAME
EXPECT US TO MINGLE WITH THE CHRISTIANS? . . . We know
our problem, we know men, don't be misled by "Mu Yomeru Hagoyim"
[what the gentiles will say] let us hearken to the call of the men and that
of Judaism.[73]

JWB executives advocated policies that protected certain types of religious difference, while always promoting the goal of social integration.
The men in the camps had other ideas. In their limited hours of free
time, they had little interest in learning to see non-Jewish soldiers as
their brothers, nor did they believe that non-Jewish soldiers had any
genuine interest in them. The JWB argued for a religiously pluralistic
America that recognized the essential sameness of Jew and Christian.
Many of the soldiers and JWB field-workers, however, insisted that they
required a degree of separation from non-Jews in order to freely express
their identities as Jews.

The WWI military thus became not just a site for Jewish integration
into American society but a space in which the boundaries of religious
pluralism had to be negotiated. JWB executives had assumed that by
winning a place for Judaism within the military and the War Department's policies and programs, they could effectively assert that Jews
possessed a faith as authentically American as Protestants or Catholics.
This logic became the basis of the sort of tri-faith religious pluralism
that many Americans came to embrace by the middle of the twentieth
century. WWI Jewish soldiers, however, seemed to want something different. Unconvinced that their comrades would ever truly view them
simply as fellow Americans, and perhaps uninterested in achieving this
goal, Jewish soldiers wanted the JWB and the military to find ways to
accommodate their distinctiveness, rather than celebrate the things that
made them the same as other soldiers. By demanding separate spaces
in which to pray and socialize, these soldiers offered a different model
for how religion shaped men's character and morals. They agreed that
Judaism was crucial to the welfare of Jewish soldiers but insisted that in
order for it to help Jewish men embrace a sense of pride and honor, they

had to be protected from the scrutiny of non-Jews. If the JWB focused on the assertion of Jewish equality within the institutions of the state and the policies of the military, these soldiers demanded the right to embrace their Judaism in private. The conflict over Jewish welfare huts increasingly became a debate about the differences between private and public spaces and about how far American Jews were willing to go in their pursuit of recognition from Protestant America.

6

Good Fences Make Good Americans

Speaking at the annual meeting of the Jewish Welfare Board (JWB) in early 1919, just months after the end of the war, Raymond Fosdick, chairman of the Commission on Training Camp Activities, offered the following assessment of the work of the CTCA's civilian partners:

> I know that some of you here have had the privilege of going up in an aeroplane and you know just exactly how the ground recedes as the machine rises and how the details and unimportant things tend to disappear. You know that as you get higher the fundamental things become very plain, but the fences all disappear. I can't help thinking that this has been the result of this work in connection with these three great organizations—the fences have disappeared, the sectarian lines have vanished, and this work that has been carried on has not been carried on as Jewish work or Protestant work or Catholic work; it has been fundamentally an American work carried on for all the troops in the camps without regard to faith.[1]

Fosdick's speech offered an image of tri-faith cooperation and even integration—at least when seen from a distance. He glossed over the touchier subjects of how it was that these three faiths came to work together and what those fences looked like when then were examined from close up, rather than from the sky. Jewish soldiers' demands for separate huts in which they would not have to socialize with non-Jewish men makes it clear that while the war and the soldiers' welfare programs created spaces in which Protestants, Catholics, and Jews worked side by side as Americans, American Jews also wanted some spaces kept separate and distinctly Jewish. For the JWB, this meant figuring out which fences it truly wanted to dismantle, which it wanted to strengthen, and how it could explain the differences between them.

The fence that JWB leaders had most wanted to take down was the one separating them from the power and influence wielded by the

CTCA through its soldiers' welfare programs. With this goal largely accomplished, JWB leaders also wanted to be sure that the public knew that there was no difference between what Jews and Judaism contributed to the war effort and what Protestants and Catholics offered. To this end, the JWB kept careful watch over publicity materials and public statements about the government's efforts to promote the welfare of American soldiers. In these public proclamations, JWB leaders and supporters strove to erase any trace of fences that might divide Jews from non-Jews. Indeed, Fosdick's speech, with its strategic avoidance of any discussion of what happened on the ground, was very much in keeping with the image that the JWB wanted to see projected. After having secured its position as a CTCA partner, the JWB fought to promote images of tri-faith partnership and integration in the public sphere, but it worked simultaneously to make sure that the Jewish private sphere remained carefully fenced in.

Fundraising and the American Public

The JWB defended its hard-won position under the CTCA with care, and although it sometimes required prodding, the War Department supported the JWB's efforts. Having accepted the JWB as one of its supposedly nonsectarian civilian partners, the War Department publically endorsed its work and stressed the cooperation and lack of sectarian division among its civilian agencies and in its soldiers' welfare programs. JWB leaders, however, were diligent about monitoring CTCA publicity materials to assure that their organization's role in the provision of soldiers' welfare services received equal billing to that of the Young Men's Christian Association (YMCA) and the Knights of Columbus. JWB chairman Harry Cutler and executive director Chester Teller wrote to CTCA chairman Fosdick and director of publicity John Colter about any failures to include mention of the JWB in pamphlets, films, and publications on soldiers' welfare work and expressed dissatisfaction with anything less than full inclusion and recognition within all CTCA events and programs, especially those pertaining to fundraising.[2]

The issue of fundraising came to the fore in August 1918, when the CTCA began organizing one of its largest campaigns to support soldiers' welfare work. By this time, there were seven civilian agencies working under the auspices of the CTCA: the YMCA, the Young Women's Christian Association (YWCA), the Knights of Columbus, the Salvation Army, the American Library Association, the War Camp Community Service, and the JWB. Leaders of both the JWB and the Knights of Columbus assumed that all seven of these agencies for soldiers' welfare work would participate in the upcoming fundraising campaign, but the YMCA objected. In a letter to Raymond Fosdick, John Mott, chairman of the YMCA's National War Work Council, protested the idea of combined fundraising. He claimed that the YMCA and its sister organization, the YWCA, should be allowed to organize and schedule funding drives on their own terms and without inclusion of all the other agencies. Mott argued that the YMCA did the majority of the work, shouldered the majority of the financial burden, and had already put mechanisms in place to begin fundraising immediately. To force it to wait for the other agencies and fundraise together would, in his words, "be absolutely disastrous."[3]

JWB Executive Committee member and prominent lawyer Louis Marshall received word of the YMCA's protest and of reports that, in order to appease the YMCA, the CTCA had decided to schedule separate campaigns. The first fundraising drive, planned for November 1918, would include the YMCA, the YWCA, the American Library Association, and the War Camp Community Service. A second one, Marshall learned, would be held for the Knights of Columbus, the Salvation Army, and the Jewish Welfare Board in January 1919.

Marshall immediately wrote to Colonel Cutler at the JWB to object: "It is highly desirable that the people shall now, more than ever, act as one, that all differences of creed shall be disregarded, that all shall work for one and one for all. To place in one class the Protestant Christians and in another the Catholics, the Jews and the members of the Salvation Army, cannot fail to stimulate class prejudice and to arouse jealousies and animosities."[4] Moreover, by holding the YMCA's drive first, Marshall noted, it would almost guarantee that the YMCA would continue to bring in the lion's share of funds raised, while the JWB, the Knights of Columbus, and the Salvation Army divided whatever was left.

Cutler wrote to Fosdick and included Marshall's letter with his own. He reemphasized Marshall's point about the desirability of acting as one, without regard for creed, and added that "the classification [of the different] agencies will have the effect of impressing on the public mind a separatism which, especially in these critical days we are all striving to obviate. It smacks too much of caste distinction."[5] Fosdick responded sympathetically but denied the charge of sectarian bias. No one, he argued, could possibly see sectarian preference or segregation in the decision to run two separate war work drives merely because the YMCA and YWCA would participate in one and the Knights of Columbus and JWB in the other. Fosdick did note, however, that "without considerable public education," an "amalgamated drive" would never work anyway because of the "extreme" opposition to the idea from "conservative elements" of the various organizations, especially their branches in the "south and middle-west."[6]

Cutler must have reported Fosdick's reply to Marshall, because Marshall soon wrote again, in stronger terms, to disagree with Fosdick's assurances that no one would perceive any difference between the two groupings of soldiers' welfare organizations. He explained,

> Mr. Fosdick's idea is that there is nothing in the creation of the two groups which he proposes that will emphasize the idea of sectarian segregation, and his reason for this statement is that in the first group there are two Protestant organizations and two non-sectarian organizations, while in the second group there is one Protestant, one Catholic, and one Jewish organization. I assume that by the Protestant organization in the second group he refers to the Salvation Army [which is] not looked upon as specifically Protestant. The two non-sectarian societies which are in the first group are conducted under Protestant auspices. At all events Protestantism is predominant in that group. That fact in itself amounts to sectarian segregation.[7]

Marshall argued that seemingly nonsectarian agencies, such as the American Library Association and the War Camp Community Service, actually represented the Protestant establishment, and he was sure that the public would notice this. He argued, moreover, that the presence of a group such as the Salvation Army, which ministered primarily to the poor, could hardly undo the impression that the proposed structure of the war work drives reinforced, intentionally or not, the assumed neutrality of Protestantism and the sectarian nature of the JWB and the

Knights of Columbus—an idea both groups had struggled against since the start of the war.[8] The Knights, in fact, for reasons similar to those of the JWB, also opposed dividing the funding drive. To bolster his claims, Marshall quoted from an article that had appeared in the Sunday *New York Times*, under the headline "K. of C. Opposes Plan for 2 Fund Drives," in which James Flaherty, Supreme Knight, implored Secretary Baker and Chairman Fosdick to reconsider their plans: "This [proposed grouping] is drawing a line between the Protestants, on the one side, and the Catholics, the Jews and the Salvation Army on the other; a line which we have been seeking to have wiped out in war activities and surely in so far as welfare of the boys in the service is concerned." Unwillingness to change the plan, Flaherty warned, "cannot fail to cause great criticism and disturbance throughout the country."[9]

Cutler once again forwarded Marshall's letter to Fosdick and urged him to press the issue of a combined drive with both Secretary of War Baker and President Wilson, if necessary. Without change to the proposed plan, Cutler warned, "the present rumblings will become loud thunder bursts, and none of us will be able to dissipate the harm unwarranted sectarian prejudice will create." Cutler also appended a note from Dr. Cyrus Adler, in which Adler lamented that "in my opinion it [the proposed drive] is a plain case of the dictation of the stronger religious elements, which represent the majority and it is a bad augury for the treatment of minorities on the new earth which optimists hope to construct after the war."[10] Financier Jacob Schiff lent his support to his JWB colleagues' arguments in a telegram to Fosdick, in which he asserted, "It is my honest opinion that proposition to make separate campaigns for practically all Protestant associations is likely to be followed by most undesirable consequences. This cannot but create deep feeling and anew start prejudices which had begun to disappear and give setback to the mutual confidence that was so satisfactorily growing as one of the more fortunate consequences of our entrance into the war."[11]

It is unclear whether Fosdick feared the "undesirable consequences" that both Jews and Catholics predicted if the plan for separate funding drives was allowed to stand or whether he too desired to build upon the feelings of "mutual confidence" fostered by the combined work of the welfare agencies. But on September 3, 1918, against the wishes of the YMCA, President Wilson announced that there would be a United

War Work campaign during the week of November 11 and that all soldiers' welfare agencies would participate. Cutler telegrammed Fosdick to congratulate him on his role in making the united campaign possible, writing that "while the practical and economic advantages are apparent, these are materially superceded by the ethical standing which as American citizens displays a spirit of cooperation regardless of creed, which will go far in impressing upon our men at the front that the nation as a whole is behind them in this war for victory."[12]

Cutler, Marshall, Adler, Schiff, and Flaherty all framed their protests against the proposal to separate the funding drives in terms of sectarian segregation, and these complaints seem to have worked. The CTCA and the War Department had resisted accepting the JWB and the Knights of Columbus as civilian partners because they had viewed the JWB and the Knights as sectarian agencies whose presence would promote unwanted division among the troops. Having agreed to work with them under the rhetorical banner of nonsectarianism, however, the War Department stood behind its decision. It promoted the collaboration between Protestant, Catholic, and Jewish agencies and worked to mute any suggestion of sectarian bias in its programs. Flaherty's and Marshall's accusations that the War Department's plan to hold two separate funding drives reinforced sectarianism and disadvantaged Catholics and Jews could not go unanswered without damaging the unified, nonsectarian image of soldiers' welfare work that the War Department and the CTCA wished to promote. Public and private warnings that, having achieved recognition as CTCA partners, Jews and Catholics would not quietly accept being placed in a different category than Protestants, proved compelling enough to make the War Department change course. Fosdick and Baker may have started the war assuming that the ecumenical Protestantism of the YMCA was simply American rather than sectarian. However, by the end of the war and in spite of its original intentions, the promotion of tri-faith unity and cooperation had become part of War Department policy.

In many areas, the CTCA saw the transcendence of differences and the promotion of a more unified sense of Americanism as crucial components of its work with soldiers and the welfare agencies serving them. It encouraged sports and athletic competitions in the belief that they provided a safe physical outlet for the men while encouraging healthy competition and a sense of teamwork and fair play.[13] Even more than sports, it promoted sing-alongs as crucial to uniting the men and inculcating in them a sense of patriotism, national pride, and shared culture. To promote singing, the CTCA assembled songbooks containing an assortment of popular patriotic songs and Christian spirituals for use in the camps, and it appointed song leaders to gather the men and lead them in song.[14] Secretary of War Baker, in a speech marking the First National Community Song Day in December 1917, exalted the power of song to lead men to victory and to teach the virtue of "subordinat[ing] the personal purpose to the common purpose, where individual success of any one must be forgotten in the common good of all."[15]

Baker and Fosdick intended the spirit of celebrating the common good and forgetting individual difference to animate all of the CTCA's programs. They saw the process of forging a common identity as critical to their plans for using the military to improve the characters of American soldiers and create a better, more moral, more fully American citizenry. Often, they defined the differences they planned to help the men "subordinate" in cultural or linguistic terms. So in addition to singing, all of the CTCA's civilian partner agencies taught classes to help immigrant soldiers learn English, study American history, and understand the principles of American government.[16] The CTCA expected that religious differences would also be subordinated in the interest of national unity. Not religious faith per se but rather the types of denominational differences that kept men from perceiving their common values and their shared responsibility as Americans. It was this sense of identity Fosdick invoked in his image of fences disappearing when viewed from the skies.

The JWB largely supported this idea of transcending denominational fences. While the preservation and protection of Judaism motivated much of the work it did in the camps, the JWB also touted the ways that working and serving together erased the insignificant differences between men, between welfare workers, and even, to some extent, between religions themselves. All of these divisions seemed less important in light of the unifying effects of military service and American citizenship. The conviction that shared military service would allow men to respect the religious differences between them, while seeing beyond them, perhaps offers an explanation for the JWB's apparent lack of protest at the inclusion of Christian hymns at soldiers' sing-alongs. So long as Jewish soldiers had access to Jewish religious services and the promise of mutual respect, the JWB appeared willing to accept displays of Christianity within the men's shared social activities, without seeing them as signs of sectarian discrimination. As Jewish military chaplain Lee Levinger wrote, "The men who have been under fire together have grown to overlook difference as barrier between man and man. . . . So the welfare workers and the chaplains overlook one distinction after another, at the end serving all alike and regarding their status as soldiers alone."[17] Or as Louis Marshall, raising funds for the JWB, proclaimed to his audience,

> Our sons are fighting side by side for the preservation of liberty. They recognize no distinction of person, faith or pedigree. As companions in arms they know of but one test, that of loyalty to the flag. Impressed by this lesson heralded from the battlefield, Protestant, Catholic, and Jew have joined hands. . . . We now understand, better than ever before, that the prosperity and happiness of a nation depend upon the complete unity of its citizens, and that it can only attain its highest development when all prejudices have been banished and when loyalty and devotion to the national ideals, which alone constitute good citizenship, shall be the supreme test by which men are judged.[18]

Chaplain Morris Lazaron echoed these sentiments in a book of prayers and meditations he wrote for the troops, in which offered his thoughts on the underlying unity of all men. He proclaimed that shared service had the power to break down all barriers and differences, including those of race, in spite of the fact that the US military was still racially segregated.[19] For Lazaron, who became deeply involved with interfaith work during the interwar period, it seemed obvious that the war had revealed the artifice of divisions between religions:

> Oh, my lads, you have worked, trained, served, suffered, sacrificed together! . . . What effect is all this to have on you? You've be thrown all together in a jumble; black, white, yellow, brown, and red! French, Italian, English, Russian, Jap, Chinese, Portuguese, American! You've eaten and lived with Mohammedan, Confucian, Buddhist, Catholic, Protestant

and Jew. Haven't you found some good in all? . . . Think, each of you, of some pal you had who was Catholic, Jew or Protestant. It's the man that counts! . . . Break down the artificial barriers of ecclesiastical denomination! Demand that in the world you've saved for democracy, democracy be practiced![20]

Head JWB camp worker Alex Steinbach reported on his service with pride: "We co-operate with the idea in mind that while we all constitute a single welfare agency, we are all spokes in the great wheel of progress that turns for the betterment not of Catholic or of Protestant, or of Jew, but for the betterment of all soldiers in Camp Meade as true Americans. We are all a fabric of the great whole, a spoke in the great wheel, and our work is for the same one big purpose."[21] Rabbi Horace Wolf, Reform leader of the formerly Orthodox Temple B'rith Kodesh in Rochester, New York, reported in the *American Hebrew and Jewish Messenger* that "khaki obliterates all the artificial distinctions of civil life."[22]

Of course, the obliteration of "artificial distinctions" was tricky business. The JWB did not hope for the abandonment of Judaism or the blurring of religious identities. Rather, it aspired to use soldiers' welfare work as a catalyst for allowing men to see beyond sectarian divisions and prejudices in order to build a stronger Jewish future—one in which Jews, Catholics, and Protestants could stand side by side, knowing that each of their traditions shared seemingly fundamental American values, such as honesty, cooperation, bravery, self-control, and love of country. Judaism, like Protestantism and Catholicism, the JWB argued, could keep American soldiers safe from temptation and transform them into better citizens. Inclusion in public events and publicity materials, as well as in the policies and programs of the US military and the War Department, conveyed the endorsement of the state for this vision of tri-faith unity and cooperation and represented a real victory for the JWB's agenda. But which distinctions were merely artificial? How far should—or could—Jewish soldiers be pushed to lay these aside in favor of true Americanness? The provision of kosher food on US military bases had proved too divisive and smacked of sectarian segregation rather than national unity. The need for separate Jewish social spaces, however, proved more difficult to dismiss, both for soldiers and for JWB leaders.

Building Jewish Homes

While many JWB executives remained steadfast in their conviction that erecting separate Jewish welfare huts would create unwanted and unproductive segregation, this did not mean that they saw no limits on the desirability of interaction between Jews and Christians. They may have been happy to see the fences between men disappear, but they had no desire to see Judaism itself disappear. For many, the preservation of Judaism required the protection of Jewish homes. In the military, the JWB argued that it could provide the Jewish influences that would lead men to honorable behavior and responsible citizenship, but outside of the military, the positive influence of Jewish tradition needed to come to the man though his home. The CTCA shared this belief in the importance of the home as a civilizing force, and it became part of the justification for why all soldiers needed welfare huts.

Both the CTCA and its civilian partners depicted welfare huts as more than places in which welfare work took place. The huts, they argued, served as substitutes for home, oases of normalcy and domesticity in the midst of the military camp, and they praised these military homes as crucial to the work of inculcating and reinforcing high moral standards in the men. YMCA chroniclers wrote of their huts and their work in the camps:

> The homing instinct of the Association has been almost universally noted by observers. If it began as an instinct, it was developed deliberately. The camp "sing-songs," the entertainments, the canteens, the writing rooms, the religious services, were all directed definitely to draw men's thoughts away from the hard business of fighting and to remind them of home. . . . [T]he "hut" presented a golden opportunity to leave behind the hardships and brutalities and meannesses of war and become again a part of the collective conscience of the nation."[23]

The CTCA particularly praised the YWCA for creating welcoming "hostess houses" where men could get a cup of hot chocolate, have their clothing mended, and indulge in conversation with women. Descriptions of these hostess houses drew heavily on late nineteenth- and early twentieth-century conceptions of women as moral guardians of the home and family. Commission member Joseph Lee of the War Camp Community Service argued that women had a particular responsibility in building the "invisible armor" that Secretary of War Baker wanted all American men to carry into battle. Lee wrote, "The effect of the society of good women is wholly good. . . . [O]ne of the best influences in our lives is the desire to merit their esteem, and . . . the strongest influence of purity in the life of a young man is the hope of being someday worthy of the love of a good woman."[24] As historian Nancy Bristow notes, this line of argument seems to suggest that the CTCA believed that men "did not naturally aspire to goodness, but they might be prompted to do so through exposure to upstanding woman."[25] The efforts of the Young Women's Christian Association in helping men remember a domestic sphere defined by the presence of women were thus seen as vital to maintaining soldiers' moral health and protecting the "collective conscience of the nation."[26]

YWCA hostess houses provided a "homelike presence" and a "safe and wholesome atmosphere" in which American soldiers could relax, socialize, and commit themselves to the types of virtuous behavior that would make them worthy of an upstanding woman's love.[27] Mrs. Philip North Moore, chairperson of the Department of Health and Recreation of the Women's Committee of the Council of National Defense and a member of the War Camp Community Service, described the work done on behalf of American soldiers by a special committee from the women's colleges of Massachusetts:

[They] provided club houses and homes outside the camp. Their purpose was to have as many homes as possible where soldiers would find recreation, friendly interest and refined surroundings; the kind of homes from which the majority of them had come. Each home . . . had a college "mother." The college mother was permanent or nearly so as possible, but the helpers varied from week to week. A few gave their services in the home itself and others provided the things needed to make the home attractive—furnishings, games, books, pianos, victrolas.[28]

These outposts of home made assumptions about soldiers' civilian lives. They presumed that most American men lived in tidy, "attractive" houses filled with the trappings of middle-class domesticity. More than anything else, however, these ideas of home assumed the presence of women who expected men's behavior to conform to the ideals of masculine self-control, discipline, and moral virtue that pervaded the CTCA's soldiers' welfare program. For soldiers whose actual homes resembled the one Mrs. Moore described, hostess houses and huts may indeed have reminded them of their civilian lives. For others, teatimes and social functions at hostess houses provided "first time experience in high standards of social intercourse" and further education in the sort of American values and standards of behavior that the CTCA wished to instill in the men.[29]

The idea that the welfare huts and hostess houses should serve as homes for the soldiers and that the soldiers needed these substitute homes in order to maintain their morale and their moral standards, became a powerful line of argument in the debate over whether or not Jewish soldiers should have huts of their own. Longing for home and the need for home appeared repeatedly in JWB reports and letters from soldiers asking for the provision of separate Jewish huts. "We must have a place where we as Jews may find and meet sympathetic Jewish souls and Jewish hearts. In short, we are aching for a Jewish environment in fact as well as in name," wrote George Cohen, a soldier stationed at Camp Devens.[30] "There is not the least doubt in the world but that the [Jewish] men want a building of their own. A place where they are positive they are at 'home,'" agreed Adolph Shirpser, JWB worker at Camp Fremont.[31] Writing in the *Hebrew Union College Monthly*, enlisted man Jacob Rader Marcus argued, "A Jewish shack is needed where Jews may congregate, feel at home, develop themselves along social lines. Jewish social development will mean Jewish religious development—the two are interwoven and inseparable."[32] And JWB worker Cyrus Janover, writing from Camp Dix, offered a cautionary tale of what can happen to men deprived of "the home atmosphere": "A national guard regiment [that] was encamped in this town left recently and over 400 girls have gotten into difficulty about 200 are pregnant, some mere children 15 years of age. The Jewish community, however, feels that a Jewish national army man taken into a Jewish home will do the right thing every time. This home atmosphere more than any other thing will re-create the man."[33]

Jewish homes, these men argued, could make or break the man. Given a home in which to "develop themselves," Jewish men would "do the right thing every time." But too long deprived of the influence of home, Janover warned, the average soldier became depraved. Without the civilizing and uplifting influence of home, he ran the risk of forgetting the demands of honor and morality that the CTCA sought to inculcate in American men. Without a home, men—even Jewish men, Janover cautioned—sometimes gave in to the lure of licentiousness, promiscuity, and even violence against women and children. Fosdick had witnessed such behavior on the Mexican border in 1916, and he and Baker had established the CTCA to stamp out its occurrence among World War I troops. Men, they believed, needed homes to keep them tethered to the values of American civilization. In order to truly feel at home, Janover, Marcus, Cohen, and Shirpser argued, Jewish men needed Jewish homes.

In the interest of providing Jewish servicemen with appropriate home influences, local Jewish communities often worked in concert with the JWB to provide soldiers with home hospitality on Shabbat, Jewish holidays, or days when soldiers had leave.[34] Local branches of both the Young Men's Hebrew Association and the Independent Order of B'nai B'rith opened their doors to Jewish soldiers looking for temptation-free activities to fill the time when they were allowed out of the military camps. These groups and local communities also sponsored social events that brought the men into contact with "good Jewish girls" and kept them away from less desirable female companions.[35]

Chaperoned dances and social events with carefully selected Jewish women served an important function within JWB programming. Dances with young, eligible Jewish women offered the men both the possibility of communally sanctioned romantic involvement, and a reminder of the types of home life they could hope to build for themselves after the war's end. Opportunities for tea and conversation with older, married Jewish women gave them the opportunity to think about their own mothers, to enjoy a bit of maternal care, and to remember the values and standards of behavior that they had either learned at home or that the JWB hoped they would aspire to. Jewish women played a crucial role in reminding the men of communal expectations for their behavior and of what they stood to lose if they deviated from those expectations.[36]

The other welfare organizations agreed that bringing the men into contact with appropriate women, and keeping them away from inappropriate women, was vital to maintaining moral standards and keeping the men out of trouble.[37] Mrs. Moore of the War Camp Community Service noted in her essay that "it becomes the peculiar function of women to prevent the destruction of the moral and spiritual forces of our nation. . . . It rests with good people, and in no small measure with good women, to create an atmosphere conducive to moral and spiritual growth. . . . The moral standard of a nation can be no higher than that of its women."[38] In his book *Morale and Its Enemies*, William Ernest Hocking—an idealist philosopher and, by his own estimation, an expert on soldiers' morale—wrote, "The young women of a community are perhaps chiefly responsible for the quality of the self-esteem of enlisted men. It is a fair, and not unanswerable question for each community whether on the whole it is aiding soldierly sobriety of self-judgment."[39]

All of the welfare agencies, as well as the CTCA itself, stressed the need for soldiers to exercise sexual restraint and to limit their contact with women to those who reminded them of the values of home. But while the War Department intended its campaign primarily to prevent the debilitating spread of venereal disease among the troops, the JWB approached its own attempts to keep the men away from inappropriate women with an additional concern in mind: the threat of intermarriage.[40]

Intermarriage rates among Jews remained extremely low in the early part of the twentieth century.[41] Nevertheless, JWB workers and rabbis did encounter some instances in which Jewish soldiers became involved with Christian girls—or Christian soldiers with local Jewish girls—and turned to the local JWB representative to ask for advice either on conversion to Judaism or on how to break the news to the families at home.[42] The number of these cases was fairly small, but the threat they represented was perceived as severe enough to warrant action. The JWB did its best to ward off these inappropriate matches by distributing an informative pamphlet for soldiers on the subject of intermarriage. In a pamphlet simply titled *Intermarriage*, Rabbi David de Sola Pool warned servicemen of the hidden dangers of marrying outside of the Jewish community. The JWB sent off at least twenty thousand copies to assure wide distribution among the men.[43]

De Sola Pool had opposed the construction of separate Jewish recreational huts, arguing that they would retard the soldiers' embrace of the finer aspects of "Americanization" and "Judaisation" and instead promote undesirable "Yiddishisation" among the men. He claimed that, for educational purposes, no meaningful differences existed between Jewish and non-Jewish soldiers and argued that separate huts would be little more than "ghettos." In his letter to Mortimer Schiff on recreational huts, de Sola Pool embraced the JWB's assertions of the fundamental sameness of the men, of Judaism's ability to foster a shared sense of Americanism, and of military camps as places where religious pluralism should allow men of different faiths to stand side by side as brothers.[44] But when he turned to the issue of homes, de Sola Pool had a different opinion about the compatibility of Jew and non-Jew.

In his pamphlet on intermarriage, Rabbi de Sola Pool set aside the rhetoric of sameness and compatibility and argued instead that "an ineradicable race feeling" created "fundamental differences between Jew and non-Jew which lurk beneath the surface, watching and working for the opportunity which friction brings to break through and aggravate any discord which may arise in a home based on the union of Jew and Gentile."[45] This "race feeling," he warned, had nothing to do with religious practice or observance. It remained equally present in the most and in the least religious Jew. Nor did it require the awareness of the couple involved, for it could exist as a "latent feeling . . . though perhaps neither [husband nor wife] will suspect its existence."[46] Sooner or later, de Sola Pool cautioned, these fundamental differences would assure that every union based on intermarriage would end in conflict and strife.

According to de Sola Pool, a Jewish man could never truly build a home with a Christian woman. They might marry, but a Christian wife could never create the sort of uplifting Jewish home that could lead her husband to the high moral standards expected of him as a Jew and as an American. She would always be tied to a faith, and a race, foreign to her husband and would never be able to imbue their home with the "Jewish spirit" he needed to make him a better man and a better citizen. Worse still, de Sola Pool claimed, the willingness to intermarry and forfeit the creation of a Jewish home indicated a fatal flaw in the character of a man:

> No man worthy of the name will, without further thought, enter into a union which he knows will mean a lifelong sorrow to his parents, and

which may result in a complete break between him and the father and mother who have given him life. . . .[47]

It is no feeling of narrow separatism, racial pride of unreasoning exclusiveness that makes the Jew oppose mixed marriage. . . . The man who will be untrue to his people and its ideal and will desert it in its hour of need, is one whom the conscience of Jewry rightly excludes from fellowship, equality and honor. He is one who is denying his parents and all the past which has made him what he is; he is sacrificing the happiness of years for momentary happiness, and he is cutting off from himself his own natural future and accepting a future bound up with a faith that is not his own.[48]

The JWB celebrated the possibilities that military service and welfare work created for Jewish and non-Jewish men to form meaningful bonds between them, but it did not view relationships between Jewish men and non-Jewish women in the same light. For de Sola Pool and for the JWB, intermarriage fell outside of the boundaries of acceptable Jewish-Christian relationships, and the home represented a sphere into which nonsectarian sensibilities must not be permitted to enter. Such restrictions, de Sola Pool stressed, should not be seen as evidence of Jewish exclusivity or remove from American society but instead as necessary to building character. According to de Sola Pool, the man who intermarried gave in to his own short-term sexual and romantic desires, betrayed his "race" and his heritage, cut himself off from the only true path toward self-improvement, and brought pain and suffering to his parents. Nothing could be further from the ideals of manhood that the War Department and the JWB hoped to instill in American soldiers. Building a generation of trustworthy, steadfast, and disciplined Jewish men able to associate freely with their non-Jewish countrymen, he argued, required the preservation and promotion of Jewish traditions in the home—and that placed relationships between Jewish men and non-Jewish women beyond the pale.

The JWB's discourse around intermarriage also reveals lingering questions about the nature of Jewish identity and the possibilities for Jewish and Christian integration. While JWB executives and field agents generally spoke about Jewish men as members of an American religious community, intermarriage led them to the language of race. In the public arenas of civil and military life, they were eager to argue for the sameness of Jewish and Christian men. When the domestic sphere became the focus, however, they embraced an idea of intrinsic differences between Jews and other Americans. De Sola Pool and other JWB leaders were hardly alone in their feelings of ambivalence over the extent and implications of Jewish distinctiveness. American Jews had long wrestled with questions about whether race or religion represented the salient factor of Jewish identity. While some soldiers and many of their critics in the Jewish press argued for Jewish racial and ethnic difference, the acculturated and Americanized men at the helm of the JWB fell firmly within the camp of those who argued that Judaism was primarily a religion rather than a category of racial distinctiveness. Men such as Schiff and Marshall rejected claims of inherent Jewish difference, which they saw as potentially undermining the political rights and social standing of Jews in America. But like others before and after them, they stumbled on the question of intermarriage, which appeared to lead too far down a path of Jewish self-destruction.[49] In public, they seemed to argue, no differences existed between the Jewish man and his compatriots. However, they remained uneasy about the effects of unchecked integration between Jews and Christians in private and at home. If Jewish men needed Judaism in order to fulfill their potential as soldiers and citizens, then Jewish marriages and homes needed to be preserved as a bulwark against the threat to their Jewish sense of self and their moral compass.

Ideas about the importance of home shaped the argument in favor of building separate Jewish welfare huts. Eventually, even the JWB embraced the idea that separate huts were necessary to protect the character of Jewish serviceman and to ensure the future creation of Jewish homes. Colonel Harry Cutler, speaking at the JWB's annual meeting in 1919, explained that he had not initially seen separate Jewish welfare huts as necessary but had changed his mind when "it became evident that this Board must erect at least some buildings of its own. The housing of our workers, the administration of our work, and the self-respect of the Jewish men in the camps demanded it."[50]

In April 1918, the CTCA recommended to the War Department that both the JWB and the Knights of Columbus be "authorized to erect buildings in the national Army and National Guard training camps and at ports of embarkation."[51] On May 22, 1918, Colonel Cutler received word from F. P. Keppel, third assistant secretary of state, that "the Jewish Welfare board, which . . . is recognized for religious social, and recreational work in the camps" would be allowed to "erect buildings under the regulations governing the YMCA, YWCA and Knights of Columbus."[52] In July 1918, Congressman Isaac Siegel wrote to JWB headquarters in New York to confirm that he had also seen to it "that under the Military Appropriation Bill, which will become law within a few days, at my suggestion, provision has been made for light and heat being furnished by the Government the same as has been done for the YMCA since 1902."[53]

By the end of the war, the JWB had received authorization to erect fifty-one buildings in training camps across the country and had completed construction on thirty-five of them. The JWB advertised its new soldiers' welfare huts to the Jewish public with a poster depicting a confident JWB worker ushering an older man, perhaps a concerned father, into a homey JWB building filled with soldiers in uniform. Some of the soldiers stood singing around a piano played by a young woman, while others gathered around a table studying a text. In the background, a stylish couple, representing the kind of respectable unions such huts would generate, looked on. The poster spoke to the families of those soldiers that Marcus and other observers pronounced least able to adapt to American norms or to socialize with non-Jewish Americans. Under the JWB seal, it announced in Yiddish, "Mir haben fur ze a heim geboit" (We have built them a home).[54]

The decision to provide separate Jewish welfare huts demonstrated not only the limits of the JWB's ability to impose its vision of American Judaism on Jewish soldiers but also the boundary to which it wanted to push interfaith cooperation. In the case of kosher food, the JWB decided to resist the demands of traditional Judaism and of Orthodox-leaning soldiers and civilians. In the case of Jewish welfare huts, however, the board bent to the will of the men. Perhaps this was a reflection of greater demand among the soldiers for Jewish huts than for kosher food, but it could also be further evidence of the ways in which the Protestant YMCA continued to define the norms of soldiers' welfare services. After all, the War Department immediately granted the YMCA permission to build welfare huts. The JWB, thus, asked only for equal treatment, not for something that challenged the standards set by the YMCA. But the debate over JWB huts also reveals the types of fences that both Jewish and national leaders saw as surmountable and insurmountable during the Progressive Era. JWB leaders had hoped to persuade both soldiers and civilians that religious difference could be transcended in the interest of building an American society in which Protestant, Catholic, and Jew stood side by side as soldiers and citizens. However, home and marriage represented another sort of difference altogether—one that could not be set aside and that no honorable American man would attempt to ignore. To JWB leaders, maintaining the home as a separate Jewish space played such a crucial part in their vision of vital American Jewish manhood that, unlike in the case of kosher food, they risked accusations of sectarian segregation in order to preserve it.

The War Department also must have agreed that the private space of the home stood apart from the public spaces created by government and military policy. Certainly, Fosdick and Baker had the power to prevent the construction of separate Jewish buildings. The fact that the JWB secured permission to build its own huts, with heat and light provided by the government, indicated that they also believed that limits existed on how far nonsectarian unity among the men should be enforced. Some forms of segregation appeared necessary to protect both the morals and the morale of American servicemen. A circular sent to all General Staff military morale officers argued as much when it explained that morale could be negatively affected by "maladjustments in the organization," including the "intermixture of fundamentally antagonistic groups, racial, religious, or other."[55] Or as Jewish soldier George Cohen wrote to Colonel Cutler from Camp Devens,

> The U.S. War Department has deeply considered the fact that it is very necessary for the mental, moral and religious welfare of the soldier that there be provided for him a suitable place, where he may spend his leisure time in a proper environment. It has realized that the general morale of the soldier is raised in this way. It has also apparently concluded that although pleasure and recreation do not depend on religion, and although a division on the basis of religion might to a certain extent tend to segregate various groups, after all, religious environment is the key to each man's heart.[56]

Men's hearts evidently stood outside of the framework of the tri-faith cooperation that took hold in the public structures of the American government and armed forces by the end of World War I. Intermarriage, moreover, proved to be a boundary that even Jews committed to a vision of tri-faith religious pluralism did not want to cross. In public, men were to act as equals and to be treated as such, regardless of religion. In private and in their dealings with women, however, honor demanded that some divisions remain intact.

Conclusion

World War I came to an end on November 11, 1918. With the armistice signed, combatant nations came to Paris to negotiate the terms of the peace, and they worked to dismantle and send home their fighting forces. In a speech entitled "Standing behind the Service Star," the Jewish Welfare Board (JWB) chairman, Colonel Harry Cutler, promised that "the Jewish Welfare Board will stand at its post until the last man has been mustered out of service."[1] During the period of demobilization, the JWB expanded its operations in Europe. While the war was still being fought, the military had refused to fill space on transport ships with representatives of the civilian soldiers' welfare agencies, but by the fall of 1918, the JWB had representatives in headquarters in Paris, Le Mans, Saint-Nazaire, Dijon, Alençon, Tours, Brest, Bordeaux, and Coblenz, all charged with keeping demobilized American servicemen out of trouble and occupied with educational and recreational programming. Working in concert with Jewish chaplains, JWB representatives ran religious services on holidays and the Sabbath, counseled servicemen on their postwar employment options, visited the sick and wounded in hospitals, and tracked down the graves of Jewish soldiers to assure they were marked with a Jewish star rather than a cross. Describing this postwar work, Cutler proclaimed,

> Three and one half million American Jews are banded together, by the Jewish Welfare Board, and through it they have written a record of service that has won commendation of all their fellow citizens. While it has contributed toward winning the war, as a Jewish institution, the Jewish Welfare Board has been nonsectarian in all of its activities save the matter of religious ministration. It has worked harmoniously with the Y.M.C.A. [Young Men's Christian Association], Knights of Columbus, and other war welfare agencies, with a spirit of co-operation which will go far toward a better understanding between members of differing religions faiths in the future.[2]

Cutler saw the end of the war as just the beginning of the JWB's work. Having secured the endorsement of the US government, compelled the support of the Jewish public, and settled upon strategies through which the JWB could balance the demand for Americanization with the desire for Jewish distinctiveness, Cutler envisioned a future in which the board would continue to advocate for American Judaism while shaping the characters of American Jews. Such a future was not meant to be. In 1919, Secretary of War Newton Baker presented Cutler with the Distinguished Service Medal in recognition of his work with the JWB, but the years following the armistice were marked by disappointment.[3]

While the government publically thanked the civilian welfare agencies for their service, behind the scenes Raymond Fosdick, chairman of the Commission on Training Camp Activities (CTCA), prepared his recommendations for future soldiers' welfare. In spite of Fosdick's initial reluctance to admit a Jewish agency to the CTCA, his official report offered only praise for the JWB: "The Jewish Welfare Board is admirable in every respect and is working under able leadership. Like the huts of the Y.M.C.A. and of the Knights of Columbus, its buildings serve all troops regardless of faith, and I was greatly interested to note in a recent trip to the Le Mans area, how widely its facilities were employed by Jew and Gentile alike."[4] The report as a whole, however, took issue with the need for civilian religious agencies in the business of soldiers' welfare. Fosdick argued,

> To have Protestant huts, Catholic huts and Jewish huts in the same camp or operating in the same area not only is wrong in principle, but represents waste of overhead and a duplication of personnel. . . . A baseball is a baseball to the soldiers no matter whether it is presented by the Y.M.C.A., the Knights of Columbus or the Jewish Welfare Board. The same is true of huts, chocolate, entertainment, stationery or good advice. . . . The religious interests of the Army are wisely committed to the Chaplains, and with an ample number of Chaplains, no need appears for further emphasis along this line.[5]

In a version of the report intended only for War Department personnel, dated July 27, 1918, and marked "Strictly Confidential," Fosdick did not even mention the JWB. He spared few words in criticizing the Salvation Army, the Knights of Columbus, and particularly the YMCA for what he saw as petty competition, lack of oversight, and an abundance of unqualified representatives more interested in evangelism than soldiers' welfare. He noted that the Salvation Army was at least popular among the troops for its ready supply of free doughnuts. While he accused the Knights of Columbus of placing too much emphasis on "religious work," he did admit that this emphasis was "more or less a matter of self defense" against the missionizing efforts of the YMCA. Overall, in both his confidential and his public reports, he recommended that the military take over the business of soldiers' welfare and leave matters of religion strictly to the chaplaincy.[6]

Fosdick's report, with its unequivocal rejection of the benefit of religiously affiliated soldiers' welfare agencies, had ominous implications for the JWB. Indeed, in the years following the end of WWI, the board floundered and lost its sense of purpose. It retained its position as the organization responsible for the Jewish military chaplaincy and the particular care of Jewish soldiers. However, as the process of demobilization was completed and the number of Jewish servicemen plummeted, the government saw little need for a Jewish representative to its peacetime soldiers' welfare programs.

In June 1919, Chairman Cutler wrote to California congressman Julius Kahn to plead for an extension of the JWB's official commission. He argued that including the JWB in the military's ongoing soldiers' morale and educational activities was crucial not just to the Jewish men but to maintaining the spirit of American unity that had prevailed during the war. To eliminate the role of the JWB simply because there were fewer Jewish soldiers in service would, he warned, undo "the harmonious cooperation [between agencies that] obtained during the period of wartime" and instead engender "rivalries and prejudice . . . which . . . all American citizens would rightly deplore."[7] His plea was of little use. By the summer of 1920, Cutler found that not only would the JWB have virtually no role to play in the peacetime military, but the War Department had decided upon a plan for the redistribution of the chaplaincy that would bring the number of commissioned Jewish chaplains down from its wartime high of twenty-six to a peacetime total of zero. Cutler wrote to the secretary of war and argued that if Baker were to "order into actual service the Jewish Welfare Board on all matters relating to the morale of the men in the peace army . . . [it would] spell a new Americanism, in which there will be no room for real or imaginary discrimination on account of class or race."[8] Baker, seemingly reaching for a return to prewar Protestant norms, assured Cutler that he remained happy to hear the views of the JWB on "any matter involving the spiritual or physical welfare of our soldiers of Jewish faith," but he offered no indication that the government saw a need for a Jewish contribution to the welfare of American soldiers in general.[9]

As the United States entered the 1920s, the JWB had little choice but to face the fact that its broad mission to the US military was over. The board maintained its Army-Navy Division but drastically reduced its staff and focused its efforts on caring for the nearly 1,200 disabled Jewish veterans in military hospitals and providing holiday leave and Sabbath services for the approximately 4,000 Jewish men who remained in service after the war.

Board leaders remained convinced, however, that the JWB still had a crucial role to play among American Jewry and within American society, and they retained their commitment to the larger mission of the JWB, which had never been just about the welfare of soldiers. During the war, the board's position as an official agent of the War Department's soldiers' welfare programs had provided it with a unique chance to integrate Jews and Judaism into the structures and culture of the American military. The JWB had charged its representatives not only with ministering to Jewish men but with positively representing Judaism and Jewish manhood to all American servicemen. It had ensured the recognition of Jewish holidays and the provision of Jewish religious services in US military camps. And at least for the period of mobilization, the JWB had managed to position Judaism, alongside Protestantism and Catholicism, as one of the three faiths recognized by the United States government for the vital contributions they made to the morale and the moral and spiritual welfare of American servicemen. For the duration of the war, the JWB had helped to turn the US military into an unprecedented experiment in American religious pluralism and had advanced the creation of a tri-faith vision of American society.

Cut off from its military mission, the JWB partnered with the Young Men's Hebrew Association and devoted most of its energies during the interwar period to building the Jewish Community Center (JCC) movement. It worked to finance and coordinate the programs of affiliated JCCs, to build and staff new JCCs, and to run summer camps, athletic teams, lecture series, and educational and social programming. In the aftermath of the war and throughout the Depression, it focused on vocational training for young men and women. As German Jewish refugees from the Nazi regime began arriving in the United States in the 1930s, the JWB sought to create programs that would help these new immigrants adjust to life in America. But no amount of enthusiasm for community service could distract from the fact that the JWB was no longer pursuing its broader national agenda. During the war, Secretary Baker's imprimatur had allowed the JWB to assert its status as the representative of American Jewry and to transcend the limits of sectarianism and demonstrate that both Jews and Judaism had something of value to contribute to the good of the nation. Without the War Department behind it, the JWB lost its access to national power. It found itself relegated back to the Jewish community and dependent upon the unsteady cooperation of the Jewish public.

The JWB's exile from the national stage did not, however, mean that the country entirely retreated from its wartime move toward a tri-faith model of religious pluralism. While the country gave in to isolationism, anti-Catholicism, and anti-Semitism in many public arenas, commitments to tri-faith religious pluralism continued and even grew during the interwar period. Reform rabbis and liberal Jewish leaders, some of whom had partnered with the JWB during the war, worked to craft a public Jewish presence that both Americanized Jews and promoted Judaism as an American religion.[10] Protestant, Catholic, and Jewish chaplains who had worked together during the war founded the Military Chaplains Association, which focused on interfaith cooperation among chaplains. The military itself continued to showcase the shared contribution of Protestants, Catholics, and Jews to the American war effort. In 1921, at the burial of the Unknown Soldier in Arlington National Cemetery, Rabbi Morris Lazaron represented American Judaism as one of four officiating chaplains.[11] Perhaps the most significant expression of ongoing engagement in interfaith cooperation was the establishment of the National Conference of Christians and Jews in 1927 to combat the rising tides of nativist hostility and to "promote justice, amity, and cooperation among Protestants, Catholics, and Jews."[12] The group was organized through the collaborative efforts of cochairmen from each of the different faiths represented. Former secretary of war Newton Baker served as the first Protestant cochair.[13]

But while efforts at moving Catholics and Jews into positions of partnership with Protestants continued, the JWB remained sidelined. JWB Army-Navy Division chairman Cyrus Adler wrote in his annual report of 1938, "The pattern of our program of welfare activities in peace time changes but little from year to year. It is adjusted to and governed by the regularized routine of military life. . . . The work is carried on as the simple discharge of an obligation which we assumed in time of war and which we have continued as a duty thereafter."[14] Indeed JWB army-navy expenses, services, and programs—and even the number of Jewish men in veterans' hospitals and on active duty—remained static throughout the 1920s and 1930s.[15] According to JWB historian Oscar Janowsky, by the late 1930s, the JWB had lost its sense of relevance, and its work was "wanting both in glamor to tempt new men to active interest, and in the sense of urgency to stir the old leaders."[16]

Even without the "glamor" of war, the JWB continued to represent the well-established leaders of the American Jewish community: Felix Warburg, Cyrus Adler, Irving Lehman, and Henry Morgenthau all sat alongside other members of the Jewish elite on the JWB Executive Committee. In 1938, when Adler reported that nothing much was going on in their army-navy program, these financially and politically active men certainly knew a great deal about what was going on in Europe as the Nazi regime expanded its territorial reach and its oppression of Jews under its control. Some of these men were in fact directly engaged in lobbying the Roosevelt administration for greater attention to the plight of German Jews under Nazism, and all of them were well aware of the rising threat of war. Yet in its public records from this period, the JWB—the only Jewish agency with any claim to connection with the US military—seemed to avoid discussion of possible changes to the military and stressed only its deep commitments to peace and Jewish communal service.

Perhaps this was intentional. Fosdick had left little room for civilian agencies, even those he praised, to reenter the field of soldiers' welfare work, and the War Department had effectively cut them out of its programs. According Janowsky, JWB executive director Louis Kraft began outlining plans for the possible expansion of military programs as early as the summer of 1939 but did not want to appear presumptuous about the role the JWB might play in a future conflict.[17] When discussing the matter, Kraft, Lehman, and Adler all agreed that it was better to wait for more information from the War Department rather than risk unwanted attention or the appearance that they were planning for war ahead of the American government.[18]

In the summer of 1940, the situation changed. Congress approved the Selective Service Act to implement the country's first peacetime draft. As this piece of legislation made its way to President Roosevelt, newly appointed JWB president Frank Weil convened a meeting with a representative from the YMCA and then another with representatives from the Knights of Columbus and the Salvation Army.[19] At these meetings, Weil set into motion a plan not only to revive the JWB's army-navy work but to realize the board's vision of more a religiously pluralistic America. He helped to lay the groundwork of a new organization in which they would all collaborate. It became known as the United Service Organizations, or USO.

The USO was never a Jewish organization, but that was what allowed it to achieve the goals the JWB had established back in WWI. It was designed as a cooperative venture between the various sectarian societies that was dedicated to raising the morale of members of the armed forces. It assumed that the distinct religious perspectives of all member organizations would be present in the work of the USO but that they would function together, under a single umbrella organization, for the good of the military and the country.[20] As Weil explained in a talk in 1943, the philosophy of the USO was "that the three great faiths represented in the member organizations had been drawn together by the fact that they share certain basic beliefs— . . . in a supernatural power . . . the brotherhood of man . . . the individual dignity of man . . . [and] the existence of positive ethical standards of right and wrong." They were united by these ideas and yet, Weil noted, they "found [that they] were strengthened by their differences in religious belief . . . observance, and . . . heritage. . . . It is these common faiths and this strength from differences that we propose to bring to our young men in the programs we are to carry on under the United Service Organizations."[21]

For the agencies sidelined by the rejection of sectarian religious influences in the military, the USO was a stroke of genius. For the JWB, it guaranteed that Jewish soldiers mustered into the WWII military would have access to the services of the JWB as an integral part of the country's larger program of soldiers' services. It represented an opportunity to once again serve as a central player in a major American wartime institution, but this time without confronting concerns about sectarianism. More than this, however, the JWB's position of shared leadership in the USO reaffirmed that Jews and Judaism had something of crucial value to contribute to the welfare of the country as whole, and that Protestant, Catholics, and Jews stood side by side as equally valuable contributors to the moral welfare of the country. Perhaps a lasting irony of Fosdick's post-World War I rejection of the services of *all* of the religiously affiliated soldiers' welfare services, including the YMCA, was that it forced them to band together as equal partners in the creation of World War II soldiers' welfare programs.

Through the USO, the JWB was once again able to break out of the sectarian confines of Jewish service and community. Through government recognition of the importance of the USO's service to all American soldiers, the JWB was able to assert that the inclusion of Jews and Judaism was not merely a nod to narrow Jewish interests but a recognition of tri-faith religious pluralism as a fundamentally American value. Indeed, USO president Chester Barnard described the unity of purpose and harmony between the religious groups behind the USO as "the highest expression of the Bill of Rights that has occurred in the United States of America."[22] As the JWB geared up for service in WWII, it was thus able to fulfill the grandest part of its WWI mission: establishing Judaism as one of what social scientist Will Herberg described as "the three faces of American religion."[23]

Herberg's popular book, *Protestant, Catholic, Jew*, published in 1955, argued that "these three communities stand on the same level, recognized as equi-legitimate subdivisions of the American people."[24] His widely read work explored the social and demographic differences that persisted among these groups and yet concluded that "all these differences remain differences *within* the over-all structure of American religious life. For all their particularities of background and development, American Protestants, Catholics, and Jews are basically Americans and reflect the common pattern of American religion."[25] It had taken until the 1950s for the idea of a "tri-faith" religious heritage to be embraced by the broader American public. Its acceptance was aided by the experiences of World War II, in which shared military service again forged bonds between men of different faiths and led them, sometime begrudgingly, to perceive one another as fellow Americans. It was accelerated by wartime rhetoric about the evils of "godless" Nazism, and later communism, which helped to shape the idea of a Judeo-Christian basis for American democracy.[26] But when the United States entered World War II, the need for Jewish military chaplains and a Jewish religious presence in the US military was simply assumed as a part of the moral- and morale-building services that all American servicemen needed. The battle for American religious pluralism was waged by the Jewish Welfare Board during World War I, and, against unlikely odds, the JWB won.

ACKNOWLEDGEMENTS

I benefitted more than I can say from the generous advice and encouragement of friends, colleagues, and mentors as I worked on this project. I owe perhaps the largest debt of gratitude to Hasia Diner. Hasia's wisdom, support, and example have been invaluable to me as a scholar and as a person.

As this book developed, I was also extremely fortunate to be able to learn from comments by and conversations with Deborah Dash Moore, Laura Levitt, Pamela Nadell, Derek Penslar, Marsha Rozenblit, Jonathan Sarna, and Kevin Schultz—who suggested the title of this book.

Dina Danon, Jodi Eichler-Levine, Kirsten Fermaglich, Shira Kohn, and Ronit Stahl have all shared their work and genuinely helpful suggestions on how to frame and develop the ideas and arguments in this book. I am deeply grateful to each of them.

I received support for this project from the Center for Jewish History in New York City and the American Jewish Archives in Cincinnati, Ohio. I am indebted to the patient and talented archival staff at the American Jewish Historical Society, and to Gary Zola, Dana Herman, and the staff of the American Jewish Archives for all of their help. Particular thanks go to Elisa Ho at the American Jewish Archives and Benjamin Guidot at the University of Maryland for their last minute archival sleuthing.

All of my colleagues at Muhlenberg College have been an unfailing source of support and good humor throughout this process. My deepest thanks to Sharon Albert, Thomas Cragin, William "Chip" Gruen, Dustin Nash, Lorena Nash, Purvi Parikh, Peter Pettit, Charles Richter, Kammie Takahashi, and Sara Vigneri. Thanks also to the many students who have cheered me on towards completion of this book, particularly to Forrest Kentwell for his enthusiasm and helpful research assistance.

My thanks and appreciation to Jennifer Hammer and everyone at NYU Press, including the anonymous readers who offered observations and suggestions that vastly improved the quality of this book and the attentive copy editor, Joshua Boydstun, who made it much more readable.

I owe many, many thanks to the dear friends who have shared all the ups and downs of life that happen while working on any project: Marc, Ivy, and Lillian Bernstein, Marc Michael Epstein and Ágnes Vető, Michael Gasper (for his kind and forgiving nature!), Mia Lipsit, Lisa and Moshe Markowitz, Mark and Alice Notis (for being the best cheerleader), Virginia Picchetti, Joanna and Jonathan Powers, and Josh and Lise Schreier. Thank you all so much! Thank you as well to Rabbi Eliav Bock, Heather and Marcus Oginsky, Scott Spitzer and Marsha Tilchin, and the entire staff of Camp Ramah in the Rockies who have offered friendship, hospitality, and a beautiful place to work and think.

Thanks finally to my family. First to my husband Hartley Lachter, who read drafts, debated ideas, and makes me laugh all the time. Being with you makes absolutely everything better. To Bernice and Leslie Cooperman, Allison Cooperman and Paul and Russell Chappell, Edward Sherman, Sandra Lachter, Martin and Naomi Lachter, Allison, Michael, Rachel, and Noah Richter, thank you for all of your love, support, and hours of childcare. I could not have finished this project without you. And to my beautiful, smart, talented, wonderful daughters, Zoe and Mollie Lachter, I love every bit of you and everything about you. You are the best. Thank you all so much.

NOTES

INTRODUCTION

1 Chester Teller, address to the 31st Annual Meeting to the Jewish Publication Society of America, March 24, 1918, 4 (emphasis in original), National Jewish Welfare Board, Army-Navy Division [JWB Army-Navy] Records, I-180, box 337, folder "Reports 1917–1918" (3 of 3), American Jewish Historical Society, New York, NY (hereafter AJHS).

2 Earlier versions of this argument appeared in Jessica Cooperman, "Unintentional Pluralists: Military Policy, Jewish Servicemen, and the Development of Tri-faith America during World War I," in *World War I and the Jews: Conflict and Transformation in Europe, the Middle East, and America*, ed. Marsha L. Rozenblit and Jonathan Karp (New York: Berghahn Books, 2017), 263–278; and Cooperman, "The Jewish Welfare Board and Religious Pluralism in the American Military of World War I," *American Jewish History* 98, no. 4 (October 2014): 237–261.

3 On American war goals and engagement in World War I, see Adam Tooze, *The Deluge: The Great War, America, and the Remaking of the Global Order, 1916–1931* (New York: Viking, 2014); and David M. Kennedy, *Over Here: The First World War and American Society* (New York: Oxford University Press, 1980).

4 Woodrow Wilson, "Joint Address to Congress Leading to a Declaration of War against Germany," April 2, 1917, Our Documents, www.ourdocuments.gov.

5 On the challenges facing both women and African Americans during the Progressive Era, see Nell Irvin Painter, *Standing at Armageddon: A Grassroots History of the Progressive Era* (New York: W. W. Norton, 2008); and Steven Diner, *A Very Different Age: Americans of the Progressive Era* (New York: Hill and Wang, 1998).

6 On nativism and anti-immigrant sentiment, see John Higham's classic text, *Strangers in the Land: Patterns of American Nativism, 1860–1925* (Westport, CT: Greenwood, 1981).

7 While Congress voted in support of Wilson's war declaration, the American public remained skeptical of the wisdom of joining the war. The Wilson administration thus adopted both persuasive and coercive measures designed to sway public opinion. On some of the persuasive measures taken, see David M. Kennedy, "The War for the American Mind," chap. 1 in *Over Here*. On coercive measures, see Christopher Capozzola, *Uncle Sam Wants You: World War I and the Making of the Modern American Citizen* (New York: Oxford University Press, 2008).

8 Chad Williams, *Torchbearers of Democracy: African American Soldiers in the World War I Era* (Chapel Hill: University of North Carolina Press, 2010), 4–5.

9 On the history of Jewish life in the United States, see Hasia Diner, *The Jews of the United States, 1654–2000* (Berkeley: University of California Press, 2004).

10 There is an extensive body of literature on race in America. In particular, see Eric Goldstein, *The Price of Whiteness: Jews, Race, and American Identity* (Princeton, NJ: Princeton University Press, 2006); Matthew Frye Jacobson, *Whiteness of a Different Color: European Immigrants and the Alchemy of Race* (Cambridge, MA: Harvard University Press, 1999); and David Roediger, *Working toward Whiteness: How America's Immigrants Became White: The Strange Journey from Ellis Island to the Suburbs* (New York: Basic Books, 2006).

11 Tracy Fessenden, *Culture and Redemption: Religion, the Secular, and American Literature* (Princeton, NJ: Princeton University Press, 2007), 3–4.

12 William R. Hutchison, *Religious Pluralism in America: The Contentious History of a Founding Ideal* (New Haven, CT: Yale University Press, 2003), 61.

13 Cara Lea Burnidge, *A Peaceful Conquest: Woodrow Wilson, Religion, and the New World Order* (Chicago: University of Chicago Press, 2016), 52.

14 Burnidge, *Peaceful Conquest*, 76.

15 Burnidge, *Peaceful Conquest*, 52–53.

16 On intelligence testing in the World War I military, see Stephen J. Gould, "The Hereditarian Theory of IQ: An American Invention," chap. 5 in *The Mismeasure of Man*, rev. ed. (New York: W. W. Norton, 1996).

17 Capozzola, *Uncle Sam Wants You*; Nancy Gentile Ford, *Americans All! Foreign-Born Soldiers in World War I* (College Station: Texas A&M University Press, 2001); and Nancy Bristow, *Making Men Moral: Social Engineering during the Great War* (New York: New York University Press, 1996).

18 Kevin M. Schultz and Paul Harvey, "Everywhere and Nowhere: Recent Trends in American Religious History and Historiography," *Journal of the American Academy of Religion* 78, no. 1 (March 2010): 129–162. For an example of recent scholarship taking up this challenge and arguing for the relationship between religion and the state, see Ronit Y. Stahl, *Enlisting Faith: How the Military Chaplaincy Shaped Religion and State in Modern America* (Cambridge, MA: Harvard University Press, 2017).

19 Jonathan Ebel, *Faith in the Fight: Religion and the American Soldier in the Great War* (Princeton, NJ: Princeton University Press, 2010), 3.

20 Mark Silk, "Defining Religious Pluralism in America: A Regional Analysis," *Annals of the American Academy of Political and Social Science* 612 (July 2007): 66.

21 Talal Asad, "Thinking about Religion, Belief, and Politics," in *The Cambridge Companion to Religious Studies*, ed. Robert Orsi (New York: Cambridge University Press, 2012), 39.

22 Christopher Sterba, *Good Americans: Italian and Jewish Immigrants during the First World War* (New York: Oxford University Press, 2003); and Jennifer D.

Keene, *Doughboys, the Great War, and the Remaking of America* (Baltimore: Johns Hopkins University Press, 2001).

23 For an examination of the development of tri-faith religious pluralism later in the twentieth century, particularly following World War II, see Deborah Dash Moore, "Jewish GIs and the Creation of the Judeo-Christian Tradition," *Religion and American Culture: A Journal of Interpretation* 8, no. 1 (Winter 1998): 31–53; Moore, *GI Jews: How World War II Changed a Generation* (Cambridge, MA: Belknap Press of Harvard University Press, 2006); Kevin Schultz, *Tri-Faith America: How Catholics and Jews Held America to Its Protestant Promise* (New York: Oxford University Press, 2011); and Mark Silk, *Spiritual Politics: Religion and America since World War II* (New York: Simon and Schuster, 1988).

CHAPTER 1. BORDER CONFLICTS

1 John J. Pershing, "We Could Have Lost 'Over There,'" *Saturday Evening Post*, July/August 1976, 46. Originally published on March 10, 1922.

2 See Tooze, *Deluge*, esp. 3–67; and Kennedy, *Over Here*, esp. 296–347.

3 On the antiwar movement, see Michael Kazin, *War against War: The American Fight for Peace, 1914–1918* (New York: Simon and Schuster, 2017). On the women's peace movement, see Melissa Klapper, "'We United with Our Sisters of Other Faiths in Petitioning for Peace': Jewish Women, Peace Activism, and Acculturation," chap. 3 in *Ballots, Babies, and Banners of Peace: American Jewish Women's Activism, 1890–1940* (New York: New York University Press, 2013).

4 On the military preparedness movement, see John Patrick Finnegan, *Against the Specter of a Dragon: The Campaign for American Military Preparedness, 1914–1917* (Westport, CT: Greenwood Press, 1974).

5 Howard Gross (president of the Universal Military Training League), quoted in Michael Pearlman, *To Make Democracy Safe for America: Patricians and Preparedness in the Progressive Era* (Chicago: University of Illinois Press, 1984), 37–38 (Pearlman's brackets).

6 Nancy Gentile Ford, *The Great War and America: Civil-Military Relations during World War I* (Westport, CT: Praeger Security International, 2008), 1–25.

7 Gail Bederman, *Manliness and Civilization: A Cultural History of Gender and Race in the United States, 1880–1917* (Chicago: University of Chicago Press, 1995), esp. chap. 5, "Theodore Roosevelt: Manhood, Nation and Civilization."

8 See Burnidge, *Peaceful Conquest*, esp. 54–105.

9 Diner, *Very Different Age*, 201. For other perspectives on Progressive reform, see Michael McGerr, *A Fierce Discontent: The Rise and Fall of the Progressive Movement in America, 1870–1920* (New York: Oxford University Press, 2003); and Painter, *Standing at Armageddon*.

10 Quoted in "Congress Backs Pursuit of Villa," *New York Times*, March 11, 1916, 3.

11 See Mark Gilderhus, "Revolution, War, and Expansion: Woodrow Wilson in Latin America," in *Reconsidering Woodrow Wilson: Progressivism, Internationalism,*

War, and Peace, ed. John Milton Cooper Jr. (Baltimore: Johns Hopkins University Press, 2008), 165–188.

12 For more on the Mexican Revolution and US intervention in Mexico, see Lloyd Gardner, "Woodrow Wilson and the Mexican Revolution," in *Woodrow Wilson and a Revolutionary World, 1913–1921*, ed. Arthur S. Link (Chapel Hill: University of North Carolina Press, 1982), 3–48; Manuel Plana, *Pancho Villa and the Mexican Revolution* (New York: Interlink Books, 2002); Joseph A. Stout Jr., *Border Conflict: Villistas, Carrancistas, and the Punitive Expedition, 1915–1920* (Fort Worth: Texas Christian University Press, 1999); Michael Tate, "Pershing's Punitive Expedition: Pursuer of Bandits or Presidential Panacea?," *Americas* 32, no. 1 (July 1975): 46–71; and John J. Pershing, *My Experiences in the World War*, 2 vols. (New York: Frederick A. Stokes, 1931).

13 On Pershing's early career, see Donald Smythe, *Guerrilla Warrior: The Early Life of John J. Pershing* (New York: Charles Scribner's Sons, 1973).

14 Jeff Jore, "Pershing's Mission in Mexico: Logistics and Preparation for the War in Europe," *Military Affairs* 52, no. 3 (July 1988): 117–121.

15 Ford, *Great War and America*, 22.

16 On Baker's career and policies, see Douglas B. Craig, *Progressives at War: William G. McAdoo and Newton D. Baker, 1863–1941* (Baltimore: Johns Hopkins University Press, 1913); Frederick Palmer, *Newton D. Baker: America at War*, 2 vols. (New York: Dodd, Mead, 1931); Daniel Beaver, *Newton D. Baker and the American War Effort, 1917–1919* (Lincoln: University of Nebraska Press, 1966); and C. H. Cramer, *Newton D. Baker: A Biography* (Cleveland: World Publishing, 1961).

17 Palmer, *Newton D. Baker*, 1:296–297. See also Bristow, *Making Men Moral*, 4–6. For a brief history of the American Social Hygiene Association, see C. Walter Clarke, "The American Social Hygiene Association," *Public Health Reports* 70, no. 4 (April 1955): 421–427.

18 For discussions of the impact of venereal disease on World War I troops, see Donald Smythe, "Venereal Disease: The AEF's Experience," *Prologue* 9, no. 2 (Summer 1977): 65–74; Fred Baldwin, "The Invisible Armor," *American Quarterly* 16, no. 3 (Autumn 1964): 432–444; and Allan Brandt, *No Magic Bullet: A Social History of Venereal Disease in the United States since 1880*, 2nd ed. (New York: Oxford University Press, 1987).

19 Quoted in Robert Moats Miller, *Harry Emerson Fosdick: Preacher, Pastor, Prophet* (New York: Oxford University Press, 1985), 7.

20 See Charles E. Harvey, "John D. Rockefeller Jr. and the Interchurch World Movement of 1919–1920: A Different Angle on the Ecumenical Movement," *Church History* 51, no. 2 (June 1982): 198–209.

21 The first of these studies was published before the war as *European Police Systems* (New York: Century, 1915); the second was published after the war as *American Police Systems* (New York: Century, 1920). Fosdick also authored a number of other books, including *Toward Liquor Control* (New York: Harpers and Brothers, 1933); *The Story of the Rockefeller Foundation* (New York: Harper and Brothers, 1952); Ad-

ventures in Giving: The Story of the General Education Board, a Foundation Established by John D. Rockefeller (New York: Harper and Row, 1962); *John D. Rockefeller: A Portrait* (New York: Harper and Brothers, 1956); and his memoirs, *Chronicle of a Generation: An Autobiography* (New York: Harper and Brothers, 1958).

22 Fosdick, *Chronicle of a Generation*, 136.

23 Palmer, *Newton D. Baker*, 1:296.

24 Fosdick, *Chronicle of a Generation*, 137.

25 Quoted in Palmer, *Newton D. Baker*, 1:307.

26 Quoted in Beaver, *Newton D. Baker*, 221.

27 Fosdick, *Chronicle of a Generation*, 138–141.

28 See Bristow, *Making Men Moral*, 6; Fosdick, *Chronicle of a Generation*, 139, 141; and Palmer, *Newton D. Baker*, 1:296–324.

29 On the history of the US military chaplaincy, see Richard M. Budd, *Serving Two Masters: The Development of American Military Chaplaincy, 1860–1920* (Lincoln: University of Nebraska Press, 2002). For a study the military chaplaincy from WWI through the present, see Stahl, *Enlisting Faith.*

30 Frederick Harris, ed., *Service with Fighting Men: An Account of the Work of the Young Men's Christian Associations in the World War*, 2 vols. (New York: Association Press, 1922), 1:170–216.

31 Harris, *Service with Fighting Men*, 1:208.

32 Maurice Francis Egan and John B. Kennedy, *The Knights of Columbus in Peace and War*, 2 vols. (New Haven, CT: Knights of Columbus, 1920), 1:202.

33 Egan and Kennedy, *Knights of Columbus*, 1:204.

34 Egan and Kennedy, *Knights of Columbus*, 1:205.

35 Egan and Kennedy, *Knights of Columbus*, 1:203.

36 Isaac Landman, "Services for Soldiers on the Border," *Yearbook of the Central Conference of American Rabbis* 27 (1917): 167.

37 For a history of the Young Men's Hebrew Association, see Benjamin Rabinowitz, "The Young Men's Hebrew Associations, 1854–1913," *Publications of the American Jewish Historical Society*, no. 37 (1947): 221–326; and David Kaufman, "YMHA: The Jewish Associations of Young Men and Young Women," in *Shul with a Pool: The "Synagogue-Center" in American Jewish History* (Hanover, NH: Brandeis University Press / University Press of New England, 1999), 51–88.

38 Jonathan Sarna, "Appendix: American Jewish Population Estimates 1660–2000," in *American Judaism: A History* (New Haven, CT: Yale University Press, 2004), 375.

39 On Jewish socialists in America, see Tony Michels, *A Fire in their Hearts: Yiddish Socialists in New York* (Cambridge, MA: Harvard University Press, 2005).

40 On shifting institutions and expressions of American Judaism, see Sarna, "Two Worlds of American Judaism," chap. 4 in *American Judaism.*

41 See Goldstein, *Price of Whiteness*, esp. 91–115; and Noam Pianko, "'The True Liberalism of Zionism': Horace Kallen, Jewish Nationalism, and the Limits of American Pluralism," *American Jewish History* 94, no. 4 (December 2008): 299–329.

42 See Pearlman, *Make Democracy Safe*, 129, 150.

43 For a comprehensive discussion of patterns and changes in the history of Jewish life in the Unites States, see Diner, *Jews of the United States*.

44 Quoted in Oscar Janowsky, *Change and Challenge: A History of 50 Years of JWB* (New York: National Jewish Welfare Board, 1966), 3.

45 *YMHA Bulletin* 17, no. 12 (December 1916): 1.

46 YMHA concerns about the possibility that Christian organizations would use their contact with Jewish soldiers as opportunities for proselytizing were not ill founded. See Yaakov Ariel, "The Rise of the Movement to Evangelize the Jews, 1880–1920," pt. 1 in *Evangelizing the Chosen People: Missions to the Jews in America, 1880–2000* (Chapel Hill: University of North Carolina Press, 2000), for a discussion of increased efforts to convert Jews during World War I.

47 *YMHA Bulletin* 18, no. 9 (September 1917): 5–6.

48 The *YMHA Bulletin*'s description of the work on the border indicates that there were likely other, perhaps smaller, bases, but the sources are unclear on this point. The headquarters, however, was in Douglas, in a building taken over from a local Elks club.

49 *YMHA Bulletin* 18, no. 6 (June 1917): 6. Younker apparently died of illness while returning to New York from Arizona in the spring of 1917. The *YMHA Bulletin* carried numerous tributes to him, describing his work among the soldiers. Younker organized the programs in conjunction with Army and Navy YMHA secretary Lewis Landes.

50 *YMHA Bulletin* 18, no. 6 (June 1917): 6.

51 Percy Weisman to D. L. Spero (chairman, YMHA Civilian Advisory Committee), October 1916, "Army Navy Branch—YMHA, 1915–1916," Council of Young Men's Hebrew and Kindred Associations Collection, 1912–1921, 92nd Street Y Archives, New York, New York.

52 On Mott, see C. Howard Hopkins, *John R. Mott, 1865–1955: A Biography* (Grand Rapids, MI: Eerdmans, 1979). On Mott's relationship with the Wilson administration, see Richard Gamble, *The War for Righteousness: Progressive Christianity, the Great War, and the Rise of the Messianic Nation* (Wilmington, DE: ISI Books, 2003).

53 On President Lincoln's decision, see Jonathan Sarna and Benjamin Shapell, *Lincoln and the Jews: A History* (New York: Thomas Dunne Books, 2015); Gary Phillip Zola, *We Called Him Rabbi Abraham: Lincoln and American Jewry, a Documentary History* (Carbondale: Southern Illinois University Press, 2014), 80–86; and Bertram Korn, "Jewish Chaplains during the Civil War," in *Jews and the Civil War: A Reader*, ed. Jonathan Sarna and Adam Mendelsohn (New York: New York University Press, 2010), 335–352.

54 For the pre-WWI history of the American Jewish military chaplaincy, see Albert Isaac Slomovitz, *The Fighting Rabbis: Jewish Military Chaplains and American History* (New York: New York University Press, 1999), 1–42; Bertram Wallace Korn, *American Jewry and the Civil War* (Philadelphia: Jewish Publication Society of

America, 1951), 56–97; and David Eichhorn, "A History of American Jewish Military Chaplaincy," in *Rabbis in Uniform: The Story of the American Jewish Military Chaplain*, ed. Louis Barish (New York: J. David, 1962), 1–33.

55 See the newspaper articles found in Central Conference of American Rabbis [CCAR] Records, MS-34, series A, box 10, folder 17, "Mexican Campaign. Publicity, 1916," American Jewish Archives, Cincinnati, OH (hereafter AJA), esp. "Central Conference and Religious Services at the Border," *Jewish Exponent*, September 15, 1916, 9.

56 Landman's obituary, listing his many publications and accomplishments, can be found in the *New York Times*, September 5, 1946, 20.

57 William Rosenau to Samuel Grabfelder of Atlantic City, NJ, September 1, 1916, CCAR Records, MS-34, series A, box 10, folder 11, "Mexican Campaign. Army Prayer Book, 1916," AJA.

58 Samuel Marks to Isaac Landman, August 25, 1916, CCAR Records, MS-34, series A, box 10, folder 14, "Mexican Campaign. C–M, General, 1916," AJA. Marks states that there was an "Army Navy Department of Federation" at work on the Mexican front, but I have found no other evidence of this. Janowsky also mentions that there were three Jewish agencies in Mexico (*Change and Challenge*, 4) but does not give the names of the agencies or sources. It is possible that Marks simply confused the name of the YMHA's army and navy branch.

59 Marks to Landman, August 28, 1916, CCAR Records, MS-34, series A, box 10, folder 14, "Mexican Campaign. C–M, General, 1916," AJA.

60 William Rosenau to Morris Stern, September 2, 1916, CCAR Records, MS-34, series A, box 10, folder 24, "Mexican Campaign. YMHA, 1916," AJA.

61 Morris Stern to William Rosenau, September 1916, CCAR Records, MS-34, series A, box 10, folder 24, "Mexican Campaign. YMHA, 1916," AJA.

62 Leon Franklin to Isaac Landman (CCAR Recording Secretary), August 28, 1916, CCAR Records, MS-34, series A, box 10, folder 11, "Mexican Campaign. Army Prayer Book, 1916," AJA. Indeed, even Rabbi Marks, who was so anxious for the CCAR to block the influence of the "New York divines," was initially resistant to the CCAR's plans because of his own work with Jewish soldiers, which was conducted under the auspices of the Department of Synagogue and School Extension Branch of the Union of American Hebrew Congregations. See Slomovitz, *Fighting Rabbis*, 39.

63 Newspaper copy, n.d., CCAR Records, MS-34, series A, box 10, folder 17, "Mexican Campaign. Publicity, 1916," AJA.

64 "Yom Kippur Services in Mexico: Rabbi Landman Conducts Service with Pershing's Column at Colonia Dublan," *Jewish Exponent*, Oct. 27, 1916, 9, CCAR Records, MS-34, series A, box 10, folder 17, "Mexican Campaign. Publicity, 1916," AJA.

65 Fosdick, *Chronicle of a Generation*, 140.

66 Raymond Fosdick, address to the JWB annual meeting, in Jewish Welfare Board, *First Annual Report* (New York, 1919), 10–11.

67 Quoted in Weldon Durham, "'Big Brother' and the 'Seven Sisters': Camp Life Reforms in World War I," *Military Affairs* 42, no. 2 (April 1978): 57–60.

68 Fosdick, address to the JWB annual meeting, 11.

69 Raymond Fosdick, "The War and Navy Departments Commissions on Training Camp Activities," *Annals of the American Academy of Political and Social Science* 79 (September 1918): 130.

70 Fosdick, "War and Navy Departments," 131.

71 Pershing, *My Experiences*, 1:281–282.

72 Pershing, *My Experiences*, 1:281–282.

73 Fosdick, *Chronicle of a Generation*, 143.

74 Quoted in Palmer, *Newton D. Baker*, 1:308–309.

75 The CTCA served only army training camps, but shortly after its establishment, Secretary of the Navy Josephus Daniels ordered the creation of a separate commission to serve the navy, with Fosdick as its chairman. There were, therefore, two CTCAs, but Fosdick chaired both and, as he notes in his autobiography, the two organizations had many of the same members and functioned largely as one. Fosdick, *Chronicle*, 143–144. For a history of the CTCA, see Bristow, *Making Men Moral*. For additional secondary information on the CTCA's programs, see Ford, *Americans All*, 88–111; Schaffer, *America in the Great War*, 96–108; and Keene, *Doughboys*, 24–25, 40–41.

76 On the members of the committee, see Fosdick, *Chronicle of a Generation*, 143; and Durham, "Big Brother," 57–60.

CHAPTER 2. GOING TO WAR

1 Cyrus Adler to Harry Davidowitz, October 15, 1918, JWB Army-Navy Records, I-180, box 326, folder "Adler, Correspondence," AJHS.

2 Wilson, "Joint Address."

3 Capozzola, *Uncle Sam Wants You*, 17–18.

4 For more on how civilian volunteers became agents of the state, see Capozzola, *Uncle Sam Wants You*, esp. 117–205. There is a vast body of scholarship on the Progressive Era and the war. For some examples, see Craig, *Progressives at War*; Painter, *Standing at Armageddon*; Kennedy, *Over Here*; Alan Dawley, *Changing the World: American Progressives in War and Revolution* (Princeton, NJ: Princeton University Press, 2003); McGerr, *Fierce Discontent*; Ronald Schaffer, *America in the Great War: The Rise of the War Welfare State* (New York: Oxford University Press, 1994); Robert Wiebe, *The Search for Order, 1877–1920* (New York: Hill and Wang, 1967); and Richard Hofstadter, *The Age of Reform* (New York: Vintage, 1960).

5 On the structure of the CTCA, see Bristow, *Making Men Moral*, 4–17; and Fosdick, "War and Navy Departments."

6 For more on the CTCA's policies on vice suppression, see Bristow, "Building a National Community: The Complexities of Gender," chap. 4 in *Making Men Moral*. See also Ann Gabbert, "Prostitution and Moral Reform in the Borderlands:

El Paso, 1890–1920," *Journal of the History of Sexuality* 12, no. 4 (October 2003): 575–604.

7 For a discussion of the Selective Service Act, see Keene, *Doughboys*, 8–34; and Kennedy, *Over Here*, 147–155.

8 John Mott, "The War Work of the Young Men's Christian Associations of the United States," *Annals of the Academy of Political and Social Science* 79 (September 1918): 204. The May order pertained specifically to the US Army. A second order was issued in July, granting the YMCA similar status in the US Navy.

9 Mott, "War Work," 206.

10 See John Donald Gustav-Wrathall, *Take the Young Stranger by the Hand: Same-Sex Relationships and the YMCA* (Chicago: University of Chicago Press, 1998), esp. 9–44; and Thomas Winter, *Making Men, Making Class: The YMCA and Workingmen, 1877–1920* (Chicago: University of Chicago Press, 2002), esp. 1–27. For a history of the YMCA, see C. Howard Hopkins, *The History of the YMCA in North America* (New York: Association Press, 1951). On the connections between evangelical Christianity and physical fitness, see Tony Ladd and James Mathisen, *Muscular Christianity: Evangelical Protestants and the Development of American Sport* (Grand Rapids, MI: Baker Books, 1999), esp. 22–94; Clifford Putney, *Muscular Christianity: Manhood and Sports in Protestant America, 1880–1920* (Cambridge: Harvard University Press, 2001), esp. 1–72; and Alexandra Lord, "Models of Masculinity: Sex Education, the United States Public Health Service, and the YMCA, 1919–1924," *Journal of the History of Medicine* 58, no 2 (April 2003): 123–158.

11 On efforts to evangelize Jews, see Ariel, *Evangelizing the Chosen People*. On Jewish responses to Christian missionary work, see Jonathan Sarna, "The American Jewish Response to Nineteenth-Century Christian Missions," *Journal of American History* 68, no. 1 (June 1981): 35–51; Sarna, "The Impact of Nineteenth-Century Christian Missionaries on American Jews," in *Jewish Apostasy in the Modern World*, ed. Todd Endelman (New York: Holmes and Meier, 1987), 232–254; and Sarah Imhoff, *Masculinity and the Making of American Judaism* (Bloomington: University of Indiana Press, 2017), esp. 62–91.

12 For a biography of Mott, see Hopkins, *John R. Mott*.

13 Fosdick, *Chronicle of a Generation*, 149. According to an editorial by B'nai B'rith leader George Fox printed in the *Jewish Monitor* of Fort Worth, Texas, both Catholics and Jews were also rejected as YMCA workers. George Fox, "In or Out of the Camps," editorial, *Jewish Monitor*, September 3, 1918, enclosed in George Fox to Raymond Fosdick, Fort Worth, TX, September 3, 1918; File 38505; General Correspondence, 1917–1921; Commission on Training Camp Activities; Education and Recreation Branch; Records of the War Plans Division, 1910–1942; Records of the War Department General and Special Staffs, Record Group 165; NACP.

14 Janet Jakobsen and Ann Pellegrini, *Love the Sin: Sexual Regulation and the Limits of Religious Tolerance* (New York: New York University Press, 2003), 114. See esp. chap. 1, "Getting Religion," for their discussion of the enduring influence of Protestantism on American law.

15 Steven Green, *The Bible, the School, and the Constitution: The Clash that Shaped Modern Church-State Doctrine* (New York: Oxford University Press, 2012), 12.

16 Noah Feldman, "Non-sectarianism Reconsidered," *Journal of Law and Politics* 18 (Winter 2002): 65–117.

17 See Kevin Schultz, "'Favoritism Cannot Be Tolerated': Challenging Protestantism in America's Public Schools and Promoting the Neutral State," *American Quarterly* 59, no. 3 (September 2007): 565–591.

18 For a discussion of the YMCA's involvement with Progressive Era projects of "democratic social engineering," see the introduction and first chapter of William Graebner, *The Engineering of Consent: Democracy and Authority in Twentieth-Century America* (Madison: University of Wisconsin Press, 1987). For further discussion of the YMCA's campaigns for social and moral reform, see Gustav-Wrathall, *Take the Young Stranger*, 9–44; Thomas Winter, "Personality, Character, and Self-Expression: The YMCA and the Construction of Manhood and Class, 1877–1920," *Men and Masculinities* 2, no. 3 (January 2000): 272–285; and Winter, *Making Men, Making Class*, 47–64.

19 James J. Hennesey, *American Catholics: A History of the Roman Catholic Community in the United States* (New York: Oxford University Press, 1983), 225–226.

20 On the Knights of Columbus, see John J. Burke, "Special Catholic Activities in War Service," *Annals of the American Academy of Political and Social Science* 79 (September 1918): 213–220; Christopher Kauffman, *Faith and Fraternalism: The History of the Knights of Columbus, 1882–1982* (New York: Harper and Row, 1982), esp. 190–260; and Michael Williams, *American Catholics in the War: National Catholic War Council, 1917–1921* (New York Macmillan, 1921), esp. 88–116.

21 Fosdick, *Chronicle of a Generation*, 149.

22 Janowsky, *Change and Challenge*, 7. The original name of the organization was the Jewish Board for Welfare Work, but it was changed, in early 1918, to the Jewish Welfare Board as a result of concerns that the acronym JWW might be confused with that of the Industrial Workers of the World (IWW), or "Wobblies." Cyrus Adler, "An Account of the Origin of the Jewish Welfare Board," in *Lectures, Selected Papers, Addresses* (Philadelphia: Privately printed, 1933), 227.

23 For some of the intracommunal battles over the founding of the American Jewish Committee, see M. M. Silver, *Louis Marshall and the Rise of Jewish Ethnicity in America: A Biography* (Syracuse, NY: Syracuse University Press, 2013), 79–134.

24 For more on Adler, see Ira Robinson, "Cyrus Adler: Toward the Biography of an American Jew," pt. 1 in *Translating a Tradition: Studies in American Jewish History* (Boston: Academic Studies Press, 2008); and Adler's autobiography, *I Have Considered the Days* (Philadelphia: Jewish Publication Society of America, 1941).

25 See Adler, "Account of the Origin," 219; and Janowsky, "The Origins of the National Jewish Welfare Board," chap. 1 in *The JWB Survey* (New York: The Dial Press, 1948).

26 Adler, "Account of the Origin," 220. In Jewish Welfare Board, *Final Report of War Emergency Activities* (New York, 1920), 113, the Executive Committee members

listed are: Harry Cutler, chairman (until his death in 1920); Cyrus Adler, acting chairman; Joseph Rosenzweig, secretary; Walter Sachs, treasurer; and Henry J. Bernheim, Boris Bogen, Carl Dreyfus, Abram Elkus, William Fischman, I. Edwin Goldwasser, Maurice Harris, Charles Hartman, Louis Kirstein, Irving Lehman, M. S. Margolies, Louis Marshall, David de Sola Pool, William Rosenau, Morris Rothenberg, Mortimer Schiff, Bernard Semel, Israel Unterberg, and Morris Wolf. An additional Advisory Committee was also established. Its members are listed as: Jacob Billikopf, Henry Cohen, Joseph H, Cohen, Julius Eiseman, Sidney Hillman, Jacob Kohn, Nathan Krass, Sam A. Lewisohn, Henry Morgenthau, David Phillipson, Max Pine, Joseph M. Proskauer, Julius Rosenwald, Jacob H. Schiff, Benjamin Schlesenger, Isaac Siegel, Maurice Stern, Oscar S, Straus, Mayer Sulzberger, and Felix M. Warburg.

27 Chester Teller, "The Jewish Welfare Board," *American Jewish Year Book* 20 (1918–1919): 89.
28 Teller, "Jewish Welfare Board," 99.
29 In 1919, the Office of Jewish War Records of the American Jewish Committee estimated that between 150,000 and 200,000 Jewish men served in the US Armed Forces in World War I. The report took care to stress that these figures indicated that Jews made up approximately 4 percent of the United States' wartime military force, even though they constituted only 3 percent of the national population. See Julian Leavitt, "The Collection of Jewish War Statistics," *American Jewish Year Book* 20 (1918–1919): 103–112. Later reports claimed that there were approximately 250,000 Jewish American soldiers. See Eichhorn, "American Jewish Military Chaplaincy," 1–33.
30 On foreign-born soldiers, see Ford, *Americans All*, esp. chap. 2, "Drafting Foreign-Born Doughboys into the American Army."
31 Janowsky, *Change and Challenge*, 7.
32 Felix Warburg to Raymond Fosdick, July 12, 1917, JWB Army-Navy Records, I-180, box 343, folder "War Department" (2 of 2), AJHS.
33 According to Adler, all members of the YMHA's Army and Navy Committee agreed to resign in order to make way for the formation of the JWB. Adler, "Account of the Origin," 220.
34 Cutler is sometimes cited as having hosted Taft at his home for a Passover seder, but I did not find evidence to confirm this story.
35 Stephen Wise to Captain F. P. Adams, October 5, 1918, Stephen Wise Papers, P-134, box 77, folder 3, "Baker, Newton," AJHS.
36 Eleanor Horvitz, "Old Bottles, Rags Junk! The Story of the Jews of South Providence," in *The Jews of Rhode Island*, ed. George Goodwin and Ellen Smith (Hanover, NH: Brandeis University Press / University Press of New England, 2004), 40–53; and "Colonel Cutler Honored," *Jewelers' Circular* 78, no. 22 (July 2, 1919): 90. Obituaries for Cutler can be found in the *New York Times*, August 29, 1920, 20; and the *American Hebrew and Jewish Messenger*, September 24, 1920, 564–565.

37 The earlier, informal arrangement is mentioned in a letter from Raymond Fosdick to Harry Cutler, September 20, 1917, JWB Army-Navy Records, I-180, box 343, folder "War Department 1917–1920" (1 of 2), AJHS.

38 Albert Hurwitz to Harry Cutler, January 2, 1918, JWB Army-Navy Records, I-180, box 343, folder "War Department 1919" (1 of 2), AJHS.

39 See "American Soldiers and Sailors Welfare League of the Independent Order of B'nai B'rith," 1917, JWB Army-Navy Records, I-180, box 326, folder "B'nai B'rith," AJHS; Harry Cutler to Raymond Fosdick, December 26, 1917 and December 28, 1917, JWB Army-Navy Records, I-180, box 326, folder "B'nai B'rith," AJHS; and Harry Cutler to Raymond Fosdick, November 8, 1917, Jacob H. Schiff Papers, MS-456, series A, box 453, folder 10, "Jewish Welfare Board," AJA.

40 Warburg to Fosdick, July 12, 1917.

41 See Silver, *Louis Marshall*, 114–118.

42 On the letterhead controversy, see Adolph Kraus to Felix Warburg, November 8, 1917, JWB Army-Navy Records, I-180, box 326, folder "B'nai B'rith," AJHS.

43 Harry Cutler to Julius Rosenwald, August 24, 1917, JWB Army-Navy Records, I-180, box 336, folder "R-Miscellaneous Correspondence," AJHS.

44 Harry Cutler to Jacob Schiff, September 6, 1917, Schiff Papers, MS-456, series A, box 453, folder 10, "Jewish Welfare Board," AJA.

45 Rabbi Isaac E. Marcuson to Harry Cutler, Terre Haute, IN, September 3, 1917, JWB Army-Navy Records, I-180, box 326, folder, "B'nai B'rith," AJHS.

46 Letter by a Rabbi Warsaw, quoted in Harry Cutler to Adolph Kraus, September 27, 1917, Schiff Papers, MS-456, series A, box 453, folder 10, "Jewish Welfare Board. 1917–1918," AJA.

47 Letter by a Rabbi Davis, quoted in Cutler to Kraus, September 27, 1917, Schiff Papers, MS-456, series A, box 453, folder 10, "Jewish Welfare Board. 1917–1918," AJA. The letter lists Rabbi Davis's location as "Fort Meyer," but it seems likely that this refers to Fort Myer in Virginia.

48 Rabbi Franklin to Harry Cutler, September 14, 1917, JWB Army-Navy Records, I-180, box 326, folder "B'nai B'rith," AJHS. This is the same Rabbi George Fox mentioned in the letter from Waco, Texas. He appears to have traveled to several cities on behalf of the B'nai B'rith, seeking to turn local communities away from the JWB.

49 Cutler to Kraus, September 27, 1917.

50 Raymond Fosdick to Judge Strasburger, September 3, 1917, JWB Army-Navy Records, I-180, box 343, folder "War Department 1917–1920" (1 of 2), AJHS. The letter is dated September 3 but makes reference to a memo of September 5. Presumably the date is incorrect and the letter was written sometime after the fifth.

51 Fosdick to Cutler, September 20, 1917.

52 Raymond Fosdick to Harry Cutler, September 29, 1917, JWB Army-Navy Records, I-180, box 343, folder "War Department 1917–1920" (1 of 2), AJHS.

53 M. R., "B'nai B'rith Breaks Away from Welfare Board," *American Jewish Chronicle*, December 7, 1917, 159.

54 Cyrus Adler to Jacob Schiff, October 31, 1917, Schiff Papers, MS-456, series A, box 451, folder 4, "Adler, Cyrus. 1917," AJA.

55 Leon Goldrich (JWB field secretary), report, November 13, 1917, JWB Army-Navy Records, I-180, box 326, folder "Affiliated Organizations," AJHS.

56 For discussion of anti-Semitism during the war, see Leonard Dinnerstein, *Antisemitism in America* (New York: Oxford University Press, 1994), 58–77. For discussion of attitudes toward Jews in military circles, see Joseph Bendersky, *The "Jewish Threat": Anti-Semitic Politics of the U.S. Army* (New York: Basic Books, 2000), esp. 1–166. For a discussion of nativism and wartime suspicion directed toward all minority and immigrant groups, including Jews, see Higham, *Strangers in the Land*; and Gary Gerstle, *American Crucible: Race and Nation in the Twentieth Century* (Princeton, NJ: Princeton University Press, 2001), esp. 44–127.

57 *Die Warheit* (The truth) was a socialist, Yiddish-language newspaper published in New York City from 1905 to 1919.

58 Harry Cutler to Raymond Fosdick, November 8, 1917, Schiff Papers, MS-456, series A, box 453, folder 10, "Jewish Welfare Board," AJA.

59 Raymond Fosdick to Harry Cutler, November 10, 1917, JWB Army-Navy Records, I-180, box 343, folder "War Department 1917–1920," AJHS.

60 Newton D. Baker to Harry Cutler, November 20, 1917, facsimile printed in Jewish Welfare Board, *Purpose, Scope, Achievements* (New York: Jewish Welfare Board, 1918).

61 Raymond Fosdick to Adolf Kraus, November 20, 1917, JWB Army-Navy Records, I-180, box 326, folder "B'nai B'rith," AJHS.

62 Adolph Kraus to Harry Cutler, January 29, 1918, JWB Army-Navy Records, I-180, box 326, folder "B'nai B'rith," AJHS. For further discussion of fraternal orders on military bases, see General Orders No. 2, War Department, Washington, DC, January 7, 1918, Raymond Blaine Fosdick Papers, MC055, Seeley G. Mudd Manuscript Library, Princeton University, Princeton, NJ.

63 As described on the committee's letterhead. For examples, see JWB Army-Navy Records, I-180, box 328, folder "Committee of Six," AJHS.

64 For example, the minutes of the JWB's first annual meeting record a battle over the composition of the Executive Committee, in which members of the nominating committee voiced complaints that even they had no say over the election of the Executive Committee. See Jewish Welfare Board, *First Report of War Emergency Activities* (New York, 1919), 53–66.

65 Janowsky, *Change and Challenge*, 5.

66 Bernard Richards, "The Problem of Welfare Work," *American Jewish Chronicle*, December 14, 1917, 167.

67 *Die Warheit*, June 27, 1918, JWB Army-Navy Records, I-180, box 341, folder "Translations 1918," AJHS. Translations from Yiddish were done by a newspaper clipping and translation service employed by the JWB. Unless otherwise indicated, the translations cited here are those found in JWB files.

68 Joel Entin, "Poor Jewish Soldiers, Why Were You Not Born Idolaters," *Die War-heit*, June 29, 1918, JWB Army-Navy Records, I-180, box 341, folder "Translations 1918," AJHS.

69 Harry Cutler to Lieutenant Colonel Mastiller (National Army, General Staff Corps, War Department), July 11, 1918, JWB Army-Navy Records, I-180, box 343, folder "War Department 1919" (2 of 2), AJHS. On a subsequent letter, Lieutenant Colonel Mastiller is addressed as "Colonel K. C. Masteller, Military Intelligence Bureau."

70 For more on the work of the Committee on Public Information, see Stephen Vaughn, *Holding Fast the Inner Lines: Democracy, Nationalism, and the Committee on Public Information* (Chapel Hill: University of North Carolina Press, 1980); and Kennedy, *Over Here*, 61–66. See also committee chairman George Creel's account of his experiences in *How We Advertised America: The First Telling of the Amazing Story of the Committee on Public Information that Carried the Gospel of American-ism to Every Corner of the Globe* (New York: Harper and Brothers, 1920).

71 Guy Stanton Ford to Harry Cutler, received July 16, 1918, JWB Army-Navy Re-cords, I-180, box 343, folder "War Department 1919," AJHS.

72 Frederick P. Keppel to Harry Cutler, July 24, 1918, JWB Army-Navy Records, I-180, box 343, folder "War Department 1918–1920," AJHS.

73 Frederick P. Keppel to Harry Cutler, August 15, 1918, JWB Army-Navy Records, I-180, box 343, folder "War Department 1918–1920," AJHS.

74 Colonel Masteller to Harry Cutler, August 16, 1918, JWB Army-Navy Records, I-180, box 343, folder "War Department 1919" (2 of 2), AJHS.

75 "Untermyer Denies Aiding Propaganda; Examination Rigid," *New York Times*, December 18, 1918, 1.

76 "Jewish Papers Unite: The Day and the Warheit to be Published as One," *New York Times*, February 28, 1919, 6.

CHAPTER 3. MAKING JUDAISM SAFE FOR AMERICA

1 Newton D Baker, "Invisible Armor," in *Frontiers of Freedom* (New York: George H. Doran, 1918), 94.

2 The War Camp Community Service was a group established by the Playground Association of America to organize communities adjacent to military camps to provide servicemen with home hospitality and wholesome entertainment. For more on the organization, see Joseph Lee, "War Camp Community Service," *An-nals of the American Academy of Political and Social Science* 79 (September 1918): 189–194.

3 For more details on soldiers' welfare work inside the camps, see Bristow, *Making Men Moral*; Ford, *Americans All*, esp. 88–112; Fosdick, "War and Navy Depart-ments"; Baldwin, "Invisible Armor"; Allen F. Davis, "Welfare, Reform and World War I," *American Quarterly* 19, no. 3 (Autumn 1967): 516–533; Thomas M. Cam-field, "'Will to Win'—The US Army Troop Morale Program of World War I," *Mili-tary Affairs* 41, no. 3 (October 1977): 125–128; Durham, "Big Brother," 57–60; and

Steven Pope, "An Army of Athletes: Playing Fields, Battlefields, and the American Military Sporting Experience, 1890–1920," *Journal of American Military History* 59, no. 3 (July 1995): 435–456.

4 Baker, "Invisible Armor," 94–95.

5 Edward Frank Allen, written with the cooperation of Raymond B. Fosdick, *Keeping Our Fighters Fit for War and After* (New York: Century Company, 1918), 207.

6 Newton Baker, speech to the National Conference on War Camp Recreation Service, October 1917, cited in Bristow, *Making Men Moral*, 15.

7 Allen and Fosdick, *Keeping Our Fighters Fit*, 207. For more on the CTCA's programs and Americanization, see Bristow, *Making Men Moral*; and Ford, *Americans All*. On World War I and the ways that immigrants—Jewish and Italian—navigated the demands and rewards of patriotism and Americanization policies, see Sterba, *Good Americans*. For more on the war, Americanization, and concerns about immigrants, see Gerstle, *American Crucible*, 81–114.

8 Bristow, *Making Men Moral*, 182.

9 Allen and Fosdick, *Keeping Our Fighters Fit*, 12.

10 On the experiences of African American soldiers in the US military during World War I, see Williams, *Torchbearers of Democracy*; Richard Slotkin, *Lost Battalions: The Great War and the Crisis of American Nationality* (New York: Henry Holt, 2005); Gerald W. Patton, *War and Race: The Black Officer in the American Military, 1915–1941* (Westport, CT: Greenwood Press, 1981), 3–116; and Arthur Barbeau and Florette Henri, *The Unknown Soldiers: Black American Troops in World War I* (Philadelphia: Temple University Press, 1974). On YMCA services offered to African American soldiers, see Frank E. Roberts, *The American Foreign Legion: Black Soldiers of the 93d in World War I* (Annapolis, MD: Naval Institute Press, 2004), 188–189; and Keene, *Doughboys*, 94–98.

11 Fessenden, *Culture and Redemption*, 12.

12 Meeting of the Committee of Eleven (a subcommittee of the CTCA), September 4, 1918, Fosdick Papers, MC055, box 24, folder 7, "Reports—Commission on Training Camp Activities," Mudd Manuscript Library, Princeton University.

13 Quoted in Raymond Fosdick, *Strictly Confidential Report on Non-military Organizations Serving with the AEF* (Washington, DC: Commission on Training Camp Activities, 1918), 25.

14 Quoted in Fosdick, *Strictly Confidential Report*, 25.

15 Harris, *Service with Fighting Men*, 1:297–298.

16 Fosdick, *Strictly Confidential Report*, 2–3.

17 Kauffman, *Faith and Fraternalism*, 209, 211.

18 JWB, *Final Report*, 13.

19 For more on the history of American Jews' belief in the reinforcing nature of Judaism and Americanism, see Jonathan Sarna, "The Cult of Synthesis in American Jewish Culture," *Jewish Social Studies*, n.s., 5, no. 1/2 (Autumn 1998–Winter 1999): 52–79; and Imhoff, *Masculinity*, 31–61.

20 Rabbi Louis Grossman, "Message of the President to the Twenty-Ninth Annual Convention of the Central Conference of American Rabbis, Chicago, Illinois," *Reform Advocate*, July 13, 1918, 547–548.

21 Rabbi Hyman Gerson Enelow, *The Allied Countries and the Jews: A Series of Addresses* (New York: Temple Emanu-El, 1918), 90.

22 Harry Cutler, address to the JWB Worker Training School, [July 1918?], JWB Army-Navy Records, I-180, box 333, folder "History 1918–1920," AJHS.

23 Irving Lehman, "Our Duty as Americans," *Menorah Journal* 4, no. 1 (February 1918): 6. "May the words of my mouth and the meditations of my heart be acceptable unto you" is from Psalms 19:14.

24 For example, see Marie Trommer, "Jews in America's Wars," *American Hebrew and Jewish Messenger* 101, no. 13 (August 3, 1917): 1.

25 Henry Pereira Mendes, "The Jew to the Bar of the World," *American Hebrew and Jewish Messenger*, June 29, 1917, 209.

26 Joseph Silverman, "Jews and the War: American Israel's Hope and Opportunity," *American Hebrew and Jewish Messenger*, September 14, 1917, 478.

27 Each of the men cited above belonged to constituent agencies of the JWB—in these cases, the YMHA and Reform or Orthodox rabbinical organizations.

28 UAHC Department of Synagogue and School Extension, "Educating 150,000 Jewish Children in New York," submitted to the *American Hebrew and Jewish Messenger* with a note asking that it be published in that paper, Union for Reform Judaism [URJ] Records, MS-72, series A, subseries 1, box 41, folder 3, "Cincinnati, Ohio—Department of Synagogue and School Extension. 1917," AJA. There was also the unstated assumption that Jewish men had been called into the military, making them unable to fulfill their traditional duty of educating their sons and leaving their children without moral guidance or education. This was, of course, not the only time in which the perceived lack of Jewish education was considered a threat to the welfare of Jewish youth. For examples, see Dianne Ashton, *Rebecca Gratz: Women and Judaism in Antebellum America* (Detroit: Wayne State University Press, 1997), 121–148; or Marianne Sanua, *Going Greek: Jewish College Fraternities in the United States, 1895–1945* (Detroit: Wayne State University Press, 2003), 31–46.

29 UAHC Department of Synagogue and School Extension, form letter, December 1917, URJ Records, MS-72, series A, subseries 1, box 41, folder 2, "Cincinnati, Ohio—Department of Synagogue and School Extension. 1917," AJA.

30 "Memorandum on Religious Services in Camp," August 16, 1918, 6, George W. Rabinoff Papers, P-58, box 1, folder "JWB 1918–1919," AJHS.

31 David de Sola Pool, "In Defense of the Jewish Welfare Board," *American Jewish Chronicle*, September 13, 1918, 462–464.

32 Cutler, address to the JWB Worker Training School.

33 Teller, "Jewish Welfare Board," 91 (emphasis in original).

34 Imhoff, *Masculinity*, 12–23.

35 On discussion of kosher food in the Russian military, see Yohanan Petrovsky-Shtern, *Jews in the Russian Army, 1827–1917: Drafted into Modernity* (New York:

Cambridge University Press, 2009), 191–196; and Rabbi Moses Yoshor, *Israel in the Ranks: A Religious Guide of Faith and Practice for the Jewish Soldier* (New York: Yeshivah Chofetz Chaim, 1943), 66–71.

36 For a discussion of controversies concerning kosher food, see Harold Gastwirt, *Fraud, Corruption, and Holiness: The Controversy over the Supervision of Jewish Dietary Practice in New York City, 1881–1940* (Port Washington, NY: Kennikat Press, 1974).

37 Unsigned letter to Rabbi George Zepin regarding a meeting of the Jewish Welfare Board Executive Committee, May 17, 1917, URJ Records, MS-72, series A, subseries 1, box 41, folder 2, "Cincinnati, Ohio—Department of Synagogue and School Extension. 1917," AJA.

38 According to historian Marsha Rozenblit, it is not clear whether kosher field kitchens ever operated on a regular basis in the Austrian army, but in 1916, Austrian officials did order that "Jewish soldiers behind the lines could have separate kosher kitchens if at least 100 men in a given unit wanted kosher food." Marsha Rozenblit, *Reconstructing a National Identity: The Jews of Habsburg Austria during World War I* (New York: Oxford University Press, 2001), 97. American Jewish newspapers kept abreast of events in Europe pertaining to Jews. Rozenblit indicates that this decision was widely covered in the Austrian Jewish press, making it likely that reports appeared in the American Jewish press as well.

39 Bendersky, *Jewish Threat*, 62–74.

40 David Goldberg, "A Chaplain's Arraignment of the Army Prayer Book," pt. 2, *Reform Advocate*, March 9, 1918.

41 For the debates concerning kosher food in early twentieth-century American Jewish communities, see Hasia Diner, *Hungering for America: Italian, Irish, and Jewish Foodways in the Age of Migration* (Cambridge: Harvard University Press, 2001), 180–188; Jeffrey Gurock, *Orthodox Jews in America* (Bloomington: Indiana University Press, 2009), 151–156; and Timothy Lytton, "Jewish Foodways and Religious Self-Governance in America: The Failure of Communal Kashrut Regulation and the Rise of Private Kosher Certification," *Jewish Quarterly Review* 104, no. 1 (Winter 2014): 38–45.

42 Draft of letter from Harry Cutler to the paymaster general, Office of the Department of the Navy, August 21, 1917, JWB Army-Navy Records, I-180, box 334, folder "Kashrut," AJHS.

43 Cyrus J. Janover, report on conditions at Camp Dix, NJ, n.d., JWB Army-Navy Records, I-180, box 337, folder "Reports 1917, 1918" (1 of 3), AJHS. See also "What the Jewish Soldiers of Camp Upton Have to Say about the Jewish Welfare Board," *Der Morgen Zhurnal*, July 30, 1918, JWB Army-Navy Records, I-180, box 339, folder "Translations," AJHS.

44 Albert Lucas to Harry Cutler, October 5, 1917, JWB Army-Navy Records, I-180, box 334, folder "Kashruth," AJHS. On Albert Lucas, see Gurock, *Orthodox Jews in America*, 130–132.

45 Presumably, Catholic leaders considered similar questions as neither military nor CTCA archives contain records of Catholic requests for meat-free meals in observance of Lent.

46 For a history of the Zionist Organization of America, see Melvin Urofsky, *American Zionism from Herzl to the Holocaust* (Lincoln: University of Nebraska Press, 1995).

47 Cyrus Adler to Harry Cutler, November 12, 1917, JWB Army-Navy Records, I-180, box 326, folder "Adler, Correspondence, 1917," AJHS.

48 Cyrus Adler to Harry Cutler, November 14, 1917, JWB Army-Navy Records, I-180, box 326, folder "Adler, Correspondence, 1917," AJHS.

49 On the relationship and conflicts between Marshall and Brandeis, see Jonathan Sarna, "Two Lawyers Named Louis," *American Jewish History* 94, no. 1/2, Special Issue: Louis Marshall and American Jewish Leadership (March/June 2008): 1–19.

50 Cyrus Adler to Harry Cutler, November 12, 1917, JWB Army-Navy Records, I-180, box 326, folder "Adler, Correspondence, 1917," AJHS.

51 On Brandeis, see Melvin Urofsky, *Louis D. Brandeis and the Progressive Tradition* (Boston: Little, Brown, 1981).

52 The Union of Orthodox Jewish Congregations proposed setting up kosher kitchens at their own expense and under their own supervision. See George A. Kohut to Chester Teller, December 18, 1917, JWB Army-Navy Records, I-180, box 334, folder "Kashrut," AJHS. The Agudath ha-Rabbonim proposed a plan to have nonperishable kosher food available for sale at all military post exchanges. See memo signed by Chester Teller (JWB executive director) and Harry Glucksman (assistant executive director) and sent to all JWB field representatives, March 1, 1918, JWB Army-Navy Records, I-180, box 334, folder "Kashrut," AJHS.

53 Harry Cutler to Jacob Schiff, September 29, 1917, JWB Army-Navy Records, I-180, box 339, folder "Schiff, Jacob, 1917–1918," AJHS.

54 Jacob Schiff to Harry Cutler, October 23, 1917, JWB Army-Navy Records, I-180, box 339, folder "Schiff, Jacob, 1917–1918," AJHS.

55 "Report of Captain N. Horowitz, U.S. Army on Work of the Y.M.H.A. and Kindred Associations in Mobilization Camps," n.d., JWB Army-Navy Records, I-180, box 337, folder "Reports 1917, 1918" (1of 3), AJHS.

56 Jason Kirschenbaum, "What General Bell Thought of the Jewish Welfare Board," *Der Morgen Zhurnal*, August 1, 1918, JWB Army-Navy Records, I-180, box 339, folder "Translations," AJHS.

57 Cutler, address to the JWB Worker Training School.

58 Teller, "Jewish Welfare Board," 92.

59 On designation of religion for Jewish soldiers on their dog tags during World War II, see Moore, *GI Jews*, 73–74.

60 Joseph Hyman to Samuel Goldsmith (JWB secretary), October 9, 1917, JWB Army-Navy Records, I-180, box 334, folder "Kashrut," AJHS.

61 Hyman to Goldsmith, October 9, 1917.

62 Joseph C. Hyman, report on conditions at Camp Upton, Yaphank, NY, n.d., JWB Army-Navy Records I-180, box 337, folder "Reports 1917, 1918" (1 of 3), AJHS. Regarding the claim that Secretary Baker himself had decided against the provision of kosher food, neither the records of the CTCA nor of the Office of the Secretary of War contain copies of this communication, so we have only Bell's say-so and Cutler's disavowal of the attempt to provide kosher food as evidence.

63 Hyman, report on conditions at Camp Upton.

64 David de Sola Pool to Mortimer Schiff, report on conditions at Camp Upton, Yaphank, NY, December 10, 1917, JWB Army-Navy Records, I-180, box 339, folder "Buildings Schiff, M.L. 1917–1920," AJHS.

CHAPTER 4. AMERICAN JUDAISM AND AMERICAN JEWS

1 Pershing, *My Experiences*, 1:284.

2 John J. Pershing to Newton D. Baker, January 17, 1918, in Pershing, *My Experiences*, 1:284.

3 For a history of the development of the US military chaplaincy in this period, see Budd, *Serving Two Masters*, esp. 92–155; John Piper, "American Churches in World War I," *Journal of the American Academy of Religion* 38, no. 2 (June 1970): 147–155; Earl F. Stover, *Up from Handymen: The United States Army Chaplaincy, 1865–1920* (Washington, DC: Office of the Chief of Chaplains, Department of the Army, 1978), 186–237; and Stahl, *Enlisting Faith*, esp. 15–43.

4 On the career of Bishop Brent, see Alexander Zabriskie, *Bishop Brent: Crusader for Christian Unity* (Philadelphia: Westminster, 1948). Brent, an Episcopal minister, served as first missionary bishop of the Philippine Islands from 1901 to 1917. He began his work with soldier and sailors while in the Philippines and continued his work with servicemen in 1917–1918 as a representative of the YMCA in France.

5 Budd, *Serving Two Masters*, 124. The number of naval chaplains grew to five times its prewar size.

6 Stahl, *Enlisting Faith*, 29–31.

7 Stahl, *Enlisting Faith*, 9.

8 On anti-Semitism in American, see Dinnerstein, *Antisemitism in America*; and the essays in David Gerber, ed., *Anti-Semitism in American History* (Chicago: University of Illinois Press, 1986). On physical stereotypes of Jews, see Sander Gilman, *The Jew's Body* (New York: Routledge, 1991).

9 For an exploration of the ways that military service has been used historically as a tool to assert Jewish masculinity and rights as citizens, see Derek Penslar, *Jews and the Military: A History* (Princeton, NJ: Princeton University Press, 2013), esp. 35–82; and Petrovsky-Shtern, *Jews in the Russian Army*.

10 Teller, "Jewish Welfare Board," 99.

11 George Mason, "Army Chaplain Bill a Law," *American Hebrew and Jewish Messenger*, October 12, 1919, 638.

12 According to Cyrus Adler, the Senate bill was drafted by himself and Secretary Baker and was intended to meet the religious needs of Jews and Christians from

minority groups, particularly Unitarians and Christian Scientists. See Adler, "Account of the Origin," 224.

13 Mason, "Army Chaplain Bill," 638. See also Slomovitz, *Fighting Rabbis*, 49, although he claims that the bills were passed in October 1917.

14 "Special Regulations No. 3: Appointment of Chaplains in the Regular Army and the National Army of the United States," 1917 (Washington, DC: Government Printing Office 1918), 6.

15 See Zola, *Rabbi Abraham*, 80–97; Sarna and Shapell, *Lincoln and the Jews*, 100–110; and Korn, "Jewish Chaplains," 335–352.

16 Cyrus Adler to Harry Cutler, October 21, 1917, JWB Army-Navy Records, I-180, box 326, folder "Adler, Correspondence, 1917," AJHS.

17 Lee Levinger, *A Jewish Chaplain in France* (New York: Macmillan, 1921), 93.

18 "Special Regulations No. 3: Appointment of Chaplains in the Regular Army and the National Army of the United States," 1917 (Washington, DC: Government Printing Office 1918), 8.

19 "Special Regulations No. 3," 9. Also see Budd, *Serving Two Masters*, 8–92.

20 "JWB Memorandum with Regard to the Appointment of Chaplains in the United States Army," JWB Army-Navy Records, I-180, box 326, folder "Adler Correspondence, 1917," AJHS.

21 Sarna, *American Judaism*, 192–193. For a history of Yeshiva University, of which the seminary is a part, see Jeffrey Gurock, *The Men and Women of Yeshiva: Higher Education, Orthodoxy, and American Judaism* (New York: Columbia University Press, 1988).

22 Cyrus Adler to Isaac Siegel, July 19, 1917, Siegel Papers, P-33, box 1, folder "JWB."

23 Cyrus Adler to Harry Cutler, August 27, 1918, JWB Army-Navy Records, I-180, box 326, folder "Adler, Cyrus Correspondence 1917–1921," AJHS.

24 Hasia Diner, "Like the Antelope and the Badger: The Founding and Early Years of the Jewish Theological Seminary, 1886–1902," in *Tradition Renewed: A History of the Jewish Theological Seminary*, ed. Jack Wertheimer, 2 vols. (New York: Jewish Theological Seminary of America, 1997), 1:6–7. For the origin of the phrase "stupid Orthodoxy and insane Reform," Diner cites *American Hebrew*, November 29, 1886, 34.

25 For a history of the Conservative movement, see Michael Cohen, *The Birth of Conservative Judaism: Solomon Schechter's Disciples and the Creation of an American Religious Movement* (New York: Columbia University Press, 2012); and Daniel Elazar and Rela Mintz Geffen, *The Conservative Movement in Judaism: Dilemmas and Opportunities* (New York: State University of New York Press, 2000), esp. 13–28. On the history of the Jewish Theological Seminary of America, see Wertheimer, *Tradition Renewed*.

26 Harry Davidowitz to Cyrus Adler, August 4, 1918 (ellipsis in original), JWB Army-Navy Records, I-180, box 326, folder "Adler, Cyrus Correspondence 1917–1921," AJHS.

27 JWB Committee on Chaplaincies in the US Army, meeting minutes, December 4, 1917, JWB Army-Navy Records, I-180, box 328, folder "Chaplains 1918," AJHS.

28 JWB Committee on Chaplaincies, meeting minutes, December 4, 1917.

29 "Getting Broadminded: Our Chaplains Gain from Contact with Our Soldiers," *New York Times*, July 3, 1918, 7.

30 Quoted in "Pershing Requests More Chaplains: Seeks to Surround Fighters at the Front with the Best Possible Influences," *New York Times*, February 14, 1918, 2.

31 JWB Committee on Chaplaincies, minutes, December 4, 1917.

32 See JWB Committee on Chaplaincies in the US Army, meeting minutes, August 14, 1918, JWB Army-Navy Records, I-180, box 328, folder "Chaplains 1918," AJHS.; and Cyrus Adler's correspondence with Harry Cutler, JWB Army-Navy Records, I-180, box 326, folder "Adler, Correspondence," AJHS.

33 Levinger, *Jewish Chaplain*, 85–86, 93. Looking through lists of graduating classes for both Hebrew Union College and the Jewish Theological Seminary it appears that at least eighteen of the chaplains were graduates of HUC; five, of JTS. Rabbis David Tannenbaum, Samuel Fredman, and Max Felshin's names did not appear on the lists of graduates from either institution. Tannenbaum, however, was well acquainted with Cyrus Adler, the seminary's acting president, making it possible that he graduated from JTS. Nine other rabbis—William Ackerman, Fred Braun, Hyman Enelow, Louis Gross, Joseph Rauch, Samuel Rosinger, Joseph Sarachek, George Solomon, and Nathan Stern—were also recommended by the JWB for appointments as chaplains, but the armistice was signed before they received commissions. JWB, *First Annual Report*, 104.

34 Chaplain David Goldberg served on the USS *President Grant* and maintained strained relations with the JWB throughout the war. For more information on Goldberg, see the David J. Goldberg Papers, MS-432, AJA.

35 Statistics from JWB, *First Annual Report*, 85–86. According to the JWB, there were also 178 male and female overseas workers stationed in 57 different centers, some of whom were controlled directly by the JWB, others by either the army itself, the Red Cross, the Knights of Columbus, the YMCA, or, in one case, the Belgian government. JWB, *Final Report*, 37.

36 Harry Cutler to Chester Teller, April 17, 1918, JWB Army-Navy Records, I-180, box 329, folder "Miscellaneous Correspondence, Col. Cutler, 1918," AJHS.

37 JWB memo, May 6, 1918, Rabinoff Papers, P-58, box 1, folder "JWB 1918–1919," AJHS.

38 "Sermon Suggestions for Sabbath *Chayye Sarah*," November 2, 1918, Rabinoff Papers, P-58, box 1, folder "JWB 1918–1919," AJHS.

39 "Comments on *Sedra Veyera*," October 26, 1918, Rabinoff Papers, P-58, box 1, folder "JWB 1918–1919," AJHS.

40 "Sermon Outline for Shabbat *Toledoth*, November 9, 1918, Esau and Jacob—Character Types," Rabinoff Papers, P-58, box 1, folder "JWB 1918–1919," AJHS.

41 Rabbi Moses Hyamson, *"Golden Rule" Hillel* (New York: Jewish Welfare Board, 1918), 1–5.

42 William Rosenau, "Ten Commandments for the Soldier," *Welfare Board Sentinel* 1, no. 1 (March 1, 1918): 3. The article reprinted an address that Dr. Rosenau had delivered to the soldiers at Camp Meade.

43 On statistics regarding foreign-born soldiers, see Ford, *Americans All*, esp. 45–66. For statistics on Jewish soldiers, see Julian Leavitt, "American Jews in the World War," *American Jewish Year Book* 21 (1919–1920), 141–155; Leavitt, "Collection of Jewish War Statistics"; and American Jewish Committee, *The War Record of American Jews: First Report of the Office of War Records* (New York: American Jewish Committee, 1919). On nativism, Americanization of immigrants, and concerns about the impact of immigrants on American society, see Higham, *Strangers in the Land*, esp. 234–299.

44 Allen and Fosdick, *Keeping Our Fighters Fit*, 207.

45 On nineteenth- and early twentieth-century American conceptions of manhood, see Bederman, *Manliness and Civilization*; E. Anthony Rotundo, *American Manhood: Transformation in Masculinity from the Revolution to the Modern Era* (New York: Basic Books, 1993); and the essays in Mark C. Carnes and Clyde Griffen, eds., *Meanings for Manhood: Constructions of Masculinity in Victorian America* (Chicago: University of Chicago Press, 1990), esp. Margaret Marsh, "Suburban Men and Masculine Domesticity, 1870–1915," 111–127, and Clyde Griffen, "Reconstructing Masculinity from the Evangelical Revival to the Waning of Progressivism: A Speculative Synthesis," 183–204. On Jewish masculinity, see Imhoff, *Masculinity*.

46 For an analysis of civilian discussions of religion, including Judaism, as the cure to crime, see Imhoff, *Masculinity*, 205–224.

47 Jewish Welfare Board, "The Sphere of the Welfare Worker," n.d., JWB Army-Navy Records, I-180, box 328, folder "Circular Letters 1917–1919," AJHS.

48 Jewish Welfare Board, "The Sphere of the Welfare Worker," n.d., JWB Army-Navy Records, I-180, box 328, folder "Circular Letters 1917–1919," AJHS.

49 Jewish Welfare Board, "General Circular No. 2 to the Representatives of the JWB," n.d. (emphasis in original), JWB Army-Navy Records, I-180, box 330, folder "Field Representatives, 1918," AJHS.

50 Cyrus Adler to Harry Cutler, May 27, 1918, JWB Army-Navy Records, I-180, box 326, folder "Adler, Correspondence," AJHS.

51 Cyrus Adler to Harry Cutler, June 3, 1918, JWB Army-Navy Records, I-180, box 326, folder "Adler, Correspondence," AJHS.

52 On Rabbi Ehrenreich, see Harold Wechsler, "Rabbi Bernard C. Ehrenreich: A Northern Progressive Goes South," *Jews of the South: Selected Essays from the Southern Jewish Historical Society*, ed. Samuel Proctor and Louis Schmier with Malcolm Stern (Macon, GA: Mercer University Press, 1984), 45–63. The website for Camp Kawaga describes "Doc. E" and his mission to help boys "develop meaningfully into manhood" but makes no mention of Judaism. "History of Kawaga," *Camp Kawaga for Boys*, http://kawaga.com. On Jewish masculinity and the attraction of Native American traditions, see Imhoff, *Masculinity*, 128–150.

53 Bernard Ehrenreich to H. L. Gluckson [read: Gluckman], March 22, 1918, Bernard C. Ehrenreich Papers, P-26, box 1, folder "National Jewish Welfare Board," AJHS.

54 "Report of Captain N. Horowitz, U.S. Army on Work of the YMHA and Kindred Associations in Mobilization Camps," n.d., JWB Army-Navy Records, I-180, box 337, folder "Reports 1917, 1918" (1of 3), AJHS.

55 Elkan Voorsanger to Harry Cutler, March 20, 1918, JWB Army-Navy Records, I-180, box 327, folder "Chaplains—1918," AJHS.

56 Janover, report on conditions at Camp Dix.

57 Cyrus Adler, "A Memorandum for Overseas Workers," enclosed in Cyrus Adler to Harry Cutler, August 16, 1918, JWB Army-Navy Records, I-180, box 326, folder "Adler, Correspondence July–December 1918," AJHS.

58 Adler to Cutler, June 3, 1918. For more on Rabbi Spitz, see Leon Spitz, *The Memoirs of a Camp Rabbi* (New York: Bloch, 1927).

59 *St. Louis Star*, May 14, 1917, Elkan Cohn Voorsanger Papers, MS-256, box 1, folder 2, "Chaplaincy," AJA. Voorsanger's obituary was printed in the *New York Times*, May 3, 1963, 31.

60 "The 'Fighting Rabbi' Goes to Poland," *American Hebrew and Jewish Messenger*, January 2, 1920, 234. For other descriptions of Voorsanger, see "A Fighting Rabbi," *New York Times*, October 12, 1919, 8; "Chaplain Voorsanger: Fighting Rabbi," *Jewish Sentinel*, July 1919, 7; and Elkan Voorsanger, "Passover Services in France," May 3, 1918, in *American Jewish History: A Primary Source Reader*, eds. Gary Philip Zola and Marc Dollinger (Waltham, MA: Brandeis University Press, 2014), 158–159.

61 Enelow, *Allied Countries*, 81–82.

CHAPTER 5. "REAL JEWS," "POOR JEHUDAS," AND RESISTANCE TO THE JWB'S AGENDA

1 For a biography of Marcus, see Jonathan Sarna, "Jacob Rader Marcus (1896–1995)," *American Jewish Year Book* 97 (1997): 633–640.

2 Jacob Rader Marcus, World War I diary, Jacob Rader Marcus Papers, MS-210, series E, box 29, folder 4, "Diary. August 1917–March 1924," AJA.

3 This was particularly true at Camp Sheridan, where—judging from Marcus's comments—he and camp rabbi Bernard Ehrenreich seem to have gotten along quite well.

4 Jacob Rader Marcus, "The Jewish Soldier," in *The Dynamics of American Jewish History: Jacob Rader Marcus's Essays on American Jewry*, ed. Gary Zola (Hanover, NH: Brandeis University Press / University Press of New England, 2004), 44. Originally published in *Hebrew Union College Monthly* 4 (1918):115–122.

5 Marcus, diary entry, Thursday, September 13, 1917.

6 These preliminary statistics are based on my analysis of 850 soldiers' surveys contained in the Records of the American Jewish Committee-Office of Jewish War Records, 1918–1921, I-9, AJHS. Foreign-born men made up approximately 18 percent of the entire American military. On foreign-born soldiers see Ford, *Americans All*.

7 Michael Aaronsohn was a friend of Marcus's from Cincinnati and a fellow student at Hebrew Union College. Aaronsohn was blinded during the war but went on to graduate from HUC and become a prominent Reform rabbi. He was also a founder of the Disabled American Veterans and of the Jewish Braille Institute. On Aaronsohn, see John S. Fine and Frederic J. Krome, *Jews of Cincinnati* (Charleston: Arcadia, 2007), 110–112; and the Michael Aaronsohn Papers, MS-511, AJA.

8 Nachman Heller to Harry Cutler, n.d., JWB Army-Navy Records, I-180, box 333, folder "Janet Harris," AJHS. Rabbi Heller had evidently expressed his wish to volunteer for the JWB in numerous letters and phone calls but had heard nothing back from the New York City office. There is no obvious connection with the Janet Harris listed on the folder.

9 David de Sola Pool, report on conditions at Camp Doniphan, Fort Sill, near Oklahoma City, March 21–23, 1918, JWB Army-Navy Records, I-180, box 338, folder "Reports 1918" (1 of 3), AJHS.

10 "Communication received from Lieutenant M.E. Gross, Base Hospital, Twenty-Ninth Division, Camp McClellan, Ala," August 26, 1918, JWB Army-Navy Records, I-180, box 328, folder "Cooperation with Agencies, 1918," AJHS. Gross appears to have written a longer letter. These quotes are taken from a section that was copied and sent, presumably, to Colonel Cutler.

11 Harry G. Fromberg to Harry Cutler, August 26, 1918, JWB Army-Navy Records, I-180, box 328, folder "Cooperation with Agencies, 1918," AJHS.

12 Fromberg to Cutler, August 26, 1918.

13 De Sola Pool, report on conditions at Camp Doniphan.

14 Cyrus Adler to Harry Cutler, dated October 21, 1917, JWB Army-Navy Records, I-180, box 326, folder "Adler, Correspondence, 1917," AJHS.

15 See de Sola Pool to Schiff, report on conditions at Camp Upton.

16 De Sola Pool to Schiff, report on conditions at Camp Upton.

17 De Sola Pool to Schiff, report on conditions at Camp Upton.

18 Hyman, report on conditions at Camp Upton.

19 David Goldberg to Harry Cutler, July 25, 1918, JWB Army-Navy Records, I-180, box 332, folder "Goldberg, David 1918," AJHS.

20 Jewish Welfare Board, *Abridged Prayer Book for Jews in the Army and Navy of the United States* (Philadelphia: Jewish Publication Society of America, 1917).

21 Goldberg to Cutler, July 25, 1918.

22 David Goldberg, "A Chaplain's Arraignment of the Army Prayer Book," pt. 1, *Reform Advocate*, March 2, 1918.

23 Goldberg, "Chaplain's Arraignment," pt. 2.

24 Marcus, diary entry, Friday, December 13, 1918.

25 Jacob Rader Marcus, "Lost: Judaism in the AEF: The Urgent Need for Welfare Workers," in *Dynamics of American Jewish History*, 57–58. Originally published in *American Hebrew and Jewish Messenger* 104 (1919): 448, 456–457.

26 Jewish Welfare Board, memo sent to all field representatives on religious service in the camps, August 16, 1918, Rabinoff Papers, P-58, box 1, folder "JWB 1918–1919," AJHS.

27 Jewish Welfare Board, report to the Central Conference of American Rabbis, July 1, 1918, JWB Army-Navy Records, I-180, box 326, folder "Adler, Correspondence, July–December 1918," AJHS.

28 Isaac First, "The Welfare Board: Its Relation to Jewish Soldiers," *Dos Yiddishe Folk*, March 6, 1918, JWB Army-Navy Records, I-180, box 339, folder "Schiff, M. L. 1917–1920," AJHS.

29 "The Crooked Path of the Welfare Board," editorial, *Yiddishes Tageblatt*, July 21, 1918, JWB Army-Navy Records, I-180, box 342, folder "Translation 1918," AJHS.

30 "Our Drafted Brethren in Camp Have a Complaint against Us and They Are Justified," editorial, *Forverts*, May 24, 1918, JWB Army-Navy Records, I-180, box 341, folder "Translation 1918" (1 of 2), AJHS.

31 "To Provide for the Jewish Soldiers," editorial, *Ha'ivri*, May, 29, 1918, JWB Army-Navy Records, I-180, box 341, folder "Translation 1918" (1 of 2), AJHS. Translation from Hebrew was done by the JWB's translation agency.

32 "Verboten," editorial, *Die Warheit*, June 27, 1918, JWB Army-Navy Records, I-180, box 341, folder "Translation 1918" (1 of 2), AJHS.

33 H. M. Kallen, "The Jewish Soldier and His Welfare," *American Jewish Chronicle*, August 23, 1918, JWB Army-Navy Records, I-180, box 333, folder "History: 1918–1919" (1 of 3), AJHS.

34 Kallen, "Jewish Solider."

35 On Kallen, see Noam Pianko, "True Liberalism of Zionism"; Daniel Greene, "A Chosen People in a Pluralist Nation: Horace Kallen and the Jewish American Experience," *Religion and American Culture* 16, no. 2 (Summer 2006): 161–194; and William Toll, "Horace M. Kallen: Pluralism and American Jewish Identity," *American Jewish History* 85, no. 1 (March 1997): 57–74.

36 Marcus, diary entry, Friday, December 6, 1918.

37 Marcus, diary entry, Tuesday, September 18, 1917.

38 Marcus, diary entry, Tuesday, September 11, 1917.

39 Marcus, diary entry, Friday, December 6, 1918.

40 Marcus, diary entry, Thursday, September 6, 1917.

41 Marcus, diary entry, Sunday, October 14, 1917.

42 Marcus, diary entry, Wednesday, April 16, 1919.

43 Marcus, diary entry, Friday, December 13, 1918.

44 The YMCA estimated that each hut would cost approximately $3,000 and spent $7,698,984.75 to build 952 huts. Harris, *Service with Fighting Men*, 1:277, 282.

45 War Department records seem to indicate the Knights of Columbus were also without their own huts for some time, as an order permitting "the erection of temporary recreation buildings by the Knights of Columbus" was issued by the Secretary of War on April 18, 1918. Major General Payton C. March (chief of staff of the army), General Order, War Department, Washington, DC, April 1918; File 24994; General Correspondence, 1917–1921; Commission on Training Camp Activities; Education and Recreation Branch; Records of the War Plans Division, 1910–1942; Records of the War Department General and Special Staffs, Record

Group 165; National Archives at College Park, College Park, MD (hereafter NACP).

46 Eustace Seligman to Jacob Schiff, n.d., JWB Army-Navy Records, I-180, box 339, folder "Schiff, Jacob, 1917–1918," AJHS.

47 Lee Levinger to Samuel Goldsmith, report on conditions at a military camp located near Waukegan, IL, June 5, 1918, JWB Army-Navy Records, I-180, box 327, folder "Buildings 1917–1920," AJHS.

48 Jacob Schiff to Harry Cutler, October 9, 1917, JWB Army-Navy Records, I-180, box 339, folder "Schiff, Jacob, 1917–1918," AJHS.

49 The camp in question was most likely Camp Upton on Long Island. The letter was written by a Mrs. Nathaniel Levy of Brooklyn. Men from New York City were generally sent to Camp Upton for basic training. Had Levy been visiting a friend or family member when she made this observation, she would most likely have gone to Camp Upton as well.

50 Hostess houses were set up near the entrance to the camps by the YWCA. They were intended to be used as places where soldiers could meet with family and friends who had come to visit, particularly with female visitors. The hostess houses were supposed to provide safe, well-chaperoned environments where a soldier could visit with a sister or a sweetheart, as it was considered inappropriate for women—particularly young, single women—to visit with men in the camps by themselves. The hostess houses thus provided a degree of protection for female visitors and assured that women who visited soldiers behaved chastely. See Bristow, *Making Men Moral*, 91–136.

51 Mortimer Schiff to Chester Teller, June 10, 1918, in response to a report given to Schiff by Mrs. Nathaniel Levy, president of the Ladies Auxiliary of the Jewish Hospital, Brooklyn, JWB Army-Navy Records, I-180, box 339, folder "Schiff, M.L." (2 of 2), AJHS.

52 De Sola Pool to Schiff, report on conditions at Camp Upton.

53 De Sola Pool to Schiff, report on conditions at Camp Upton.

54 Janover, report on conditions at Camp Dix.

55 One official report explaining the conditions under which JWB workers might use YMCA facilities declared, "This splendid cooperation on the part of the Y.M.C.A. is another evidence of the broad and brotherly spirit which animates its work. Lose no opportunity to render every possible service to the Y.M.C.A. in your camp." Jewish Welfare Board, "Bulletin #3," sent to all field representatives, January 1, 1918, Ehrenreich Papers, P-26, box 1, folder "National Jewish Welfare Board."

56 John Mott, quoted in Jewish Welfare Board, bulletin sent to all field representatives, January 1, 1918, Rabinoff Papers, P-58, box 1, folder "JWB 1918–1919," AJHS.

57 Ehrenreich to Gluckman, March 22, 1918.

58 JWB, "General Circular No. 2."

59 Quoted in A. G. Robinson to Harry Cutler, September 4, 1918, JWB Army-Navy Records, I-180, box 337, folder "Reports 1917–1918" (3 of 3), AJHS.

60 Quoted in Robinson to Cutler, September 4, 1918.

61 Adolph Shirpser to Samuel Goldsmith, June 6, 1918, JWB Army-Navy Records, I-180, box 327, folder "Buildings 1917–1920," AJHS. Rabbi Horace Wolf, reporting on Jewish life in the camps for the *American Hebrew and Jewish Messenger*, described YMCA huts in very similar terms: "I am simply pointing out that the atmosphere of the Y.M.C.A. buildings is, to a certain extent, Christian in character. The Y.M.C.A. conceives one phase of its work to be the conservation of 'Christian' manhood and it takes this work, which forms an important part of the program, very seriously." Horace Wolf, "The Y.M.C.A. at Camp Dix," *American Hebrew and Jewish Messenger* 102, no. 11 (January 18, 1918): 1.

62 Hyman, report on conditions at Camp Upton.

63 George H. Cohen to Harry Cutler, December 25, 1917, JWB Army-Navy Records, I-180, box 327, folder "Buildings 1917–1920," AJHS.

64 Cohen to Cutler, December 25, 1917.

65 See Coleman Silbert, report on conditions at Camp Devens, Ayer, MA, October 12, 1917, JWB Army-Navy Records, I-180, box 337, folder "Reports 1917, 1918" (2 of 3), AJHS; Cohen to Cutler, December 25, 1917; Hyman, report on conditions at Camp Upton; and Janover, report on conditions at Camp Dix.

66 Silbert, report on conditions at Camp Devens.

67 Hyman to Goldsmith, October 9, 1917. The term "declarants" indicates that these men were not yet American citizens but had merely filed their first papers declaring their intention to apply for citizenship.

68 Marcus, diary entry, Thursday, August 30, 1917.

69 Marcus, "Jewish Soldier," 51.

70 Silbert, report on conditions at Camp Devens (emphasis in original).

71 Hyman to Goldsmith, October 9, 1917. See also Janover, report on conditions at Camp Dix.

72 Marcus, "Jewish Soldier," 51.

73 Silbert, report on conditions at Camp Devens (emphasis in original).

CHAPTER 6. GOOD FENCES MAKE GOOD AMERICANS

1 Fosdick, address to the JWB annual meeting, in JWB, *First Annual Report*, 12.

2 See correspondence between Harry Cutler, Raymond Fosdick, and Edward S. Rochester, April 13 and 15, 1918, File 23837; between Chester Teller and John Colter, June 13 and 14, 1918, File 32271; between Ian Beith and John Colter, April 24, 1918, File 25825; between Harry Cutler and John Colter, May 31, 1918, File 31439; and between John Colter and Franklin Edwards, June 5, 1918, File No. 31439; General Correspondence, 1917–1921; Commission on Training Camp Activities; Education and Recreation Branch; Records of the War Plans Division, 1910–1942; Records of the War Department General and Special Staffs, Record Group 165; NACP.

3 John Mott to Raymond Fosdick, August 7, 1918; File 38556; General Correspondence, 1917–1921; Commission on Training Camp Activities; Education and

Recreation Branch; Records of the War Plans Division, 1910–1942; Records of the War Department General and Special Staffs, Record Group 165; NACP.

4 Louis Marshall to Harry Cutler, August 15, 1918; File 38055; General Correspondence, 1917–1921; Commission on Training Camp Activities; Education and Recreation Branch; Records of the War Plans Division, 1910–1942; Records of the War Department General and Special Staffs, Record Group 165; NACP.

5 Harry Cutler to Raymond Fosdick, August 16, 1918; File 38055; General Correspondence, 1917–1921; Commission on Training Camp Activities; Education and Recreation Branch; Records of the War Plans Division, 1910–1942; Records of the War Department General and Special Staffs, Record Group 165; NACP.

6 Raymond Fosdick to Harry Cutler, August 17, 1918; File 38055; General Correspondence, 1917–1921; Commission on Training Camp Activities; Education and Recreation Branch; Records of the War Plans Division, 1910–1942; Records of the War Department General and Special Staffs, Record Group 165; NACP.

7 Louis Marshall to Harry Cutler, August 20, 1918; File 37898; General Correspondence, 1917–1921; Commission on Training Camp Activities; Education and Recreation Branch; Records of the War Plans Division, 1910–1942; Records of the War Department General and Special Staffs, Record Group 165; NACP.

8 On the Salvation Army, see Diane Winston, *Red-Hot and Righteous: The Urban Religion of the Salvation Army* (Cambridge, MA: Harvard University Press, 1999), esp. 143–190.

9 "K. of C. Oppose Plan for 2 Fund Drives," *New York Times*, August 18, 1918, 7; and Kauffman, *Faith and Fraternalism*, 219–221.

10 Harry Cutler to Raymond Fosdick, August 21, 1918; File 37898; General Correspondence, 1917–1921; Commission on Training Camp Activities; Education and Recreation Branch; Records of the War Plans Division, 1910–1942; Records of the War Department General and Special Staffs, Record Group 165; NACP.

11 Jacob Schiff to Raymond Fosdick, telegram, August 25, 1918; File 38018; General Correspondence, 1917–1921; Commission on Training Camp Activities; Education and Recreation Branch; Records of the War Plans Division, 1910–1942; Records of the War Department General and Special Staffs, Record Group 165; NACP.

12 Harry Cutler to Raymond Fosdick, telegram, September 5, 1918, JWB Army-Navy Records, I-180, box 327, folder "Camps, 1917–1919," AJHS.

13 For a discussion of the relationship between sports and the American military, as well as the YMCA's role in developing the Army's World War I athletics program, see Pope, "Army of Athletes." See also Wanda Ellen Wakefield, *Playing to Win: Sports and the American Military, 1898–1945* (Albany: State University of the New York Press, 1997), 1–34. For the importance of sports in the programs of the YMCA, see Putney, *Muscular Christianity*, esp. 45–72, 162–194; and Ladd and Mathisen, *Muscular Christianity*, esp. 22–94.

14 See Commission on Training Camp Activities, *Camp Music Division of the War Department* (Washington, DC: Government Printing Office, 1919). For a list of songs included in the *Official Army Song Book*, see also Bristow, *Making Men Moral*, 221–224.

15 Newton D. Baker, "The Singers of Songs," in *Frontiers of Freedom*, 18–19. For a discussion, see Bristow, *Making Men Moral*, 42–43.

16 In the interest of promoting greater cultural and linguistic cohesion among the troops, the JWB, for example, offered classes on English, civics, American history, and current events, as well as special lectures in Russian and Yiddish on citizenship and naturalization. JWB, *Final Report*, 30.

17 Lee Levinger, "Christian and Jew at the Front," *Biblical World* 53, no. 5 (September 1919): 477–480.

18 Louis Marshall, fundraising speech, 1918, JWB Army-Navy Records, I-180, box 334, folder "Marshall, Louis, 1917–1918," AJHS.

19 On the treatment of African American troops, see Slotkin, *Lost Battalions*; Barbeau and Henri, *Unknown Soldiers*; Bill Harris, *The Hellfighters of Harlem* (New York: Basic Books, 2002); and Mark Ellis, *Race, War, and Surveillance: African Americans and the United States Government during World War I* (Bloomington: Indiana University Press, 2001); and Williams, *Torchbearers of Democracy*.

20 Morris Lazaron, "What Has It Meant to You?," in *Side Arms: Readings, Prayers and Meditations for Soldiers and Sailors* (Baltimore: Lord Baltimore Press, 1918), 33–34.

21 Alex Alan Steinbach, report on conditions at Camp Meade, near Baltimore, MD, March 24, 1918, JWB Army-Navy Records, I-180, box 327, folder "Camps 1917–1919," AJHS.

22 Horace J. Wolf, "A Month with the National Army," *American Hebrew and Jewish Messenger* 102, no. 10 (January 11, 1918): 1.

23 Harris, *Service with Fighting Men*, 1:71.

24 Lee, "War Camp Community Service," 193, cited in Bristow, *Making Men Moral*, 48.

25 Bristow, *Making Men Moral*, 48.

26 Harris, *Service with Fighting Men*, 2:60–61.

27 Atlanta Young Women's Christian Association, meeting minutes, June 8, 1917, quoted in Sarah Mercer Judson, "'Leisure is a Foe to Any Man': The Pleasures and Dangers of Leisure in Atlanta during World War I," *Journal of Women's History* 15, no. 1 (Spring 2003): 105.

28 Mrs. Philip North Moore, "Health and Recreation," *Annals of the American Academy of Political and Social Science* 79 (September 1918): 249. All of the welfare agencies, including the JWB, published articles in this issue of the journal, which was devoted to the theme of war relief work.

29 Atlanta YWCA, meeting minutes, April 18, 1918, May 13, 1918, quoted in Judson, "Leisure is a Foe," 92–114.

30 Cohen to Cutler, December 25, 1917.

31 Shirpser to Goldsmith, June 6, 1918.

32 Marcus, "Jewish Soldier," 51.

33 Janover, report on conditions at Camp Dix.

34 Accounts of home hospitality for Jewish soldiers can be found in the manuscript collections of the American Jewish Archives. For examples of the papers of Jewish

soldiers at the AJA, see the Aaronsohn Papers, MS-511; Irwin L. Small Papers, 1918–1920, SC-11627; and the Marcus, World War I diary. For accounts of soldiers' hospitality in the AJA collections, see the Isadore Sondheim, "Jewish Welfare Board at Camp Dodge and Fort Des Moines, Iowa, scrapbook"; and the Ehrenreich Papers, P-26, box 2, folder "WWI Correspondence, 1917").

35 Silbert, report on conditions at Camp Devens.

36 These events were considered even more important in France during the period of demobilization, as the men often had more free time and far more access to women of "ill repute." For example, see Harry Cutler to the Acting Chief of Staff, G-1, 10, "Commander-in-Chief's Report," April 5, 1919, JWB Army-Navy Records, I-180, box 333, folder "History 1919–1920" (2 of 3), AJHS.

37 For a discussion of repressive policies put into place to restrict women suspected of prostitution, promiscuity, or of carrying venereal disease, see chap. 4 in Bristow, *Making Men Moral*, 91–136.

38 Moore, "Health and Recreation," 245–253.

39 William Ernest Hocking, *Morale and Its Enemies* (New Haven, CT: Yale University Press, 1918), 146.

40 For accounts of the CTCA and the army's attempts to encourage sexual restraint—or at least to prevent the spread of venereal disease among the troops—see chap. 2 and chap. 3 in Brandt, *No Magic Bullet*, 52–121; Smythe, "Venereal Disease"; and Baldwin, "Invisible Armor."

41 The intermarriage rate for Jews in New York City, between 1908 and 1912, was estimated to be only 1.17 percent. Julius Drachsler, *Intermarriage in New York City: A Statistical Study of the Amalgamation of European Peoples* (New York: Columbia University, 1921), 48, cited in Goldstein, *The Price of Whiteness*, 98.

42 For some examples, see Alex Alan Steinbach, report on conditions at Camp Meade; Marcus, diary entry, Monday, December 31, 1917; and correspondence between camp rabbi Bernard Ehrenreich and Mr. I. Blank (whose son Max married a non-Jewish woman who was attempting to convert to Judaism under Rabbi Ehrenreich's instruction), letters dated October 17, October 21, November 1, and December 3, 1917, Ehrenreich Papers, P-26, box 2, folder "WWI Correspondence, 1917."

43 Jewish Welfare Board, *Final Report*, 62.

44 De Sola Pool to Schiff, report on conditions at Camp Upton.

45 David de Sola Pool, *Intermarriage* (New York: Jewish Welfare Board, n.d.), 6.

46 De Sola Pool, *Intermarriage*, 7.

47 De Sola Pool, *Intermarriage*, 8.

48 De Sola Pool, *Intermarriage*, 15.

49 See Goldstein, *Price of Whiteness*, esp. chap. 4, "'What Are We?': Jewishness between Race and Religion."

50 JWB, *First Annual Report*, 88–89.

51 Raymond Fosdick to Newton Baker, memo and enclosures, April 5, 1918; and Major General Payton C. March (chief of staff of the army), General Order, War Department, Washington, DC, April 1918; File 25354; General Correspondence,

1917–1921; Commission on Training Camp Activities; Education and Recreation Branch; Records of the War Plans Division, 1910–1942; Records of the War Department General and Special Staffs, Record Group 165; NACP.

52 Frederick P. Keppel to Harry Cutler, May 22, 1918, JWB Army-Navy Records, I-180, box 343, folder "War Department 1919" (1 of 2), AJHS.

53 Isaac Siegel to the Jewish Welfare Board, July 3, 1918, Siegel Papers, P-33, box 1, folder "JWB." Siegel also evidently secured the same for the Knights of Columbus, as he sent an almost identical letter to Cardinal John Farley, St. Patrick's Cathedral, on the same day.

54 Color Poster No. 4-P-47; "The Jewish Welfare Board. United War Work Campaign–Week of November 11, 1918"; World War I Posters, 1917–1919; Records of the U.S. Food Administration, 1917–1920, Record Group 4; NACP.

55 US General Staff, Morale Branch, Morale Circulars, no. 1, 1918, 8, Vertical File Manuscripts, box 13, items 196–216, folder 211, "Morale Circulars from the Morale Branch, U.S. General Staff," US Military History Institute, US Army War College, Carlisle, PA.

56 Cohen to Cutler, December 25, 1917.

CONCLUSION

1 Harry Cutler, "Standing behind the Service Star," n.d., National Jewish Welfare Board [JWB] Records, I-337, subgroup I, series C, subseries 3, box 163, folder "WWI, 1919–1920" (5 of 6), AJHS.

2 Cutler, "Standing behind the Service Star."

3 The postwar years were difficult for Cutler personally, as well as in connection with the JWB. He suffered from nephritis of the kidney, lost his wife to diabetes, and died of a blood clot while travelling to London as a member of the War Memorial Board in August 1920. Jacob Schiff, who had provided much of the financial clout behind the JWB, died shortly thereafter, in September 1920. For obituaries for Cutler, see *Jewelers' Circular* 81, no. 1 (September 15, 1920): 119; and *New York Times*, August 29, 1920, 20.

4 Raymond Fosdick, *Report to the Secretary of War on the Activities of the Welfare Organizations Serving with the A.E.F.* (Washington, DC: War Department, June 1, 1919), 8.

5 Fosdick, *Report to the Secretary of War*, 10–11.

6 Fosdick, *Strictly Confidential Report*, 18–39.

7 Harry Cutler to Julius Kahn, June 23, 1919, JWB Army-Navy Records, I-180, box 343, folder "War Dept. 1919" (2 of 2), AJHS.

8 Harry Cutler to Newton Baker, July 24, 1920, JWB Army-Navy Records, I-180, box 331, folder "Glucksman, H.L. 1919–1920," AJHS.

9 Newton Baker to Harry Cutler, July 19, 1920, JWB Army-Navy Records, I-180, box 331, folder "Glucksman, H.L. 1919–1920," AJHS.

10 See Lila Corwin Berman, *Speaking of Jews: Rabbis, Intellectuals, and the Creation of an American Public Identity* (Berkeley: University of California Press, 2009), esp. chap. 2, "Spiritual Missions after the Great War."

11 "A Finding Aid to the Morris S. Lazaron Papers," MS-71, American Jewish Archives, www.americanjewisharchives.org. See also Schultz, *Tri-Faith America*, 35–41.

12 "The Purpose and Program of the National Conference of Christians and Jews," *Journal of Educational Sociology* 16, no. 6, (February 1943): 324–326.

13 See Schultz, *Tri-Faith America*, 29–41.

14 Cyrus Adler, report of the chairman of the Army-Navy Committee, Jewish Welfare Board Annual Meeting 1938, JWB Records, I-337, subgroup I, series A, subseries 1, box 3, folder "Annual Meeting 1938," AJHS.

15 Cyrus Adler, report of the chairman of the Army-Navy Committee.

16 Janowky, *Change and Challenge*, 29.

17 Janowsky, *JWB Survey*, 107.

18 Kraft to Lehman, November 3, 1939, JWB Army-Navy Records, I-180, box 268, folder "Correspondence, Misc. 1936–1941," AJHS.

19 Janowsky, *JWB Survey*, 110.

20 Gretchen Knapp, "Experimental Policymaking during World War II: The United Service Organizations (USO) and American War Community Services (AWCS)," *Journal of Policy History* 12, no. 3 (2000): 321–338.

21 Frank Weil, "USO—Its Origin, History and Significance," May 31, 1943, 4, JWB Records, I-337, subgroup 1, series A, subseries 4, box 43, folder "Addresses, 1940–57," AJHS.

22 Weil, "USO," 8.

23 Will Herberg, *Protestant, Catholic, Jew: An Essay in American Religious Sociology* (Chicago: University of Chicago Press, 1983), 211.

24 Herberg, *Protestant, Catholic, Jew*, 211.

25 Herberg, *Protestant, Catholic, Jew*, 211.

26 See Moore, *GI Jews*, esp. 118–154, 248–264; Moore, "Jewish GIs"; Mark Silk, "Notes on the Judeo-Christian Tradition in America," *American Quarterly* 36, no. 1 (Spring 1984): 65–85; Silk, *Spiritual Politics*, esp. 40–107; and Schultz, *Tri-Faith America*, esp. 15–96.

INDEX

Aaronsohn, Michael, 109–110, 192n7

Abridged Prayer Book for Jewish in the Army and Navy of the United States, 116–119

Adler, Cyrus, 35, 41; Chairman of JWB Chaplains Committee, 88–94, 101; on conflicts between Reform and Orthodox Jews, 114, 119, 123; education and career, 41–42; goals of the JWB's soldiers' welfare program, 43, 66–67; JWB struggles for Jewish leadership, 52, 53, 56; on JWB workers, 104; on kosher food in the military, 74–80; post-war work with JWB, 163–163; on war work drive, 141–142

African Americans, 3, 10; in Chaplains Corps, 87; soldiers, 4, 9, 16, 64

Agudath ha-Rabbonim, 42; on debates over kosher food in military, 78–82; representation on JWB Chaplains Committee, 90

alcohol, as a threat to servicemen, 18, 20, 33

Allen, Edward Frank, 63, 99

American citizenship, 60, 63–64, 72, 75, 84–85, 110, 119, 143–144, 146, 195n67

American democracy: and Judaism, 67–69, 71, 74, 84, 97, 99, 119; limits on, 3–4; making the world safe for, 1–3, 68, 97; and masculinity, 105–107, 117, 127; values of, 7, 10–11, 63, 105–106, 145, 165

American Jewish Committee, 41–42, 46, 48, 79

American Jewish Congress, 46, 79

American Judaism, 9; debates over religious practices, 75–85 117–118, 123

American Library Association, 61–62, 139–140

American religion, 2, 4–8, 10–11, 79, 88, 107, 160, 164

American Soldiers and Sailors League of the Independent Order of B'nai B'rith, 48–49

American Social Hygiene Association, 18

"Americanism, 100 percent," 3, 5, 10, 192n7

Americanization, 3–5, 22–23, 44, 46, 63, 67–72, 80–84, 107, 116, 120, 123–128, 151

anti-Catholicism, 10, 21, 39–40, 161

anti-Semitism: in the military, 124, 132; in military intelligence bureau, 75; in the United States, 10, 161

armistice, 157

Aronson, David, 101

Asad, Talal, 7

Ashurst, Senator Henry Fountain, 16

Baker, Newton D.: on conditions during Punitive Expedition into Mexico, 19–21, 27–28; founding of the Commission on Training Camp Activities, 32–24; as Mayor of Cleveland, 17; on the military chaplaincy, 86; on the moral welfare of soldiers, 6–7, 10, 61–65, 147, 149, 155; Protestant biases of the CTCA, 36–39, 43–44, 71, 81–82, 141–143, 158–161; recognition of the JWB, 51–55, 60; religious pluralism, 72, 162

Jessica Cooperman is Director of Jewish Studies and Assistant Professor in the Department of Religion Studies at Muhlenberg College. She teaches courses on modern Jewish history, religion in the United States, and religion and violence. Her research focuses on American Judaism and American Jewish history. She is particularly interested in the relationship between religion and the state.